Play Production Today

Play Production Today

Fifth Edition

Jonniepat Mobley

Cuesta College
San Luis Obispo, California

National Textbook Company
a division of *NTC Publishing Group* • Lincolnwood, Illinois USA

Acknowledgments

Photography

Richard Feldman: cover, p. 63

San Diego City Schools: pp. 2, 3, 29, 30, 31, 34, 47, 48, 49, 67, 68, 69, 89, 90, 91, 139, 140, 141, 161, 162, 163, 191, 192, 193, 211, 212, 213, 227, 228, 229, 245, 246, 247, 257, 258, 259, 273, 274, 275, 291

National High School Institute, Northwestern University: pp. 7, 8, 11, 12, 17, 23, 42, 51, 80, 82, 93, 143, 151, 195, 202, 250, 268

Bradley Wilson: pp. 3, 10, 18, 29, 31, 47, 49, 55, 67, 69, 89, 91, 103, 139, 141, 161, 163, 165, 169, 175, 191, 193, 211, 213, 218, 220, 222, 227, 229, 233, 237, 245, 247, 257, 259, 261, 265, 266, 273, 275, 291

Jeff Ellis: pp. 14, 15, 37, 41, 52, 71, 79, 95, 97, 99, 100, 102, 146, 149, 171, 183, 185, 187, 197, 205, 207, 217, 232, 236, 240, 262, 279

Bettmann Archive: pp. 44, 45, 159, 225, 270

Jonniepat Mobley: pp. 76, 182

Leslie Baldwin: p. 253

The publisher is grateful to the faculty and staff of St. Scholastica High School, Chicago, Illinois, and Evanston Township High School, Evanston, Illinois, for their cooperation.

Excerpts from "Life at the *Grand Hotel*" reprinted from *TheaterWeek*, 12/11/89.

Cover and interior design: Ellen Pettengell

1997 Printing

Published by National Textbook Company, a division of NTC Publishing Group.

Library of Congress Catalog Card Number: 95–67114

7 8 9 RM 9 8 7 6 5 4 3 2

To Mort Tenenbaum, that best of all chairmen

Contents

Contents

Contents

Preface

Collaboration—the company spirit—has always been the very essence of successful theatre productions. Each person involved in a play has a unique role and makes a unique contribution. *Play Production Today* takes an in-depth look at the many jobs to be done in mounting a show, from the formation of the company through auditions and rehearsals to the final performance. The director, the technicians, the actors—the performance of each and the cooperation between them are crucial to the success of the production.

HOW THE BOOK IS ORGANIZED

Play Production Today takes you step by step through the production process. The first chapter, "Theatre: A Collaborative Art," examines the formation and organization of a theatre company, while Chapter 2, "The Time, the Place, and the Show," describes the all-important processes of choosing and casting a play. Chapter 3, "Taking On Responsibilities," explores the roles of the assistant director and stage manager, and describes blocking and other preliminary rehearsal issues. Chapters 4 and 5 examine types of performance space and explain fundamentals of set design and construction. The sixth chapter, "Reaching the Audience," details the roles of the publicity and house management crews. Chapter 7, "Creating the 'Look of the Show,'" explains some of the visual aspects of a production—props, costumes, hairstyles, and makeup—while Chapter 8, "Adding Light and Sound," discusses the design and implementation of these important components. Chapter 9, "Countdown to Performance," explores the final rehearsals and last-minute publicity that lead up to a performance. Chapters 10 and 11 examine opening night, subsequent performances, and the post-production critical evaluation of the show. The book concludes with chapters on musical theatre, one-act plays, reader's theatre, and other types of productions, plus an appendix describing hundreds of plays that are suitable for student companies.

SPECIAL FEATURES

Each chapter in *Play Production Today* begins with a Company Meeting, which previews the chapter's topics and working vocabulary. The thirteen Story of Theatre features present an overview of theatre history, from antiquity to the contemporary stage. Careers in the Theatre offers profiles of contemporary theatre professionals, including actors, designers, and even the playwright. Finally, the Theatre Workshops offer a variety of activities designed to encourage personal creativity and to foster communication and cooperation among company members.

A specific goal of this text is to help student companies overcome some frequently encountered obstacles. Too often students who want to mount a production don't even try because no formal auditorium is available for their use. *Play Production Today* suggests many alternative venues. Too often a student company wants to stage the latest plays, only to find the school lacks the budget necessary to produce them. This book urges consideration of a nonroyalty or low-royalty play, a period piece, an original work, or a theme-based collage of scenes. And too often student companies become discouraged because they are not playing to full houses. *Play Production Today* outlines plans for attracting larger audiences and bringing them back again.

I hope that *Play Production Today* will inspire you to explore the world of theatre and the wealth of experiences that are available to you in that world. Enjoy the show!

ACKNOWLEDGMENTS

Thanks go to Beverly Moerbe, Boswell High School, Fort Worth, Texas, and Suzanne Adams, former theatre department chair, New Trier Township High School, Winnetka, Illinois, for their valuable suggestions.

J. P. M.

Play Production Today

Theatre:
A Collaborative Art

Company Meeting

Theatre is a collaborative art. People form a theatrical company and work together to produce a show. You and your classmates are, in fact, a newly founded theatre company. How should you go about the planning and production of your play?

INTRODUCTIONS

Typically, the first company meeting begins with introductions. In turn, each of you should pronounce your name clearly and share a little about yourself. The director—your teacher—will offer information about himself or herself, as well. Keep in mind that in order to produce a play you can enjoy and be proud of, you must fulfill your responsibilities as a company member. A positive attitude and a genuine commitment to the production are essential.

TOPICS FOR THIS MEETING

- Company Organization
- Job Titles and Associated Responsibilities
- Scheduling Your Production
- Production Logbooks
- The Story of Theatre: Origins
- Theatre Workshop
- Careers in the Theatre: The Producer

WORKING VOCABULARY

Like other arts and areas of expertise, theatre has a unique language. Key terms in this chapter include *scene shop, technician, house, strike, blocking, blocking plot, load-in* or *set-in, props table, dress parade, dress rehearsal, lighting plot, stagehand, properties (props), properties plot, prop fabrication, straight makeup, character makeup, houseboard, prior life, line reading, off book, ensemble playing, protagonist, antagonist, catharsis,* and *deus ex machina.*

THEATRE ETIQUETTE

Because producing a play can sometimes be chaotic, rules have evolved in the theatre to help keep order and promote good working relationships among the members of the company. While most of these rules are just common sense, some do relate specifically to the theatre.

Be sure to familiarize yourself with the rules of theatre etiquette on pages 5–6. Consideration for everyone else in the company and commitment to the production will ensure good results for everyone involved.

AGENDA

At the next company meeting you'll discuss play and cast selection and receive instructions about auditions. At future meetings there will also be progress reports from the actors and various technical crews.

THE PHYSICAL PLANT

To conclude this inaugural meeting, take a company tour of the physical plant that makes up your theatre: stage, backstage areas, dressing rooms, **scene shop** (where the sets are built), house, and box office.

Theatre Etiquette

Actors:

- Be careful not to distract from another actor's lines.
- Remember that the director's word is final, as he or she has responsibility for the whole production.
- Leave the directing to the director.
- Be punctual for rehearsals.
- Learn your lines promptly.
- Remember that attracting unwarranted attention to yourself onstage is distracting and confusing both to actors and audience.
- Give the same quality of performance in the rehearsals as in the show.
- Be courteous to fellow actors offstage.
- Distracting company members—even when such actions wouldn't be seen by the audience—is unprofessional.
- Leave any critique of other actors to the director—even if other company members ask you to comment.
- Treat props, costumes, and sets with respect.
- Report, repair, or replace any damage caused to props, scenery, costumes, and so on.
- Guests should not be invited backstage or in the dressing room.
- Greeting guests while in costume or makeup spoils the illusion.
- Keep discussion of errors or mishaps inside the company.
- Remember that accepting a role indicates your willingness to play it as directed.
- Speak only positively of the play, your role, other actors, the direction, or the technical crews (the **technicians**)—even within the company.
- Readily accept assigned styles for costume, hair, or makeup—they should reflect your role rather than your personal taste.
- Remain quiet in the wings, backstage, or in the **house**—the audience seating area—while others rehearse.
- Show an uncritical and supportive attitude to all company members. Don't laugh when others make mistakes in auditions or rehearsals, and don't mock the way another actor says a line.
- In the makeup room, leave your area orderly.
- Don't try to rewrite the play.
- A serious emergency is the only valid excuse for missing a rehearsal.
- Be punctual for the performance call—the time designated for your arrival at the theatre on the nights or days of performance.
- Changes in hair length or color require prior permission of the director.

- If you have a small role, help out willingly with some technical assignment.
- Respect the technicians and recognize their contributions to the production.
- Acknowledge the hard work of the director and the assistant director with a tribute or company souvenir on closing night.
- Be gracious in accepting direction.
- Understand that the good of the show is the guiding principle in play production.

Technicians:

- When accepting an assignment, remember the requirement to attend rehearsals.
- Meet the director's deadlines for costumes, props, set, lighting, and sound.
- Watch rehearsals quietly.
- Once the lights are hung, run them at every rehearsal.
- Keep the set in good repair throughout the run of the play.
- Be at every rehearsal to set up and **strike** (clear away).
- Performance call time applies to technicians as well as actors.
- Meet all TV, radio, and newspaper publicity deadlines.
- Research the period in which the play is set.
- Don't take any aspect of the production for granted; nothing gets done by itself.
- Be courteous to all company members.
- Leave work areas neat.
- Observe all the safety precautions for your technical area.
- Speak only positively of the play, your job, actors, the direction, or other technicians—even within the company.
- Be present on closing night to do the full strike.

COMPANY ORGANIZATION

A theatrical company may work together to produce a single play or a series of plays. The members of the company include the director, the actors, and the technicians. If the play to be produced is an original work, that is, written for the occasion, the playwright may also be a member of the company. While the director has the final say in all matters, company members may be consulted on some issues. The entire company works as a team for the good of the show, recognizing the value of each person's contribution. Thus, for actors, trying to attract undue attention or to steal a scene from others—or snubbing of technicians—is unacceptable.

To help establish their identity at school or in the community, companies have selected names such as the Prairie Street Players, the Footlight Club, and the Templeton Thespians. Some companies choose to be known as the Senior Class or the

The entire company works as a team for the good of the show, recognizing the value of each person's contribution.

Drama Society, however. To build camaraderie and to serve as publicity for the show, your company may opt to create a logo—some symbol of drama, your school, or the play you're producing—to appear on programs, fliers, and correspondence. In addition, consider having T-shirts or sweatshirts printed with the company logo and performance dates. Company members can wear the shirts to create publicity for the show. Further, the shirts might be made available for sale in the lobby at performances to raise funds and provide additional publicity. If the company members wish to stand out as a group, they might choose a company color for their shirts, offering the fund-raising shirts in a different color.

JOB TITLES AND ASSOCIATED RESPONSIBILITIES

Recall some play programs you have seen. Each of the many job titles listed carries with it specific tasks. Some of the jobs require close attention to instructions. Others require initiative and cre-

The need for a unified vision is the reason the director has the final say on every aspect of the production.

ativity. As a company member, you recognize that each job is essential to the success of a production and that a failure in any area affects everyone. As you read through the following descriptions of job responsibilities, note the specific contributions each makes to the show.

Director

In educational theatre, that is, theatre connected with a school, usually the director is also the producer. The director combines who, what, where, and when into a package that reflects his or her unity of vision. The need for a unified vision is the reason the director has final say on every aspect of production. The director determines the pace or tempo of the performance; the tone and the interpretation to be used throughout; and the **blocking,** or the movement, of the actors on stage. Some directors show how they want each line read, while others prefer to allow the actor to try several variations before choosing the reading to be used.

In addition to working with the actors in rehearsal, the director confers constantly with technical personnel to ensure that their work is consistent with his or her vision for the production.

Assistant Director

The assistant director is a student who supports the director by keeping the **blocking plot** (a diagram of the stage floor with actors' movements marked); noting all script changes; helping actors to learn their lines; advising actors regarding enunciation and pronunciation; running small side rehearsals for part of the cast during the main rehearsal; prompting actors the first week they're working without scripts; and acting as messenger to backstage crews when the director is conducting rehearsals. The job of assistant director is very demanding and requires him or her to be constantly alert and to anticipate others' needs. The assistant director does not have a free hand, however, and should not make decisions without consulting the director. Nonetheless, because the assistant works so closely with the director, he or she is a good source of information for a company member who missed an announcement or failed to note some blocking or line changes.

One of the ways in which the assistant director supports the director is by helping actors learn their lines.

Stage Manager

The stage manager functions as the chief of all the backstage crews. He or she confers constantly with the set designer and builders, the stage crew, and the properties manager. After the **load-in** or **set-in,** when the set has been built and positioned on the stage, the stage manager keeps the actors backstage, just as in a performance, reminding them of the need for absolute quiet and attention to cues for entrances. A stage manager walks through the set before each performance, checking that everything is in place. He or she works with the properties manager to double-check the **props table**—the area where all the show's props are arranged. At ten minutes before curtain the stage manager confirms that the actors are in their places backstage, then follows the script throughout the performance to ensure each actor's prompt entrances. The stage manager also runs the strike after the final performance. A stage manager must have a thorough understanding of the play and its requirements. He or she must be both assertive and diplomatic in working with colleagues. In some community theatres this is one of the few paid positions because of its importance to the production of the play.

In a small company the jobs of assistant director and stage manager may be combined. In such circumstances, the student generally sits with the director until the load-in and then works backstage to run the show.

Set Designer

In educational theatre, community members and family often help with the set design and construction. If this is not true of your company, then someone will need to design the set and direct the construction crew. As with every other detail, the design and any subsequent changes must have the approval of the director. Size, shape, color, and texture all communicate information in a play. Thus, decisions about them should be made only after serious consideration.

Costume Designer

Costume designers for school plays are, in most cases, limited by time and budget. Rather than create an entire collection of new costumes, designers often use what is already in stock from previous productions, refurbishing and accessorizing the existing costumes appropriately. Another possibility is to shop thrift stores and other economical sources for clothing needed and then to adapt the garments to the play. If costumes are to be designed specifically for the play, then the time period and locality of the play and the economic status of the characters must be thoroughly researched. And, regardless of the source of the costumes, actors cannot take it upon themselves to alter the cut, fabric, color, or ornamentation of their assigned wardrobe.

Finally, if your school has a sewing class or a night program in fashion design, consider asking those students to become involved in this aspect of your production.

Designers sometimes create new costumes by refurbishing and accessorizing those used in previous productions.

Wardrobe Manager

If the costumes are not designed specifically for your company's production, then the wardrobe manager is responsible for acquiring all of them. Sources for these costumes may include

The master builder encourages safety and caution in set construction.

the actors themselves, school wardrobe stock, costume rental services (perhaps you can obtain a discount in exchange for an advertisement in the play program), community members, or economical retail outlets. As suggested earlier, it may be necessary to refurbish the costumes obtained to suit the current production.

In addition to coordinating the acquisition of the costumes, the wardrobe manager takes charge of their maintenance, checking them for tears or soiling as they are returned after **dress parade** (a wardrobe check done under stage lighting), **dress rehearsal** (the final rehearsal before performance), and each performance.

Lighting Designer

The person who designs the lighting plot (the plan detailing the intensity, color and position of the lights) probably will also run the lights for the show. Thus, the lighting designer must know the play thoroughly and ensure that the lighting not only illuminates the set and the actors, but also helps to establish mood and atmosphere and to create special effects. If one person cannot run all the lighting required, a lighting crew should assist. For example, one technician might be needed to run a follow spotlight.

Master Builder (Carpenter)

Once the set has been designed, it must be constructed. The master builder or carpenter directs the set construction crew in this work and usually in the load-in, or the placement of the set on the stage. Since construction involves potentially dangerous power tools and the like, the master builder must oversee the process and encourage safety and caution at all times. For additional assistance the master builder can ask students of a woodshop class or stagecraft class to help, if such classes are included in the school curriculum.

Stagehands

Often the members of the construction crew become **stagehands** (backstage workers) when the load-in is complete. In a single-set show, this simply involves keeping the set in good repair throughout the run of the show. When a second set is involved, however, stagehands change the scenery.

Properties Manager

Called "props" for short, **properties** are any portable objects used to decorate the set or used by actors in the performance of a play. Although props usually can be managed by one person, an elaborate **properties plot** (list of items needed), such as that of *You Can't Take It With You,* may require a whole crew to obtain and manage. A props manager is responsible for the acquisition of all props. Some play scripts include a props plot at the end of the script. If not, the properties manager must read through the script carefully, ideally with the assistant director to help, listing all props to be used. Watch rehearsals carefully to make sure no item is overlooked.

In gathering the props, appeal to the company members themselves, and, if necessary, make a general call for donations from the community. Items from the school's prop stock, from thrift stores, or from rummage sales may serve as well. If you can't locate props, you must make them. The theatre term for this is **prop fabrication.** If your school offers three-dimensional art classes, those students may be of great help to you in fabrication.

The sooner props are acquired, the better for the actors: they can stop miming actions and begin to work with real objects. If a prop is fragile or takes a lot of abuse in the play, you will need both a rehearsal prop and a performance prop. Obviously you will need duplicates of any prop that is destroyed by direction in the play, such as a letter that is torn up or a glass that is broken.

Finally, once the actors are working with props, the property manager must be present at rehearsals to hand out, reclaim, and store them after each rehearsal and performance.

Sound Engineer

The sound engineer's job can be as simple as playing audiotapes of music or sound effects from a booth or as complex as actually creating the sound effects and recording them for later play or creating them live for each performance. To do the job well, a sound engineer must thoroughly understand the action of the play, be alert and quick-witted, and have a good working knowledge of the sound equipment to be used. If sound will be coming both from the lighting booth and from backstage, a sound crew will be needed to help.

Makeup Artist

If there is a large cast, the makeup artist should have assistants to help with the making up of the actors, but actors themselves can usually be counted on to do some of their own makeup. Many professional actors prefer to do their own **straight makeup** (when they appear as someone like themselves in coloring and age), only asking for assistance when they need **character makeup** (when they are playing someone quite different in coloring or age from themselves).

A makeup artist must learn the needs of each actor in the play and the techniques used to achieve the appearance required. Maintaining a constant inventory of supplies is part of the job. In addition to making up the actors before each perfor-

The makeup artist learns the needs of each actor in the play and the techniques used to achieve the desired effects.

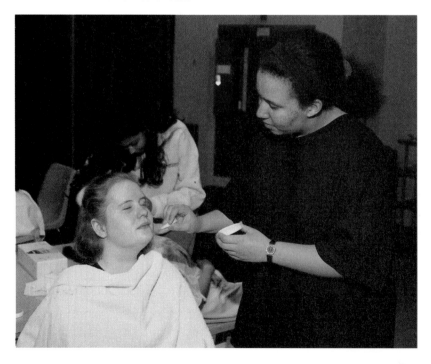

mance, repairs or changes between scenes may be needed. Also, a makeup artist must do research to ensure that the makeup suits the period in which the play is set. For example, white lipstick on a 1920s character or hard dots of rouge on a 1960s character would be inappropriate.

Hairstylist

Like the makeup artist, the company hairstylist needs to study the period in which the play is set so that the actor's hairstyles reflect the times. While the actors should be able to care for their own hair, particularly if the styles are simple and much like their own, assistants may be needed in some circumstances. Maintaining supplies and making repairs to the actors' stylings are responsibilities of the hairstylist, as well as caring for any wigs that are used in the show.

While actors can often style their own hair, an assistant can help with the more complicated hairstyles.

Graphic Artist

The graphic artist's job may include ornamentation of the completed set, such as painting a border around a fireplace or faking an "Old Master" portrait to hang in the drawing room. It may be to design the posters, fliers, and programs. Or it may include not only those tasks, but also to design a company or show T-shirt logo as well. For help in rendering the necessary designs, the graphic artist might want to appeal to students of any art classes the school offers. Note that this job requires artistic ability. The best intentions in the world will not overcome the lack of that talent. However, if someone has ideas but cannot draw them well enough, he or she can work with someone else who can do the execution under direction. As with any other aspect of production, however, the director must approve any design before it is used.

House Manager

The house manager, aided by ushers, refreshment servers, and ticket takers, oversees everything not onstage or backstage. For example, he or she heads a crew that provides hospitality—anything from a gracious welcome to intermission refreshments—for the audience. The house manager may also run the box office, although that job may be taken over by a school official. In addition, the house manager is responsible for reservation lists, purchasing or printing of the tickets themselves, ushering and distributing programs, keeping the halls or lobby quiet during performances, dispensing refreshments, and moving audience members into and out of the theatre safely and courteously. Finally, if the house manager runs the box office, he or she is also responsible for the financial statement after each performance.

Publicist

The publicist handles paid advertising, free publicity, public service announcements (PSAs), press kits, and poster and flier distribution. He or she uses clever gimmicks to grab attention and make the public eager to attend the show. To be effective, a publicist must be persistent but not annoying, be inventive but not brash, and seize every opportunity to publicize the show. A publicist should be bold enough to ask, yet gracious in express-

Publicity photos of the cast should be taken to display in the lobby or distribute with press releases to local newspapers.

ing thanks. Certainly the success of the publicist is all-important. Without his or her efforts, the planning and building and rehearsing will go for nothing.

If the theatre company is small, consider combining the house manager's job with that of publicist. The responsibilities coordinate well because both jobs require high energy and creativity. Regardless of the staffing choice, however, a crew is needed to help carry out all the duties. For additional support, ask students of a school photography class to shoot cast photos for newspaper articles or for the **houseboard** (a prominent bulletin board in the lobby).

Actor

An actor represents the work of the playwright, the director, and all the technicians. As the direct link to the audience, the actor must convincingly *become* his or her role. Far more than simply memorizing a script, acting requires you to get inside your character.

Begin by examining what the playwright has given you in your lines and in the lines of others. Then build on this under-

Actors should carry out the director's instructions in everything from line reading to movement.

standing by developing a **prior life** for your character. That is, determine everything you can about your character's life before he or she would have spoken the lines in the script. Use your understanding of your character's life experiences to make him or her real.

At rehearsals, take direction willingly. Listen carefully and carry out the director's instructions in everything from movement to **line reading** (how to say a line with the appropriate inflection, tone, pace, and volume). Be conscientious about meeting the deadline for getting **off book** (knowing your lines). Remember, other actors depend on your preparation, your attention, and your reaction in order to play their parts well. Actors should not portray their characters in isolation, however; **ensemble playing** creates a total effect, as cast members work as a group for the good of the show.

Clearly, there is a place in theatre for a variety of talents and interests. Having read these brief descriptions, do you know which job seems to best suit your own interests and abilities? Then go for it!

SCHEDULING YOUR PRODUCTION

How does a theatre company determine its production schedule? In general, take the date of opening night and work backward, taking care to allow a minimum of forty hours of rehearsal time. Your thinking might go like this: "We open Friday, May 1, so we should have dress rehearsal Thursday night, April 30. That means tech rehearsal and dress parade around April 10, or sooner if the stage is free. Props need to be ready as soon as the actors are off book—say, by April 3. That allows four weeks to work on action and reaction, to polish line readings, to get comfortable using props, to develop the right tempo—in short, to pull everything together. If we plan for a week to block and another week to get that blocking firmly set in the actors' minds, we can read through the play around March 16. That places auditions the week of March 9, and if we want prepared readings for the auditions, we'd better ask the librarian to have copies on reserve by the middle of February."

The company might then receive a schedule like the one shown. You and your parents may be asked to sign and return a copy of a more detailed schedule to indicate your commitment to it.

Ten Weeks Before the Play Opens

Play scripts on reserve in the school library

Announcements about auditions posted

Nine Weeks Before

Auditions held during Play Production class

Everyone given a chance to read for any parts, but auditioners must be familiar with the play

Eight Weeks Before

Cast and crew assignments posted in school library and outside Play Production classroom

First reading and discussion of the play and technical requirements

Seven Weeks Before

Blocking rehearsals on stage (or in rehearsal hall)

Technical crews begin assignments

Six Weeks Before

Rehearsals continue

Technical crews at work

Five Weeks Before

Rehearsals continue

Technical crews at work

Four Weeks Before

Press kits distributed

Actors off book

Lighting plot complete

Props ready

Costumes ready

Makeup and hairstyles decided

Three Weeks Before

Load-in of set

Posters and fliers ready

Lights hung

Rehearsals continue

Two Weeks Before

Program copy ready

Posters and fliers distributed

Technical rehearsal

Dress parade

Rehearsals continue

One Week Before

Final publicity campaign

Refreshments ordered

Programs printed

Dress rehearsal

Opening Night

7 PM call for everyone

8 PM curtain; break a leg!

Week between Performance Weekends

Fine-tuning and polishing rehearsals

Technicians run checks of everything

Second Week of Performances

7 PM call for everyone

8 PM curtain; break a leg!

Full strike after final performance

To make your schedule more specific, include deadlines for tasks of each of the technical crews, such as step-by-step dates for the publicity campaign. It is the responsibility of the director to provide the detailed schedule. The stage manager must then see that the deadlines are met.

PRODUCTION LOGBOOKS

Many directors—professional as well as school—require their actors to keep a logbook throughout production. Often, actors find that keeping a logbook helps them analyze and evaluate their experiences. They can document their preparation and development of a prior life for their characters, and, later, have a valuable record of that time.

Broadway actor Karen Akers kept a logbook of her work in the show *Grand Hotel*. In it she detailed the direction, advice, and inspiration provided the company by director/choreographer Tommy Tune.

Sunday, October 29

On the day which was to have been our opening, we had the best show yet. Joel Grey saw it and said it made him excited about the theater again. Lucy Arnaz said she knew that Tommy [Tune] was still revising it but that she would have like to tell him, "Don't change a thing."

Long rehearsal tonight. We were there until 11:30 P.M. with many of us dreaming of an early release. Kevin [Karen's friend] says that the way we talk of our time with Grand Hotel *makes him think of inmates in a mental institution.*

Tuesday, October 31

Morale is especially high after tonight's show. In spite of our exhaustion, the feeling that we have a strong, beautiful show keeps growing. Boston, and the mixed-to-negative press which discouraged us, seem light years away.

Thursday, November 2

Tommy said during notes today that we never took off last night. "It's the longest opening in the history of musical theatre and the only way it works is to play it fast. Don't let up. Circle is the key, you must do Circle." "Circle" is the gathering of cast members before each performance, a chance to remind ourselves of our commitment to the ensemble. Tommy feels, as I think all of us do, that we are something of a family—a group that cares for and supports one another. "I don't just do shows," said Tommy. "If this were an ordinary show we would have had a script from the beginning. Think of wholeness. Circle is so important. Do it. When I left Nine *they didn't always do it and the show suffered. This is something metaphysical, something spiritual and it's a way of our staying connected." I'm sure that Tommy believes that there is a spiritual connection between us, and when everyone is completely present in the show, I think he's right.*

Michael Bennett told him once to pretend he was deaf, and to ask himself if the story was clear, then to pretend he was blind, and ask himself if the story still made sense. Tommy says ours does.

Keeping such a log not only serves to remind you what happened during production, it encourages you to examine and learn from each experience. Remember, too, when you are writing your end-of-production report, the log will be a helpful reminder of all the ways you participated as a company member.

Daily Entry

Ideally, you will write in your production logbook every day. At the very least, keep the log on the days you rehearse. Even when you are not at rehearsal, continue to prepare by thinking about your character, reading over your lines, and considering the influence of technical details. Don't turn your logbook into a diary filled with complaints, ups and downs in your personal life, or remarks about company members.

John Corbally, who played George in the West Lost Angeles College production of Francis Swann's *Out of the Frying Pan*, wrote the following entry just after being cast in the part:

I'm having trouble figuring out how George, I mean how I feel about Kate. Marge and Tony are romantically involved from the start of the play and Dottie and Norman are involved by the end, but do I feel that way about Kate? It would make a tidy and symmetrical arrangement: three boys plus three girls equals three couples, but I don't think that's what's happening. I think Kate and I are far too serious about our careers to get sidetracked. Yes! I think we're the two who eventually succeed in the theatre! I just bet that's it. So, I like her, I like them all, but I'm too interested in making it on Broadway to see Kate as more than a friend. And that's how I'll try it next rehearsal.

Bonnie Cashell, putting together a costume portfolio in a stagecraft class for the character of Mary in Jean Kerr's *Mary, Mary* wrote:

Mary is a pretty girl, but she has not always been and is not confident about the way she looks. She grew up awkward and homely and still sees herself as such. In this scene she has been out to dinner with a glamorous movie star so she would make a special effort with her clothes. The outfit needs to be dressy, yet conservative. She wouldn't wear anything frilly or clingy, no bright colors to attract attention to herself, no excessive jewelry. Shoes the color of the dress and heels not too high. Well, that means something safe like blue, but a really nice fabric and a locket or family pearls. I'll check the fabric stores tomorrow for swatches.

Writing daily in your logbook can help you evaluate and analyze your experiences as a company member.

Character Analysis and Prior Life

If you're an actor in the theatre company, your analysis of your character should be added to your logbook. Consider the following items:

1. Birth date
2. Birthplace
3. Childhood memories, happy and sad
4. Education
5. Economic circumstances in childhood
6. Economic circumstances now
7. Other members of your family
8. Marital status
9. Pets in childhood
10. Pets now
11. Cultural interests
12. Major influences in your life
13. People you admire
14. Your temperament
15. Favorite colors
16. Favorite foods
17. Favorite pastimes
18. Favorite sports, as player or spectator
19. Favorite books
20. Favorite movies or plays
21. Clothing style
22. Home furnishings
23. What you were doing immediately before you entered
24. Your objective in the play
25. The obstacle to your objective
26. Setting for the play
27. Time period of the play
28. World events taking place at the time of the action of the play
29. Music that might have been playing before the action of the play began
30. Health
31. Voice quality. Loud? Nasal? Hushed?
32. Posture and movement
33. Occupation or profession
34. Religious or ethical values

35. Your relationship to the other characters
36. Your position in the community
37. Your response to criticism? To praise?
38. Your fate after the action of the play is over

If you consider all these influences in developing your character, you won't have to wonder how your character thinks and acts—you'll know.

SUMMARY

To promote harmony among the company members and to reduce chaos, all participants in a production need to observe the rules of theatre etiquette. Within the company itself are opportunities for a great variety of jobs. Choose those that most appeal to you and suit your abilities. To determine a workable production schedule, begin with the opening date and work backward, allowing a minimum of forty hours of rehearsal time. Remember that regular company meetings keep everyone informed and involved. Finally, in a production logbook make frequent entries about your observations and experiences as a company member.

For as long as people have gathered together to eat, to work, and to be sheltered from the weather and from other creatures, there have been elements of theatre in their lives. Imagine the gestures and expressions of the woman showing her family how she found berries or edible roots; of the man mimicking how the animals he saw walked and ran; of parents recounting their children's latest triumph; of children gleefully imitating their elders.

In acting out these activities, primitive people probably used mime techniques, dance, and monologue. Surely those first audiences sat wide-eyed and enthralled, maybe jumping to their feet to praise the "actor"—the earliest standing ovations. As one person seemed better than another at relating the day's adventures, he or she likely was singled out to be the storyteller. To enhance the story this person might have used the tusks or hide of an animal for a costume, dyes from plants as early makeup, or leaves to create a mask. These performances served not only to entertain, but to pass along tribal secrets of hunting and food gathering and to help primitive society to understand its world.

For Western civilization, the origins of theatre were in Athens, Greece, about 500 B.C. Religious festivals in honor of the god Dionysus were held every year, with a chorus of men chanting hymns. Eventually, a man named Thespis suggested his stepping forward to reply to the leader of the chorus, which produced dialogue and the opportunity for conflict. This first actor and principal character, around whom the action revolves, was called the **protagonist** of the play. Later another actor was added to oppose him, called the **antagonist**.

Early Greek theatres were vast outdoor arenas with seating for thousands. The chorus danced in the area called the *orchestra,* which was almost completely surrounded by the audience. Because theatre was considered important for all, anyone unable to pay was admitted free.

Such huge theatres required an exaggerated and presentational style of acting; the actors faced the audience rather than each other. All actors were men. They wore high boots to add height and dignity and used masks with exaggerated features and a kind of megaphone to help amplify their voices. Since there were never any more than three main actors plus the chorus, an actor could change character easily by changing his mask.

Early Greek tragedy used stories from mythology and featured a hero who lost face because of a tragic flaw—often pride—in his personality. Feeling fear and pity for the protagonist, the audience was gripped by the inevitability of the tragedy. Then, when the performance was over, the audience felt a **catharsis,** that is, a release from tension. Since the same plots were used repeatedly, there was no suspense. Despite this, the audience attended again and again for the cleansing experience of the *catharsis.*

Because the mythological subject matter frequently led to seemingly insoluble entanglements for the actors, playwrights

often used a **deus ex machina.** An actor playing a god would be lowered into the midst of the conflict to employ supernatural means to solve the problems. The term *deus ex machina* still is used today to describe an improbable solution to a play, such as a character waking to find all the action had been a dream.

Aristotle, a fourth-century-B.C. Greek philosopher and theatre critic, described the ideal tragedy as having unity of time, place, and action. In other words, the action of the play occurs within twenty-four hours, uses only one location, and is strict tragedy with no mingling of comic episodes. The chorus made the first two unities possible, as anything happening at another time or in another place could be explained or commented upon in the narration by the chorus. Since the day-long theatrical event was enlivened by short rowdy skits presented between the plays, there was no reason to dilute the tragedy with comic relief.

The three major writers of tragedy from this early period were Sophocles, Aeschylus, and Euripides. Some of their most famous plays are *Oedipus Rex* (Sophocles), the *Oresteia* trilogy (Aeschylus), and *Medea* (Euripides).

In the last scene of Sophocles' *Antigone,* Creon weeps over the body of his son Haemon.

Design Projects

1. Use what you know about your school, company, and company members to help you design a suitable company logo for use on posters, fliers, or T-shirts.
2. To better understand what performing in ancient Greece would have been like, research Greek arena theatre and make a cardboard model of the stage.
3. To imagine the earliest theatrical experiences, make a paper or fabric mask an actor could use for a hunting or tribal lore story.

Writing Projects

1. Write a proposed agenda for a company meeting during the first week of rehearsals.
2. Choose a standard play of educational theatre such as *Our Town, Charley's Aunt,* or *Arsenic and Old Lace* and develop a properties plot. Then decide where and how you would acquire the props needed for the production.
3. So that the company will have resources to consult, visit your school library, public library, and bookstore to compile a list of books dealing with one of the following areas of stagecraft:
    a. Set design
    b. Costume design
    c. Lighting
    d. Sound effects
    e. Makeup
    f. Hairstyles
    g. Publicity and public relations
4. Develop a production schedule for a play with a twelve-week rehearsal schedule.
5. Select a character from a favorite story, play, or film, and develop a prior life for him or her. Remember, any decisions you make need to be justified by information given in the text of the play, story, or film. Using a favorite childhood story for this exercise can be fun because it gives you a new look at an old friend.
6. If your community has a theatre, arrange to interview someone who has the same responsibility there that you are considering undertaking in your own company. Make a list of interesting questions before you go to the interview. If you want to tape-record the interview, be sure to obtain permission in advance.

The Producer

Every theatrical venture begins with the producer, the person who puts together the package: financing, management, publicity, and artistic teams. One of the United States' most important producers for more than twenty years has been Elizabeth Ireland McCann.

McCann has earned more than sixty Tony nominations. The Tony, named for Antoinette Perry, is Broadway's equivalent of the film industry's Oscar. McCann has produced dozens of Broadway hits, including *Dracula, The Elephant Man, Amadeus, Nicholas Nickleby, The Gin Game, Orpheus Descending, Mornings at Seven, Mass Appeal,* and *Cyrano de Bergerac.*

The daughter of a New York City subway motorman, McCann attended Manhattanville College in the late 1950s. A chance remark from one of her teachers, urging her not waste her life as a telephone operator, led her to try for a career in the theatre. She began as a box office attendant and then a producer's secretary, then became a theatre management apprentice working for Hal Prince, Maurice Evans, and Saint Subber.

At age thirty-two, convinced she was going nowhere in the theatre, she chose to study law. After graduating from Fordham Law School three years later, she decided her future did lie in the theatre after all. Hired as managing director for the Nederlander Organization, a top producer and presenter of Broadway plays, she produced *Sherlock Holmes, Otherwise Engaged,* and *My Fat Friend.*

In 1976 Elizabeth McCann formed her own producing management firm, McCann and Nugent, and in 1984 she decided she preferred a solo operation. Her successes include twenty Tony Awards, as well as several New York Drama Critics, Drama Desk, Drama League, and Outer Critics Circle Awards.

In a 1990 *TheaterWeek* interview, McCann declared that timing is a central consideration in determining whether a play will be successful. "Besides the right timing and the right play, casting is the most essential ingredient," she added. "It's not going to happen often, but the goal is to be the producer of a play in which the actor's chemistry combined with the material breaks through to the heart of the writer."

While the producer usually is not involved with the artistic direction of the production, he or she hires, and if necessary, fires the artistic personnel, and so puts a personal stamp on the finished production.

The Time, the Place, and the Show

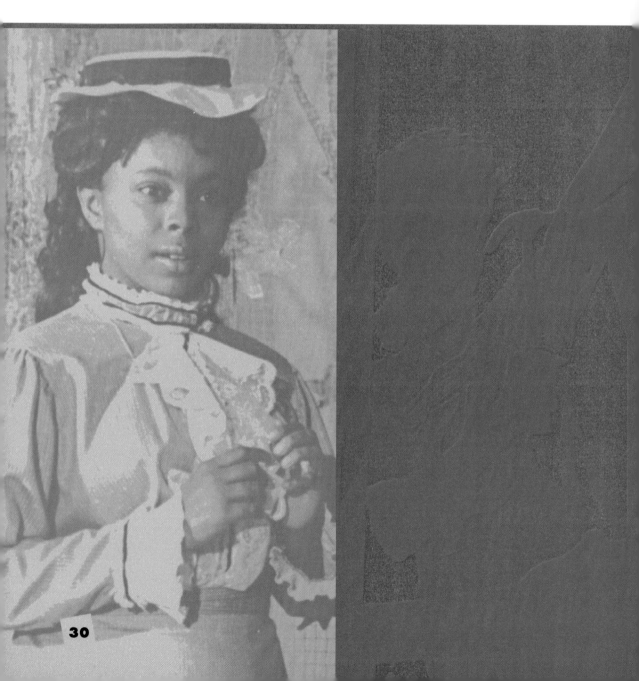

30

2

31

Company Meeting

By now you have worked together for at least a week and are gathering for your second company meeting. If there are any new members of the company, be sure they are introduced to everyone else.

TOPICS FOR THIS MEETING

- Considerations in Play Selection
- Types of Plays
- Sources of Plays
- Auditions
- The Story of Theatre: Early Developments
- Theatre Workshop
- Careers in the Theatre: The Actor

WORKING VOCABULARY

As you become involved in your production you will need to be able to communicate quickly and precisely in the working vocabulary of the theatre. Key terms in this chapter include *period piece, genre, tragedy, message plays, melodrama, stock character, comedy, farce, royalties, typecasting, character role, improvisations,* and *understudy.*

AGENDA

At the next meeting you will discuss the responsibilities of the stage manager, the preparation of a prompt script and a blocking plot, and the first reading of the play by the newly assigned cast. Afterward, company members will present progress reports. Any problems encountered can then be addressed.

CONSIDERATIONS IN PLAY SELECTION

Choosing the right play for your company may mean the difference between full and empty houses. A well-known but recently done play may not attract an audience, while an obscure play by an unknown author may depend upon clever publicity to promote attendance. Trying to do a play beyond the financial means of the company might result in costumes and scenery that are cheap, flimsy, and unimpressive in appearance. Further, if a play had characters and situations beyond the abilities of young student actors, both the company and the audience will feel frustration and disappointment. Be aware, too, that taking a famous **period piece**—a play from another decade or century that has stood the test of time and is still popular—and updating it or placing it in a different setting just for the novelty may disappoint an audience expecting the traditional version. If this is the first time the actors have performed the play or the first time many in your audience have seen the play, it makes sense to work with and thoroughly understand the traditional before attempting the experimental. In the words of West Coast theatrical producer Anet Gillespie-Carlin, "You have to know what the center is before you become eccentric." However, if your company decides it can make a strong statement or provide real entertainment by updating a theatre classic, make sure the advertising informs the public that your version is not the original. Also, at least read, discuss, and thoroughly understand the original before changing it.

If you have a small performance space, don't attempt plays with huge casts and cumbersome scenery. Consider the many delightful plays written for more intimate staging—plays that would be lost on a large stage but would be very effective in a smaller space.

In most cases your director will have chosen the play before the company ever meets, but if you are asked to help select the production, be sure to choose something that (a) meets the expectations of your potential audience; (b) suits your budget (c) gives the actors a chance to stretch and enjoy (not struggle with) the material; and (d) fits nicely in your performance space.

TYPES OF PLAYS

There are several **genres** or types of plays, including tragedy, melodrama, comedy, and farce. Each type has subgenres because of differences among time periods and production styles. By understanding the characteristics and demands of each genre you can better determine the kind of play your company would like to present.

Tragedy

Classical Tragedy. Simply defined, **tragedy** is a serious play that ends unhappily. Strictly speaking, classical tragedy comprises the tragic plays of ancient Greece or Rome, but popularly speaking, the term includes any tragedy written before this century that has continued to be recognized over time. In either case a classical tragedy is a serious play that ends unhappily. In *Oedipus Rex,* for example, Sophocles writes of a king who, hav-

Shakespeare's tragedy *Romeo and Juliet* is beloved by young actors and audiences alike.

ing learned that he has unknowingly killed his own father, puts his own eyes out and is banished into exile. Even today, in a time and place far from those of Sophocles, audiences can be moved to fear and pity at the plight of Oedipus.

Shakespeare's *Romeo and Juliet* has much appeal for young actors, and audiences continue to thrill to its plot of young lovers thwarted by their families' feud. And Henrik Ibsen's *Ghosts*, with its insistence on the inescapable consequences of sin, still has the power to hold an audience. However, such plays ask a great deal emotionally from a company and some may think it too heavy a burden to perform such material.

If you do feel equal to the challenge, however, you can perform it as close to the original as possible, or you can modernize the play by placing it in present times and using contemporary costumes. If you decide on modernization, be sure you do not dishonor the play by misinterpreting it or by holding it up to ridicule. On the other hand, if you believe you can make a point about the play's connection to contemporary times by modernizing it, it can be an exciting venture for your company. Remember, though, you do not always need to modernize a play to make its significance clear to your audience. The reason these plays have endured is because they remain relevant.

Modern Tragedy. Modern tragedy includes a range of serious plays written in this century. Unlike classical tragedy, these usually deal with domestic or social concerns. The hero is the common man or woman. While you may be eager for the challenge that such plays present, remember that most of the characters are older adults, and maintaining such characterizations is a tremendous challenge.

Drama

People often refer to a serious, though not tragic, play as drama. Although such a play may have comic moments, it is essentially a play that considers serious issues. Sometimes such plays are called **message plays** because they propose solutions to problems (unlike the classical tragedy, in which the tragic ending is inescapable). The drawback is that such plays can come across as preachy and lacking in entertainment value. That does not mean they are not worth doing, but that they require careful, skilled production.

Melodrama

Drama that relies heavily on sensationalism and sentimentality is known as **melodrama.** The characters are clearly heroes or villains, with no blurred lines or mixed motives. Melodrama frequently includes **stock characters**—roles representing a personality type or occupation like the meek clerk, the thieving landlord, or the sickly orphan. The moral is virtue rewarded and evil punished. A problem with doing melodrama is the temptation to ham it up. To be effective, melodrama must be played straight by the actors, leaving the laughter to the audience.

Mystery-Suspense

Plays of mystery or suspense have strong audience appeal and may be serious or comic. The timing of the lines and of the entrances and exits may be tricky, and special effects—secret passages, bloody corpses, gunshots—are often required. The mystery may be a "whodunit" or simply contain a suspenseful situation such as deciphering a secret code or finding a hidden will.

Comedy

Classical Comedy. A simple definition of **comedy** is "a play with a happy ending." Classical comedy, like classical tragedy, comprises the plays of ancient Greece and Rome (or comedies written before this century that have endured over time). Classical comedy continues to be popular in educational and professional theatre. In choosing such a play, your company can remain faithful to the original or update the presentation. Although much of the comedy derives from jokes about ancient times, the classical Greek or Roman comedy also includes physical humor that should work well for any audience. Many plays also include some coarseness, but this can be omitted with little damage to the plot or characterizations.

    Comedy of Manners. Comedies of manners satirize the manners and attitudes of a given segment of society. They include the witty plays of the Restoration, such as George Etherege's *The Man of Mode,* Anna Cora Mowatt's social comedies of the mid-nineteenth century, the late-nineteenth century comedies of Oscar Wilde, and, in this century, the many clever comedies of Noel Coward, Philip Barry, and Alan Ayckbourn.

Modern Comedy. Modern comedy includes all plays of a generally happy nature and ending. These may provoke laughter or simply pleasantly amuse, and they usually include romantic situations. The humor may come from the situations, the characters, the dialogue, or from a combination of these. Some people mistakenly think comedy is easier to perform than serious plays. Not so! The characters need to be very carefully developed, and timing is all-important. Poor timing of a comic line can kill the expected laugh, just as poor timing of a serious line can provoke an unwanted laugh.

Farce

Farce is an extreme form of comedy that depends on quick tempo and flawless timing by the actors. Since farce often contains improbable events and farfetched coincidences, the audience must not be allowed time to think things through. Brandon Thomas (*Charley's Aunt*) and George S. Kaufman and Moss Hart (*The Man Who Came to Dinner, You Can't Take It With You*) have provided many farces that are popular with educational, community, and professional theatre companies.

Musical

Although many musicals are also comedies, many contemporary musicals—*Les Miserables, Dream Girls, Phantom of the Opera*— are quite serious. More often, though, if you want to do a musical, you will choose the staples of the American theatre that never disappoint an audience or a company, such as *Bye Bye Birdie, Brigadoon,* and the operettas of Gilbert and Sullivan. Performing in musicals, obviously, requires singing and dancing as well as acting talent.

In addition to acting talent, performers in musicals must have dancing and singing ability.

SOURCES OF PLAYS

Once you have chosen the *type* of play you'd like to produce, you need to find the play that is right for your audience, budget, actors, and performance space.

To help you in your pursuit, look to your public school and libraries. The library may have the actual play scripts or the text of a play included in an anthology. In the latter case there may also be some commentary on the play that can help you assess what the production will require. Some books will include scenes from a variety of plays, and this textbook, as well, has a section of scenes from plays that are appropriate for educational theatre. Reading the scene can help you get a feeling for the whole play.

Another source to explore is the catalogues from play publishing companies and from bookstores that offer mail-order service. Samuel French Inc., Dramatists Play Service Inc., and the Dramatic Publishing Company hold the rights to most of the plays available for performance. Looking through their catalogues can help you make a list of possible choices for your company. The Samuel French catalogue is arranged in sections according to the number of characters required for the play. Dramatists Play Service provides a brief listing of "Character Breakdown of Plays"; to find the individual play, you can consult the index. The Dramatic Publishing Company provides an alphabetical index as well as an index organized by number of characters required in the play. In each catalogue the entries are brief but descriptive and include information such as number of sets required and type of audience and type of company for which the play is suitable.

Once the play has been chosen, your next consideration is the matter of **royalties**—the amount of money you must pay in order to perform the play. You will need to contact the publisher holding the rights to the play and ask permission to perform it. If there is another production of the same play planned for the same time in your area, the publisher may refuse permission, so don't wait until the last minute to submit your request. If the publisher grants permission, it will also quote the royalty. Keep in mind that newer plays usually have higher rates than older ones. Musicals generally have higher fees than straight (nonmusical) plays because music royalties are involved as well.

If you have a very low budget, consider a nonroyalty play such as Shakespeare or something from the nonroyalty list in the Samuel French or Dramatic Publishing catalogue. The Samuel French list includes full-length as well as one-act nonroyalty plays. As long as you buy copies of the script for every part and present a single performance, Samuel French will allow the nonroyalty play to be presented without a fee. Dramatic Publishing offers only short plays in the nonroyalty category. The only stipulation is that one script must be purchased for each cast member.

AUDITIONS

To cast the play, your director may choose to work with your class or theatre group for several weeks on theatre basics and then assign parts as they seem best suited. Sometimes, parts will be switched around in the course of early rehearsals until the director is satisfied that the best cast for the play has been assembled. Usually, those who are not assigned parts will be asked to take a technical responsibility in the production, such as running the lights or helping build the set.

Often, however, your director will hold **auditions,** or try-outs, for the parts. Auditions involve prepared readings, cold readings, or prepared monologues.

Prepared Readings

For a prepared reading audition, copies of the script are made available beforehand so you can become familiar with the plot and prepare portions to read aloud. To do well, you must read the play not only to understand the plot, but also to study the characters and the theme of the play. In other words, you must analyze what the play means as well as what happens in it. It's best if you choose a character whose physical description most closely resembles your own. This is called **typecasting,** that is, casting an actor who fits the physical type of the character to be played. Often, physical attributes of a character are important in the plot or dialogue. For example, in Shakespeare's *A Midsummer Night's Dream,* much of the quarreling between Hermia and Helena includes comments on the difference in their heights. And in Owen and Donald Davis's adaptation of *Ethan Frome,* Mattie explains that she hasn't the strength in her arms to do the household chores well.

If the character you wish to play is much older than you, you must audition with an understanding of the vocal and physical challenge that playing such a character would present. Be prepared to show how you would stand, sit, move, and speak as an older person. In holding a prepared reading audition, the director will expect to see some characterization and thought already present in your work.

Cold Readings

In a cold reading, scripts are not available ahead of time but are distributed at the audition. You will have a few minutes to glance over a part and then appear on the stage or at the front of the classroom. You will have a scene partner and be asked to read aloud from the script. To do well in this situation, you should quickly skim the material for its sense and then read with some understanding. Refrain from commenting about the quality of the play—never remark that it is hard to understand, that some words are difficult to pronounce, or that the character doesn't seem interesting. The director has chosen this play after careful consideration, may even have written it, and intends to produce it. He or she will not appreciate hearing complaints from someone hoping for a part in it.

Try to communicate that you are calm, intelligent, poised, interested, and serious about the reading. Although the director will not expect a full-blown characterization at this point, you should demonstrate a good understanding of the lines and use a clear reading voice. On the day of an audition it's best not to wear anything distracting or uncomfortable. Auditioners who are constantly tugging at or fussing with their clothing don't appear confident or ready to work. As you skim the script, note the stage directions for clues about the action of the scene. If you should mistakenly read a stage direction aloud, don't giggle, act upset, or elaborately apologize. Simply apologize briefly and calmly and continue reading.

To do well in cold readings, you need to be a good sight reader, and that skill comes only with practice. Make it a point to read aloud at least fifteen minutes a day. Sight reading is a useful ability, not only in auditions, but in any situation in which

To do well in cold readings, practice reading aloud every day for at least fifteen minutes.

you have to read aloud. Any material will do for practice—even the back of the cereal box at the breakfast table. Especially effective, however, are letters to the editor in a local newspaper. Often, those letters were written in the heat of anger, dismay, indignation, or concern. Their emotional content should be reflected in your reading. This makes them ideal material for sight reading practice. Try working with a tape recorder as well, so you can gauge your speed, enunciation, and vocal variety as you read aloud.

Prepared Monologues

The last type of audition—the prepared monologue—requires you to present a monologue that you have memorized and rehearsed. Usually, these monologues last two to five minutes. You may be asked to present two monologues, one serious and one comedic, or one modern and one classical (something from a previous century that remains relevant or noteworthy). Shakespeare is a favorite choice for the classic monologue, as are Sophocles, Aristophanes, Sheridan, Goldsmith, Molière, Shaw and Wilde.

The monologue you choose should not be studied in isolation. In other words, you should read the entire play in order to

The director may ask you to deliver a two- to five-minute memorized monologue for your audition.

fully understand your excerpt. You should analyze the character you are portraying so that if the director asks you questions you can answer knowledgeably. This is especially important if you are attempting a **character role,** that is, someone quite unlike you in age, voice, personality, or physical characteristics.

In preparing your monologue, take care to look up any unfamiliar words in a good dictionary, so that you can say them smoothly and with understanding.

Musical Auditions

If the show is a musical, you will be asked to present a song as well as a monologue during your audition. If you want piano accompaniment, provide sheet music for the pianist (unless you have been told to prepare a number from the show to be produced). Usually you will not be asked to perform a solo dance. Instead, the director or choreographer will divide the auditioners into groups of four to eight and will teach you a combination of dance steps. You will be expected to learn these quickly and perform them as part of the audition. For more on musical auditions, turn to Chapter 12.

Improvisations

After your director has heard everyone read for parts, he or she may ask you to participate in some **improvisations.** These are spontaneous episodes created by an actor or actors without using a script. This kind of exercise shows the director how quickly you can think on your feet and how well you work with other people. To do well in improvisations of any kind, you need to observe people carefully, listen to speech patterns and conversations, and read fiction and nonfiction regularly to give you a background of experiences to draw upon and use in an improvisation.

After Auditions

Probably more people will audition than there are parts available. When the cast is announced, some people will not have been given a part. If this happens to you, remember that it is not a rejection of you as a person. Sometimes, the director isn't looking for the best actor, but for the person who comes closest to the appearance and personality of the character in the play. This is typecasting—a perfectly acceptable way of casting a show. If there was no suitable part for you in this play, remember that this does not indicate that there will be no part for you at another time in another play. You may be offered an opportunity to **understudy** (learn in order to substitute) a part in case the person originally chosen cannot continue. Or, you may be offered a technical responsibility. Take it! It means being a part of the production, sharing the excitement of the performance, and, important for the next opportunity, demonstrating your dependability, positive attitude, and capabilities. Directors remember qualities such as these the next time auditions are held.

SUMMARY

There are several genres of plays; tragedy, melodrama, comedy, and farce are the four major types. In selecting a play for your company you need to consider the expectations of your potential audience, your budget, the abilities of your actors, and your performance space. To cast a play, directors hold auditions at which you may be asked to present a prepared reading, a cold reading, a prepared monologue, and, if the play is a musical, a song. If you are not cast in the play, accept a technical responsibility to participate in the production.

GREEK COMEDY

When most people think of classical Greek drama, they think of the great tragedies, but Greek drama included comedy, too. The boisterous interludes between the tragedies at a day-long festival evolved into what became known as Old Comedy, Middle Comedy, and New Comedy. Old Comedy contained elements of fantasy, music, and a plot line concerned with working out a "happy idea." The chief playwright of Old Comedy was Aristophanes, whose plays are still performed today. Middle Comedy brought a greater realism to plot and language. The role of the chorus, so important in the tragedies, dwindled, and playwriting became a profession. New Comedy was concerned with the manners and activities of the leisure class, much like the comedies of manners which followed centuries later, and it presented stock characters like the loyal slave, the foundling, the miser, and the adventurer.

CLASSICAL ROMAN COMEDY

Comedy in ancient Rome derived from Greek New Comedy. The Greek influence can be seen especially in the use of stock characters. Roman audiences liked plots that concerned mistaken identity, clever servants, young lovers, or old men with complaining wives.

As in Greece, festivals in Rome provided an occasion for play performances. The Roman theatre, like the Greek, was a vast outdoor structure that could accommodate thousands of spectators. In the second and third centuries B.C., the comedies of Plautus and Terence, based on earlier Greek models, were popular. They in turn influenced later playwrights.

OTHER ROMAN DRAMA

All classical Roman tragedy was based on Greek plays. There are many examples of both the Roman plays and their Greek originals still in existence, so we can compare them. For example, the Roman playwright and philosopher Seneca wrote an

Aristophanes (445?–380? B.C.) was the greatest writer of ancient Greek comedy.

Oedipus tragedy based on the Sophocles play, but he added a ghost scene.

All Roman performances were state-financed and free to the public. Gradually the entertainments became huge spectacles that included gladiator contests. When the amphitheatre popularly known as the Colosseum was built, it featured events filled with slaughter of humans and animals. The public lost interest in acted drama, wanting to see more battles to the death and other savagery. Shortly after, the decline of the Roman empire ended theatre and drama in the Western world for centuries. When theatre finally revived, it was once again in a religious ceremony, as in ancient Greece.

The Roman theatre was a vast outdoor structure that could seat thousands of spectators.

Research Projects

1. Even though this term's play may have been selected, you can plan for the future. In order to create a list of possibilities, turn to the section in the Samuel French catalogue listing plays for a cast of twelve. Skim the descriptions and select five plays that seem to be good possibilities for the actors in your company.

2. Check out an anthology of plays from your public or school library. Keeping in mind the expectations of your potential audience, choose one play that would meet those expectations.

3. Examine a number of acting editions of plays for the set design provided there. Then select a play that could be staged effectively in your company's performance space.

4. Choose any play by Shakespeare and make a list of the ideas, problems, and situations it contains that could apply to life today.

5. Form a team to walk all around your school listing every possible space usable for play performance. Be sure to consider outdoor as well as indoor sites.

6. Working with a theoretical budget of $500, select a play that could be produced in your theatre, for your audience, and with your company.

7. Conduct a survey in your other classes to determine specific plays or kinds of plays that your classmates would be interested in seeing for your next production.

Performance Projects

1. From a collection of comic monologues in the library or from a play you know, prepare and present a two-to-five-minute monologue suitable for an audition.

2. First, spend some time in a clinic waiting room or a senior citizens' center observing the elderly. Then, with another company member, improvise a scene between two elderly friends meeting unexpectedly and exchanging news. Be sure to use the physical and vocal characteristics you observed earlier.

3. Analyze your physical character type as an actor and then prepare and present a two-to-five-minute serious monologue that suits your character type.

The Actor

Anyone with experience in the theatre knows that every member of a company makes a valuable contribution to the production. For most audience members, however, the actors *are* the show. This places a heavy responsibility on the actor, who must give the best performance possible each time he or she steps on the stage. To ensure a superior level of performance, actor Michael Jeter says he never stops rehearsing.

Born in 1952 in Lawrenceburg, Tennessee, Jeter was one of six children. He attended the University of Memphis, first as a premedical major and then as an acting major. Following graduation he moved to New York City and almost immediately was cast in the 1978 Circle in the Square revival of Kaufman and Hart's *Once in a Lifetime*. Next he appeared in the Public Theatre's production of *The Master and Margarita*. He won a *Theatre World* Award the following year for his work as Straw in David Berry's Vietnam era play *G. R. Point*.

Jeter followed that part with a variety of roles in Elizabeth Swardo's *Alice in Concert*, a musical version of *Alice in Wonderland* that starred Meryl Streep. Next he played an Irish American police officer in *El Bravo,* a reworking of the Robin Hood legend. He worked with Tommy Tune, who would later direct him in *Grand Hotel,* when he took over a part in Caryl Churchill's *Cloud 9*. Later he took over for another actor, Jason Williams, in the Circle in the Square's production of *Greater Tuna*. Since there are only two actors in the show, Michael Jeter played eleven roles and remarked that every time he left the stage he changed clothes!

For the role of Arnold, a mentally retarded adult in Tom Griffin's *The Boys Next Door,* Jeter prepared by spending time in a group home for the mentally retarded. He found it a "joyful experience." The same year, in Jim Geoghan's *Only Kidding!,* the critic Howard Kissel called him "brilliant" as a nervous wreck of a writer.

One of his more recent Broadway appearances was as Kringelein in Luther Davis's *Grand Hotel*. Edith Oliver, stage critic for *The New Yorker,* called him a "dandy eccentric dancer," and *TheaterWeek* reviewer Ken Mandelbaum said Jeter had "walked off" with the show. Jeter won a Tony Award for that role, and in his acceptance speech, alluding to his personal struggles, he asked anyone watching the awards program who felt hopeless to see Jeter as living proof that life can change and dreams do come true.

Michael Jeter is familiar to millions of television viewers for his Emmy Award–winning role of Herman Stiles in the television comedy hit *Evening Shade*. His character was the favorite of many, but Jeter remained the true ensemble player, working always for the good of the show.

Taking On Responsibilities

3

Company Meeting

Now that the play has been chosen and cast, it's time to begin rehearsals. For several weeks the actors will be on stage while the technicians work behind the scenes. The company meeting is a chance for groups to come together, confer, raise questions, and offer solutions.

PROGRESS REPORTS

Some company members may have started their jobs even before the first rehearsal and will want to inform the company of their progress. For example, the assistant director and the stage manager may have already consulted with the director about the rehearsal schedule and can now announce any changes. The house manager may have learned of a plan to remove a row of seats in the house in order to accommodate wheelchair patrons. Not only will this change the ticket count for the house, it will give the house management/publicity crew specific information to include in their press releases. Results of any work for the show should be shared with the company at this point in the meeting.

TOPICS FOR THIS MEETING
- Rehearsing
- The Responsibilities of the Assistant Director
- The Responsibilities of the Stage Manager
- The Prompt Book
- The Read Through
- Blocking
- The Blocking Plot
- Stage Business
- Rehearsal Space
- The Story of Theatre: The Far East
- Theatre Workshop
- Careers in the Theatre: The Director

WORKING VOCABULARY

As rehearsals proceed, you will need to add to your understanding of theatre vocabulary. Key terms in this chapter are *read through, stage business, sound cue, read in, greenroom, prompt book, pickup rehearsal, objective, obstacle, proscenium stage, raked, arena stage, thrust stage, Bugaku, Noh, Kabuki,* and *Shingeki.*

AGENDA

At the next meeting you'll discuss subtext and the rehearsal technique of shadowing, theatre architecture, types of sets, and clothing styles through the ages. In addition, company members will report on their progress.

REHEARSING

Actors can hardly wait for rehearsals to begin. The first **read through,** when you know the part is yours and you sit down with the rest of the cast to read the play together, is almost as exciting as opening night. Of course, you can't expect to hold that level of excitement through weeks or months of rehearsal. There are bound to be setbacks along the way. For example, the first rehearsal off book often seems like a big step backward. The first rehearsal after the set load-in may find you bumping into walls and tripping over furniture that has suddenly appeared on the stage. Add the props, and you may find your-self continuing to mimic the action even though you now have the cup or sword at hand. Don't be discouraged though, because these things happen to every company. Instead, con-centrate even harder on keeping lines, blocking, props, the set, and, most importantly, your character, in mind.

Bring a pencil or pen to all rehearsals until you are off book. If you are told not to write in the playbook itself, then carry scratch paper, as well. If you have been instructed to highlight your part in the book, be sure you do so before the first read through.

The first read through can be almost as exciting as opening night.

Beyond a pen and some scratch paper, you may need to bring additional equipment to rehearsals. For example, occasionally the costumes for a play are so different from what you are accustomed to or present so many movement problems that the director will ask you to wear a version of the costume through rehearsals—a hoop skirt that must be danced in, a cartwheel hat that is to be held through long passages of dialogue, a leg cast or arm sling—anything that presents special challenges for maneuverability.

RESPONSIBILITIES OF THE ASSISTANT DIRECTOR

Although the assistant director (AD) does not direct the play, he or she assists the director in numerous ways. This is a fascinating job for a person who handles responsibility well and enjoys keeping details organized and running smoothly. The assistant director confers with the director before each rehearsal to confirm the plans for that session. At the company meeting the AD

The assistant director works with the actors individually to make sure every line is delivered accurately.

checks that everyone is present; if an actor is absent, the AD informs the understudy so he or she can be ready to step in. The AD makes notes of the progress reports and any problems raised to serve as a reminder for the director later. As soon as the cast and crew are determined, the AD prepares and distributes a company roster and sets up a telephone tree to pass along any emergency messages or changes in rehearsal times. During rehearsals the AD notes in his or her playbook all the director's instructions as to blocking, **stage business** (all onstage actions, except blocking), lighting changes, **sound cues** (signals for sound effects), or line readings.

The assistant director keeps the blocking plot—the diagram of the blocking or stage movement. In the early rehearsals he or she may also be responsible for simulating sound effects—the ringing of a phone, the chime or buzz of a doorbell—until the sound person has the cues ready. If the understudy is already standing in for one missing actor, the AD may need to **read in,** that is, read from the house the lines of any absent or tardy actors.

Since the director cannot direct with one eye on the book, the AD must ensure that every line is delivered accurately and every word is pronounced correctly. When an actor has trouble with a particular word or line, the AD works with that person individually until the difficulty is overcome. The AD also rehearses blocking with the understudies, since they don't get the stage time the cast does.

While the director takes the main cast through a rehearsal, the AD may take a small group through their lines in a corner of the house or backstage. At each rehearsal the AD makes notes of lines missed, words mispronounced, blocking confused, stage business forgotten—any areas that need special attention at the next rehearsal.

Clearly, the job of assistant director is demanding, but the experience is valuable for anyone considering being a director someday.

RESPONSIBILITIES OF THE STAGE MANAGER

Simply put, the stage manager (SM) runs the show from backstage. Even before the rehearsals begin, however, the stage manager is at work on the various technical aspects of the production. He or she must coordinate the director's work with that of the actors, the designers, and the technicians.

At the beginning of production the SM works with the assistant director to organize and communicate information. The rehearsal timetable is obtained from the director and conveyed to the company by way of announcements posted on the bulletin board and delivered over the school public address system, at school assemblies, and at company meetings. Once rehearsals are under way, the SM keeps his or her own blocking plot in order to anticipate problems with quick costume changes, scene shifting, coordination of lighting and sound effects with stage action, and, of course, to see that actors make their entrances on time.

Stage managers need to be decisive yet diplomatic. The area backstage must be kept orderly and quiet during rehearsal as well as performance, so everyone must recognize the authority of the SM. At the same time, the SM cannot be a dictator who orders people around with no regard for their feelings or their job difficulties. A clear understanding of theatre etiquette and respect for the chain of command will help everyone to feel a genuine company spirit.

Once the set has been loaded-in, the SM does a walk-through of stage and offstage areas before each rehearsal begins. He or she checks that the stage is properly set, with all furniture and props in their correct positions. If there is no **greenroom**— a room offstage, often with a television monitor of the stage, where the actors can wait to go on—the stage manager must arrange seating backstage or in the wings for the cast. When everything is set, the stage manager gives the signal for the curtain to be raised or the stage lights to come up so the rehearsal or performance can begin.

The stage manager needs a base behind the scenes, out of the way of entrances and exits and scene changes, but from which he or she can see everything and attend to responsibilities. This base of operations should be established from the start so that company members know where to find the SM.

As outlined in Chapter One, the stage manager is chief of all the technical crews and runs the strike after the last performance. In running the show itself, the SM uses the script on which he or she has marked all the blocking, stage business, lighting, sound, and scene change cues.

Combining Responsibilities

In a small company the jobs of assistant director and stage manager may be combined. The two positions merge well because each sees the production in its totality. One necessary adjustment, however, is that the assistant director must move from the house area to backstage once load-in has occurred. Since the understudies will sit in the house to watch rehearsal, they can act as note takers for the director and as messengers to and from the assistant director/stage manager.

THE PROMPT BOOK

Because the acting edition of a play usually is only 5" × 8" and the margins are small, the assistant director and stage manager need to prepare a book that will allow for notes. Once called a script, this now is known as a **prompt book.** To prepare the prompt book, take $8^1/_2$" × 11" sheets of paper and cut a window in each that is one-half inch smaller than the pages of the playbook. Separate the pages of the playbook and using paste or tape, mount each one on a sheet of the windowed paper. This will provide room for your notes.

In running the show, the stage manager uses a script marked up with all of the blocking, stage business, and technical cues.

Another method is to write only warnings of cues and the cues themselves in the actual book, keeping a separate blocking plot on graph paper. Since the blocking is determined well before the play opens, the SM need have only the cue-marked book backstage during performances. The assistant director can keep the blocking plot for any **pick-up rehearsals**, that is, rehearsals called after the play has opened to polish or correct problem areas.

If the blocking plot is kept separately from the prompt book, it can easily be prepared using sheets of 8½" × 11" graph paper turned horizontally. Staple the sheets to cardboard backing to

Figure 3.1.
Sample prompt book page.

Warning: *Sound*	Rob:	Get your things together, everyone; we're leaving this place!
	Ed:	(*Going through his belongings*) Hey. My buck's missing!
	John:	Your dollar?
	Ed:	No. My buck knife. I had it when we were eating.
	Rob:	It's gotta be around here somewhere.
	Sandy:	You don't think . . . ?
Sound cue	*Everyone stands frozen. In the silence there is a tapping sound at the window. People shriek and cling together.*	
Warning: *Entrance Leroy*	Rob:	(*Disgusted*) Danny.
	Sandy:	What if it's not?
	Kathy:	Ed's knife . . .
	Linda:	The escaped convict . . .
	Rob:	(*Insisting*) Danny.
	Ed:	(*Bravely*) Let's go out and see.
	All try to leave together.	
	Rob:	(*Motioning to the others to stay*) Ed and I'll go.
Entrance: *Rob, Ed, Leroy*	*Rob and Ed exit and return immediately with a protesting Leroy.*	
	Leroy:	I tell you I wasn't doing any harm out there, just trying to keep out of the wind for a bit.
	Kathy:	That wasn't you tapping at the window?
	Leroy:	'Course not. Think I wanted to attract attention?
	Sandy:	(*Shaky voice*) Are you the escaped convict?
	Leroy:	(*Insulted*) No. Certainly not.

create a pad of paper or store them in a looseleaf binder. If you are the assistant director or stage manager, first make a floor plan of the set on the graph paper, deciding on the ratio of each square to a square foot of stage space. Then make several copies so that you can have one drawing for each change in blocking. Number the pages and write the corresponding play-book page number for cross-reference. The playbook, as well, should have page numbers added to cross-reference the blocking plot. This cross-referencing saves time when the director or cast calls upon the AD or SM for information.

On the sample shown on page 56, note the warning written in the margin that a sound cue is coming up. Following the warning is a note for the cue itself. The same pattern is used for an entrance cue. (If the greenroom is some distance from the stage, however, the stage manager must mark the entrance cue earlier in the book.) Changes in the lighting should be indicated as well. For emphasis, warnings and cues are marked in red, but some stage managers choose to further highlight them by taping a small red tab to the edge of each page on which there is a cue.

THE READ THROUGH

Most directors have the blocking in mind before they begin any rehearsals. They generally begin the rehearsal schedule with a read through with all the technical personnel present, so the company can get a clear understanding of the play. Because this is the first time the actors will read knowing who they are to play, they are eager and excited. Nonetheless, this is a time to listen carefully to the others and, especially, to any instructions the director may give.

Some directors will allow the actors to read through the play without interruptions, while others will begin immediately to correct the line readings and pronunciations. After the read through the director will discuss any notes he or she has made during the reading and then open a discussion of the play: its meaning; the various characters, including their **objectives** (goals), and the **obstacles** (characters or situations that prevent or delay achievement of the objectives); the structure of the play; the background of time and place; and any other issues that will help the entire company to understand the work ahead.

Report to the first read through with a good sense of the play itself and your part in it. Ask questions and make observations in the discussion that follows. Don't wait until you are well into production to ask what the play or your character is all about!

Depending on the length of rehearsals, the read through may require several sessions. Perhaps the director will have you focus on one scene or act per session. There may be a second read through after the discussion, after which most actors are eager to move on to the stage and the process of learning the blocking.

BLOCKING

If actors just stood still, frozen in space, audiences would soon grow bored. On the other hand, if actors moved about aimlessly, audiences would soon grow annoyed. Blocking, or directions for movement on stage, must be appropriate to the characters involved, the situation, and even the genre of the play. The movement must happen for a reason—not merely because an actor is tired of standing still. The blocking may be of a practical nature: the phone rings and a character moves to answer it. It may show emotion: a character cannot resist looking out a window, eagerly anticipating someone's arrival. Blocking may be provided by the stage directions in a play, although these directions need not be followed to the letter unless the director says so. After all, the playwright may have had a much bigger stage or more elaborate set in mind. Blocking may be suggested by the actor, who feels his or her character would rise, or sit down, or pick up a prop at a given moment. Mostly, however, the blocking is supplied by the director in keeping with the play, the cast, and the set design he or she has selected.

Stage Directions

In order to understand the director's instructions, you need to know the names for the various areas of the stage. Remember, *the designations are from the actor's point of view.*

Most schools have a **proscenium stage**, a stage enclosed by a proscenium arch—the "picture frame" through which the audi-

Figure 3.2. Stage areas: (a) proscenium stage; (b) arena stage; (c) thrust stage.

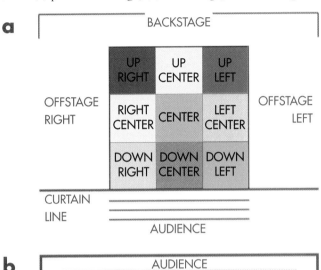

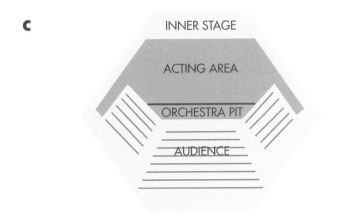

ence views the action. Figure 3.2a divides the proscenium stage into labeled sections. If, for example, you are standing at upstage left and are directed to cross to downstage right, you move diagonally across the stage from one side to the other, moving down, or toward the audience, as you cross. Although today most stages are not **raked**—that is, slanting up toward the back—the old designations of "up" and "down" still are used.

If you are working on an **arena stage** (in the round), you may find it helpful to think of the stage as a clock and designate areas by number. For instance, a stage direction might be, "Move to three o'clock." (See Figure 3.2b.) Another strategy is to use geographical designations such as north, south, southwest, and so on. A **thrust stage** (Figure 3.2c), surrounded on three sides by the audience, also lends itself to the geographic or clock designations.

Some General Reminders about Stage Movement

1. While you may move on (during) your own line, don't move on someone else's line unless you have been directed to do so to show disrespect or to attract attention.

2. If you need to turn your back on the audience for effect or because you are working on an arena stage, remember to compensate with voice projection.

3. Don't move so that an actor talking to you has to turn upstage to see you.

4. When making a turn, turn downstage, that is, into the audience's view, rather than upstage, or away from their view.

5. Adjust as needed so that you don't stand where you block another actor from view.

6. Unless otherwise indicated in a stage direction or by your director, stand with your weight firmly on both feet so that you won't sway or lose your balance.

Be warned: Blocking rehearsals go very slowly. There is much to understand and assimilate, so keep your energy up with proper rest and a healthful diet. All professional actors know the importance of doing so. In addition, don't hesitate to ask questions, but do phrase them concisely and listen to the answer so you don't have to ask again. Don't waste time with "Can I ask a question?" or "I'm sorry to have to interrupt, but . . . ." Just ask, "Is this where I cross?" Don't slow an already lengthy process with complaints or failure to bring a pencil to write down the blocking or line changes.

THE BLOCKING PLOT

To keep track of all the blocking, the assistant director and the stage manager keep the blocking plot—a series of floor plan drawings with the notations of each change in blocking clearly indicated. As shown in Figure 3.3a, each character is in position as the second act opens. In Figure 3.3b, you can see that two of the characters have changed positions.

Even though a blocking plot is being kept for the company, each actor needs to take responsibility for noting and memorizing his or her own blocking. If permitted, make notes on your own book (or use scratch paper) to help you remember during the early rehearsals. However, if you are in doubt about your position, ask a question rather than cause onstage confusion.

Figure 3.3. Sample blocking plot.

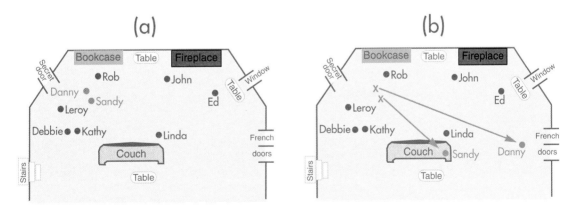

STAGE BUSINESS

Included in the action of a play is what the actors are doing while saying their lines. Are they, for example, working at some task, having a meal, reading a letter, playing cards? Again, while stage directions in the playbook provide some stage business, the lines themselves suggest other action. The actors realize as they go along that a gesture here and there can support their lines; usually, however, it is the director who assigns the stage business to each character.

As with blocking, stage business must be appropriate to the character, the type of play, and the situation. It must suit the time and place of the play, as well. Clearly, characters cannot play computerized games before they are invented or hum a tune before it is written!

REHEARSAL SPACE

Don't be disheartened if all your rehearsals can't be held on the stage. You may need to share the use of that space with other companies or groups. In fact, even the blocking rehearsals can take place in another space, as long as the stage manager measures the stage area carefully and then approximates it in the rehearsal space. If chalk or tape is not allowed on the floor of your rehearsal room, then mark boundaries by placing chairs at the four corners of your acting space and stringing ribbon or yarn to represent the walls.

SUMMARY

Once the play has been cast, the excitement and work of rehearsals begins. The assistant director prepares and keeps the prompt book, which contains all the blocking and cues for the company. The stage manager runs the show from backstage, acting as chief of all the technical crews. The read through is a chance to hear the play read and to discuss interpretation, characterization, and meaning with the company. Blocking and stage business must be appropriate and serve a purpose.

Through careful research and scholarship we are able to recreate our conception of classical Greek and Roman drama, but in Japan there are companies presenting dances and dramas today just as they were seen more than twelve centuries ago. Traditional Japanese theatre has continued uninterrupted since its beginning and has not undergone any drastic changes. The dances and dramas are intact and faithful to their origins. Traditional Japanese theatre usually has been performed by acting families—some of whom have been in the theatre for many generations. Japanese theatre also observes many conventions of stagecraft and features traditional costumes.

The earliest form of Japanese theatre, **Bugaku** began in the seventh century. It is a series of austere dances accompanied by *Gagaku,* orchestral music featuring drums, flutes, and gongs. The dances have charming and fanciful titles, such as "Dragons Basking in the Sun."

The second oldest form, **Noh** (or *No*) is about five hundred years old. It fuses dance with mime and is influenced by Zen Buddhism. The guiding principle of Noh drama is *Yugen,* meaning gracefulness, elegance, and fragility. Noh is not concerned with dramatic action. Instead, it presents a situation in lyrical form.

All Noh performers are men, and seldom is a cast larger than six characters. A chorus narrates much of the action and sings an actor's lines while he dances. The actors wear masks a little smaller than their faces, to remind the audience that what they are watching is theatre—not real life. Noh costumes are ancient ceremonial dress, rich in color and design.

Noh plays have five types of subjects: gods, warriors, women, mad people or spirits, and demons. A performance of Noh takes an entire day to present, as there is a play on each of the five subjects as well as short comedy interludes.

Kabuki, the third type of Japanese theatre, is fairly well known in the West thanks to movies and television. It began around 1600 and consists of three types of plays: historical, dance-plays, and domestic dramas. As with the other forms of traditional Japanese theatre, only men act in

In Noh theatre, actors wear masks and ceremonial dress rich in color and design.

Kabuki. They begin training at age six, appearing in children's roles at first. Kabuki theatre is largely a hereditary profession. No masks are used; instead, actors wear much colorful, elaborately patterned makeup. Some plays, *Chushingura,* for example, take all day to perform.

In addition to these classical forms of theatre, Japan has **Shingeki,** literally, "new theatre." Its playwrights deal with contemporary issues, and its actors need not come from old theatre families. Kinoshita Junji is an outstanding play-wright of the Shingeki form of theatre.

Like Japanese theatre, China's public entertainment dates back to the seventh century. It began with mime and dance. In China the classical stage has no front curtain, scenery, or realistic props. A tem-ple canopy, held up by two lacquered columns, decorates the acting area, and the backdrop is a screen or decorated cloth. The orchestra and prop man or woman are onstage and visible the whole time. Traditionally, men have played all the roles, but recently some women have taken part in the performance. An actor enters and tells the audience who he or she is and what he or she intends to do. Entering a house would be indicated by miming the opening of sliding doors. A table and chair may serve as mountains, walls, river banks, and so on. There may be a scene painted on a panel or a long pole with draped fabric. For winter the prop man or woman may shake out paper snowflakes.

There is so much singing in these plays that they are considered a kind of opera—Peking Opera, for the city most famous for this type of theatre. The dances require very stylized movements. The makeup is very vivid and uses colors sym-bolically: white for wickedness, red for loyalty, green and blue for demons, black for honesty.

Rather than having the Western divi-sions of comedy and tragedy, Chinese theatre divides into military and civilian dramas. Although the ancient forms are still popular as family entertainment, a modern theatre movement was founded in the 1930s. Its concerns are contemporary, largely influenced by Communism. Representative plays and playwrights are *Ballad of the Fair Women* by T'ien Han and *To Be a Soldier* by Hu Shao Hsuen.

Technical Preparation Projects

1. Act as a stage manager and collect names, addresses, phone numbers, homeroom numbers, and class schedules from everyone in the company. Prepare and distribute a company roster to all members. If several people want to try this project, one could handle the company while others choose a school sports team, club, or homeroom.

2. Act as an assistant director and organize a telephone tree in case a message needs to be passed along quickly. As with the previous project, if more than one person is interested in this task, organize a telephone tree for a school club or class as well.

3. Using an inexpensive copy of a play from a used-book store, do one of the following:
   a. Mark all the entrances and exits of the actors.
   b. Mark all the lighting cues.
   c. Mark all the sound and special effects cues.
   d. Mark all uses of props.
   e. Mark all examples of stage business.

4. Prepare a floor plan of your set. Make several copies, then mark the blocking on your floor plan for the first scene of your play.

5. Act as an assistant director and read through the playbook, marking any difficult wording. Check pronunciations in a dictionary so that you could prompt any actor having difficulty.

Acting Preparation Projects

1. In pairs, go through all the possible stage directions for one of the following. One partner should call out directions, and the other should follow them.
   a. An arena stage viewed like a clock.
   b. An arena stage viewed with geographical designations.
   c. A proscenium arch stage with standard designations.

2. Write a line that could be read in a variety of ways and ask your company to see how many different meanings they can give the line. Here is an example: "Bill is taking Sandy out to a movie tonight." It could be read to express jealousy of Bill or of Sandy; anger that they are seeing one another; mockery that one is going with the other; a longing to see a movie; amazement that Bill is spending some money; delight at this turn of events; disapproval of movies; and so on.

3. Select a play you know well and analyze one character's objectives, scene by scene, and the obstacles to his or her objectives. You might also try this exercise with a character from a favorite story, movie, or television program.

4. Divide the company into small groups. Then, with each member having a turn at performing while the others in the group watch, perform some of the following bits of stage business. Although these can be

mimed, most of them benefit from the actor talking about what he or she is doing. After your turn, ask the members of your small group to discuss what you were doing.

a. You enter an office to keep an appointment. No one is there. You smell smoke and notice there is a fire in the wastebasket.

b. You enter a nursery school, empty except for a crying child. You have no experience with children.

c. You enter a dark room to plant a tape recorder in order to gain evidence for a criminal investigation.

d. You are seated in a friend's living room waiting for her to come downstairs. Her very large dog approaches you.

e. You are playing cards with a friend when he is called away to the phone.

f. You decide to clean out your purse or wallet.

g. You are trying to follow a complicated recipe being given on television.

h. You are trying to give your cat her medicine, but she doesn't want to take it.

i. You are wrapping an odd-shaped gift.

j. You are styling a friend's hair for her, but it isn't turning out right.

k. You are raking leaves in a wind storm.

l. It is your first time at a self-serve gas station.

m. You are trying to take a photograph of six puppies.

5. Choosing four or five characters from your play, invent a piece of stage business for each that helps bring out some aspect of that character's personality or state of mind.

The Director

Since the director of a play is responsible for its interpretation, many directors are tempted to make all the choices for the actors. That is not the case with Tony Award–winning director Lloyd Richards, who explained in an *American Theatre* interview, "My desire is to lead the actor to discover what I want him to discover so that he feels it is his own. He has to perform it, so it should come out of him rather than out of something I said." Apparently this preference goes back to Richards's own days as an actor, when he didn't appreciate directors who gave him line readings.

Richards has served as dean of the prestigious Yale School of Drama, director of the Yale Repertory Theatre, artistic director of the National Playwrights Conference of the Eugene O'Neill Theatre Center, president of Theatre Communications Group, and the first representative from a not-for-profit professional (regional) theatre to the National Council for the Arts. His collaboration with playwright August Wilson began in 1982, and over the years the two have won an impressive array of awards, including Tonys for *Fences,* for which Wilson also won a Pulitzer Prize.

Richards was born in Toronto and raised in Detroit. His father, a Jamaican-born carpenter, died when Richards was nine, and his mother, who became blind when Richards was in his teens, raised five children alone during the Depression. Richards was a prelaw student at Wayne State University until World War II interrupted his studies. After serving in the army he returned to college, but soon acting in college productions replaced his interest in the legal profession. While still in Detroit he hosted a radio jazz show called "The Good Will Hour."

By the 1950s he had moved to New York, where he worked in radio, off Broadway, and on Broadway in *Freight*. The turning point came in 1959, when he directed his first Broadway production, Lorraine Hansberry's New York Drama Critics Circle Award–winning *A Raisin in the Sun*. After that he never returned to acting.

The entire Richards family is involved in show business. Richards is married to actor Barbara Davenport. One son, Scott, is a composer, and the other, Thomas, is a protégé of director Jerzy Grotowski.

Richards's belief in the potential of America's regional theatre is evident in his desire to share the work he does with regional theatres all over the country. He explains that when he first began as artistic director of the National Playwrights Conference he received about 300 scripts a year. Now the figure is 1,300 to 1,800 submissions, and Richards detects better writing even in the scripts he cannot accept for production. He attributes this improvement largely to the growth of the regional theatre.

67

Designers
at Work

4

69

Company Meeting

At this stage in your production almost everyone will be eager to bring the others up to date on the work under way, so it's best to establish an order for reports at the company meeting.

PROGRESS REPORTS

Once the assistant director has checked attendance, the director outlines the topics to be covered at the meeting, makes general comments on the progress of the production, and answers any pertinent questions. Next, the assistant director asks a representative of each technical area, in turn, for a report. Some technicians may not have anything to report at the time, while others will have accomplishments to share. Company members should mention any difficulties that have arisen and ask for help. It's best to call for reports in alphabetical order each meeting, ensuring no one is overlooked or has cause to feel slighted at being called late in the rotation. Under this system the assistant director, who speaks for the actors as well as him- or herself, reports first. Then, in the order shown, the following are heard from: costume designer, graphic artist, hairstylist, house manager, lighting designer-engineer, makeup artist, master builder, properties manager, publicist, set designer, sound engineer, stage crew chief, stage manager, wardrobe manager.

To save time, technicians may present combined reports. For example, publicity and graphic designer could be added to house management's report, and information from the master builder, set designer, and stage crew chief could be incorporated into the stage management report. The goal is an equitable system that allows everyone to share relevant information in an efficient manner.

TOPICS FOR THIS MEETING

- The Assistant Director At Work
- Subtext
- Shadowing
- Performance Space
- Functions of Stage Sets
- Types of Stage Sets
- Four Methods of Set Design
- Show and Tell
- Costumes Through the Ages
- The Story of Theatre: Medieval Drama
- Theatre Workshop
- Careers in the Theatre: The Costume Designer

WORKING VOCABULARY

This chapter focuses on both understanding the meaning of the play you're working on and the various types of stage sets. Key terms used in this chapter include *subtext, flat, mansion setting, exposition, theme, abstract set, arras set, box set, unit set, periaktos (prism set), ground row,* and *rear projection.*

AGENDA

At the next meeting you'll discuss line memorization techniques, voice production, housekeeping and safety, and set construction. Also, company members will present production progress reports.

THE ASSISTANT DIRECTOR AT WORK

While the designers are doing their research and making their preliminary sketches, the actors are rehearsing with the director and the assistant director. By now the read through and the blocking rehearsals are completed and the cast is on its feet, still on book, taking direction and going over and over their lines. The assistant director is at the director's side noting any changes in lines, blocking, stage business, or problem areas that may need special rehearsal. He or she is often called upon to be a messenger to the technical crews, keeping everyone up to date on schedules and developments in the production. The assistant director, like the stage manager, needs to have all the details in mind so that the director's vision of the production is carried out.

SUBTEXT

At this point in the rehearsal schedule your director may ask the actors to do some special work on **subtext.** This term refers to the thoughts, feelings, and reactions implied but never stated in the dialogue of a play. The subtext may be supplied by the

After read throughs and blocking rehearsals, cast members
continue to work on their lines with the assistant director.

actors, the director, or both as they interpret the roles of the characters. To understand a play fully, the audience must be able to infer the subtext as it is suggested by the actors' body language, facial expressions, gestures, and line readings.

The work on subtext may be a homework assignment for your production logbook or a formal exercise in class. Sometimes actors learn their lines without a full understanding of the thoughts and feelings that lie beneath the words. Exploring the subtext furthers your understanding of the characters' ambitions and personalities. You can then express that understanding in your line readings and body language as you perform.

If your director prefers you to work on subtext on your own, begin by selecting any portion of your part that you are having trouble learning or understanding. Sometimes difficulty in learning lines comes from not understanding them clearly. In your logbook, write out the first line and, below it, write what you believe the line means, or what your character is feeling and thinking when you say the line. Follow this pattern for each line in the section that has been difficult for you. If the director has not made this a specific assignment, he or she may not have time immediately to review your notes, but you can try the subtext out on a parent, friend, or company member. Ask if it seems logical and truthful to the text itself and the character you play. Even if no one else reads what you have written, the exercise itself, if carried out conscientiously, should help you in understanding your part.

SHADOWING

A formal class exercise that is helpful for understanding subtext is called shadowing. The exercise works best for monologues or two-person scenes; if more parts are involved it can get confusing. For the two-person scene, two actors stand in to recite the lines of the scene while the two actors actually cast in the parts stand behind them as "shadows." Actor One speaks the first line of dialogue and then Shadow One (the actor who actually has the part in the play) speaks what he or she feels is the subtext. Actor Two responds and Shadow Two (again, the actor actually playing the part in the play) speaks what he or she feels is the subtext of that line, and so on through the scene. Though they are on book, the substitutes should be familiar with the script so they are not fumbling when reciting lines. In addition, they must allow time for the Shadows to voice the subtext before going on to say their next line. Throughout the exercise the director can comment, suggest, and correct.

Example of Shadow Subtext

In this example the subtext is in parentheses.

Amaya: Mom, I can't find my leggings again.
(Shadow: Why is this place such a pig sty?)

Mother: They're probably right where you took them off. Look, here they are!
(Shadow: Do I have to do everything for you?)

Amaya: Not those. I need the white ones.
(Shadow: Can't you keep up on the styles?)

Mother: Oh, you're not wearing those to the dance. You'll look like your underwear's showing.
(Shadow: At least I know what looks good.)

Amaya: No one would think that. It's what they all wear.
(Shadow: You don't have a clue.)

Mother: Do you have to look like a ragamuffin just because they all do?
(Shadow: Have some originality.)

Amaya: You just don't like me to wear them because Dad bought them for me.
(Shadow: You're trying to shut him out of my life.)

Mother: I don't like you to wear them because I like to see you looking pretty.
(Shadow: Your father is always trying to undermine my authority. I have all the responsibility . . .)

Amaya: I'll wear the pink dress next time, so can I go now?
(Shadow: Let's each give in a little.)

PERFORMANCE SPACE

All the world may be a stage, as Shakespeare said, but some-times it's hard to find a place to put on your play. If you have the use of a theatre—whether it be arena, thrust, or proscenium arch—your set designer can get to work right away to create the setting for your play. However, if you need to find a space, con-sider the cafeteria, the science lab, the gym, or, if the weather permits, any cleared outdoor area of the school that can be lit. If you want to give only daytime performances, then the lighting need not be a consideration. If none of these spaces is available, try giving performances for small audiences in the largest class-room you can find. Don't give up, because there is a play for every space and a way to light and create a set on any clear area you can secure. While it's true that such "found space" tests the ingenuity of the designers, most of them welcome the challenge, and certainly the sense of accomplishment can be all the greater at managing to transform the chemistry lab into an Irish pub for John Millington Synge's *The Playboy of the Western World* or a school courtyard into the forest of Arden for Shakespeare's *As You Like It.*

Figure 4.1.   Adapting (a) the gymnasium and (b) the cafeteria for performance.

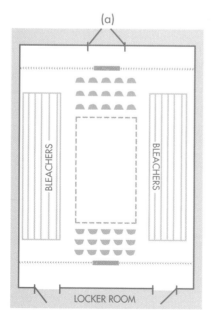

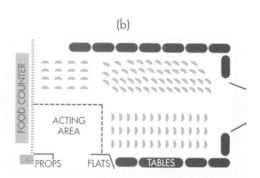

Adapting School Interiors

If you will be using a standard classroom with movable desks, first consider the location of the door. If there are two doors to the room, use one for the audience to enter and exit and the other for the actors to enter and leave the set. Set up screens in the hallway immediately outside to serve as wings or space for a quick costume change. Secure an adjoining classroom for use as offstage, so that costume changes, props, and small furnishings are immediately available during a performance. If there is only one door, obviously it needs to be used by both the audience and the actors. In that case the set can be a freestanding back-drop, a series of **flats** (fabric-covered wooden frames), or an arrangement of screens behind which there is room left for a backstage.

Remember, when you set up the chairs for the audience, you should stagger the rows so that no seat is directly behind the one in front of it. If you want to use the width of the room for the playing area, then arrange a few long rows of seats in a gen-tle curve or horseshoe. You will have created a thrust stage for your show.

If you are using the gym and it has bleachers, those will serve to seat part of the audience, while folding chairs on the gym floor itself can accommodate the rest. However, be sure to find out whether the gym floor should first be protected by some kind of covering before positioning chairs or scenery on it.

For plays performed in the cafeteria, remember that the food service counter provides a convenient storage area for props and other small items needed for quick changes of costume or set. Position screens or flats accordingly. If using a cafeteria or gym, you can borrow an idea from medieval drama—**mansion set-tings.** These are simple constructions on small platforms, repre-senting the various scenes in the play. In the medieval plays the actors moved from mansion to mansion and the audience fol-lowed them. The lighting should be directed on the set in use, then moved along to the next set as needed.

Adapting the Outdoors

While an athletic field with bleachers is fine for a large-scale production, such as a chronicle play recreating the founding of your town or the re-creation of a classical Greek tragedy, it is too vast a space for most plays. However, you can use part of the field to create an arena or central stage, or a thrust stage with the seating in a semicircle or horseshoe around the acting area. A large wooden platform, built on the site or built elsewhere in sections and then moved, can serve as a stage. Or, chairs can be placed on this platform to accommodate the audience. Test for sound and use microphones if you have to, though it's best to keep the area used small enough to project naturally.

The stadium lighting already in place may be sufficient for all but special effects. Remember, too, that portable light trees are easily assembled and used.

For any open area you choose, it's important to first investigate the surroundings for noise, passersby, and other distractions. Make the area as secure as you can, both for performances and rehearsals. In turn, make sure that your activity doesn't disturb others nearby.

The ideal outdoor performance area is free from traffic noise and other distractions.

FUNCTIONS OF STAGE SETS

Once your performance site and your play are chosen, the set designer can get to work. These are his or her major considerations: The set must serve as the scene of the action; it must help to develop the character of the person or people occupying the place represented; it must establish the time and place; it must communicate the mood of the play; and, finally, it must reinforce the theme. In order to ensure that the set does all that, the set designer must read the play carefully and confer with the director. In particular, the set designer needs to watch blocking rehearsals to determine whether a design will work for the production.

The Scene of the Action

A set crowded with furniture, no matter how lovely the pieces, is not suitable for a play in which there is a lot of physical movement. The designer needs to determine how much clear area is needed by the actors and how best to arrange the furniture to help—not impede—the flow of the action. For example, Patrick Hamilton's *Angel Street* takes place in Victorian times and its heroine feels shut in and threatened. In this case a crowded set is appropriate. But John Murray and Allen Boretz's *Room Service* has a large cast and lots of running in and out. That level of activity requires more open space.

Character Development

The set designer must create a believable environment for the character or characters who live in the setting. Unless there are some unusual circumstances indicated in the script, an underpaid clerk is not likely to have a luxurious apartment and a wealthy man-about-town won't reside in a shabbily furnished room. Yet, suppose the poor clerk has made an inexpensive attempt to beautify her surroundings, or the rich man has little regard for his possessions and treats them carelessly. By using the set to communicate this information, the set designer helps to develop the characterizations. For example, the set designer for a production of John Van Druten's *Bell, Book, and Candle* is challenged with creating a room for a modern witch who does not flaunt her sorcery, yet has a highly unusual decor.

Time and Place

A lot of **exposition**—that is, background information about things and people in a play—can be given to the audience through the set design. An art deco interior immediately tells the audience the play is set in the 1920s or 1930s. Posters of the Beatles and Rolling Stones, black lighting, and lava lamps place the play in the 1960s or 1970s. A neon light blinking onto the fire escape outside communicates a big city atmosphere. Such details of setting quickly inform the audience about time and place. Louis O. Coxe and Robert Chapman's dramatization of *Billy Budd* is set on the main deck of an eighteenth-century sailing ship. One look at a set with wooden decking, masts, sails, and other period nautical equipment can clearly communicate this to the audience.

Establishing the Mood

The look of the set creates a state of mind and evokes an emotional response in an audience. A gloomy setting can foreshadow tragedy, while a bright and sparkling color scheme sets a cheerful tone. A farcical murder mystery, though, can take place in a spooky haunted house. In such a case, the irony of the setting soon involves and informs the audience. Such a contrast of setting and mood is delightful. In *The Bat,* Mary Roberts Rinehart and Avery Hopwood combine spine-tingling mystery in a musty mysterious mansion with comical plot twists.

Reinforcing the Theme

The set designer may be able to use his or her design to help express the playwright's **theme,** that is, the meaning of the play. For example, for a play about two people who do not reach out or give to other people and who live their lives just for themselves, the designer might create a cold, sterile environment. The room represented would have no fabric, no wood, no plants or flowers, nothing living or natural. Instead, everything, including art objects and furnishings, would be of glass, chrome, or plastic—all cold to the touch. Not only would this setting characterize the people, it would reinforce the theme of the play that those who do not give of themselves will be left to themselves. Ming Cho Lee's set for Patrick Meyer's *K2* represented a wall of

The set designer creates a believable environment for the characters who "live" in the setting.

ice and snow. In its stark challenge it reminded viewers of one's freedom to choose life or death.

Research

After carefully reading the play, the set designer needs to research the time and place of the story. One approach is to consult books and magazines for photographs and descriptions of what was used in the period and the location to be represented. If the time period is not too distant, interviewing those familiar with the era or locale can help the designer gain a sense of what is appropriate.

It's wise to remember that colors popular in one period may not have been used at all a decade later. Wallpaper was not always in fashion. Ornamentation, elaborate in Victorian times, was emphasized less in other times. Sizes, shapes, and treatment of windows and doors differed from period to period. And, while furniture from an earlier time may still be in use in later times, the reverse is not true. Though fringed lampshades or floral wallpaper may seem to be of little consequence, even in a very small production it is attention to such details that makes the difference between convincing the audience and confusing them.

TYPES OF STAGE SETS

Four basic set types offer the set designer a variety of choices: abstract, arras, box, and unit. As with any technical aspect, however, there are considerations of audience, budget, actors, performance space, and, in this case, the action of the play itself.

The **abstract set** uses draperies, freestanding doors and window frames, and segments of arches to suggest a room. For example, you can suggest an elegant eighteenth-century drawing room with just portrait frames and panels of draped brocade.

The **arras set** uses curtains or drapes to enclose the entire acting area on three sides. If you don't have the budget or time

Freestanding doors and windowframes are features of an abstract set.

to build something more elaborate, the arras set works well with whatever furniture you have assembled. You can even have "set changes" by using lighting effects to change the color of the draperies. This could be especially effective if the play calls for several changes of mood throughout.

A **box set** has three walls and a ceiling, leaving the fourth wall open and to be imagined by the actors and audience. The doors and windows are "practical," that is, they actually work. As nearly as possible, the box set represents a real room. A play such as *George Washington Slept Here,* by George Kaufman and Moss Hart, really benefits from a box set since so much of the dialogue and action concern the renovation of a run-down Revolutionary War–period farmhouse.

The **unit set** uses an arrangement of scenery in which some or all of the pieces—flats, doors, windows, or draperies—can be used in different combinations for different scenes. There may be a permanent framework that stands throughout the play with the individual units brought in and taken out as needed, or the pieces of one scene may simply be reassembled differently for the next scene.

Enhancing the Set

Three methods for enhancing settings work well with the sets previously described. A **periaktos** is a three-sided prism made of flats and mounted on casters so that it can revolve and show a different background on each surface. A periaktos (or **prism set**) can be used as quick-change scenery to enhance an arras set. One side of the prism could be painted to suggest a row of trees. Then, as the action moves indoors, the periaktos could be turned to reveal a flat painted to resemble a series of bookcases. In a box set a periaktos can be first a china cabinet, then a freestanding fireplace, and finally a portrait in progress on an artist's easel.

Ground rows are small elements of scenery that stand independently on stage and represent things such as hedges, riverbanks, or boulders. Since an arena stage has audience on all sides and therefore has no back wall, you cannot use flats of any kind. But you can use furniture and ground rows. Keep in mind that the latter must be the same on all sides to satisfy all sightlines. Of course, ground rows can be used with any kind of staging.

Rear projection is a system consisting of a large screen or fabric drop at the rear of the acting area and a projector equipped with a special lens and positioned behind the screen in order to project an image onto the screen. Technology has provided this alternative to the box set on a proscenium arch stage. It is an improvement over projecting from the front, whereby the image often was cast on or shadowed the actors. An image projected from the rear can be a slide of an actual place, a drawing, or a design, such as clouds or trees or skyline. It can remain static during the play or be changed as often as needed.

Here projectors positioned behind the fabric drops create the three images you see.

FOUR METHODS OF SET DESIGN

The first method of set design is to start with a mental image or a photograph of a real place and then, as nearly as possible, to re-create it on the stage, reducing the size of the original as necessary. The result is a box set—the kind of setting most often used in a proscenium arch theatre.

The second method is to start with the needs of the actors as they move through the most important events of the play. With a unit set, flats can be added or removed as required. This will work in any acting space that has at least one side where no audience is seated.

The third method is to work with the mood of the play only. An arras set can be used to suggest a time and place. The colors chosen for the draperies can suggest something sinister or something merry. Like the unit set, this will work in a performance area that has at least one side free from audience seating.

The fourth method of set design concentrates on theme and uses the sets as symbols, to capture the inner meaning of the play. For example, if the plot concerns two children lost in the woods, the trees are made larger than life, skeletal, and with branches that seem to reach out menacingly. This kind of setting would work just as well on an arena stage as on a proscenium arch stage.

SHOW AND TELL

As soon as the preliminary set sketches have been approved by the director, the set designer should bring them to a company meeting. While displaying them, he or she should explain just how the set will work for the actors. It is not the place of the company members to find fault with the approved sketches unless some important detail has been overlooked, and even that kind of comment should be given as information—not criticism.

After the rough or preliminary sketches have been discussed, the designer should progress to a detailed and accurate scale floor plan and an elevation—a drawing that shows the vertical dimensions of the set. The next step, usually highly enjoyable, is to build a scale model. There is something intriguing to cast and

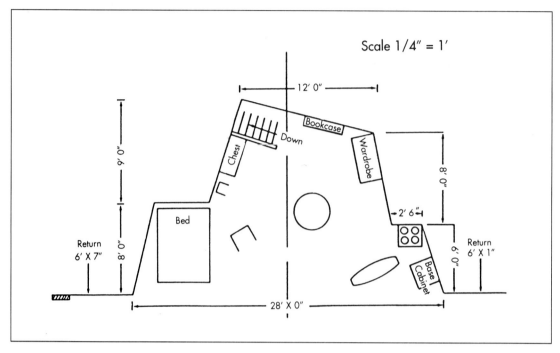

Figure 4.2.   Floor plan for *Look Back in Anger*.

crew alike about a miniature of the set they will all be working on. The model can be constructed of cardboard or wood and should include the placement of all furniture. As the model is always painted with the chosen color scheme, it is a chance to see early in production how well the proposed color scheme works.

If the set designer is to supervise the set construction, the plans and model stay with him or her for use in the scene shop; otherwise, they are turned over at this point to the master builder.

COSTUMES THROUGH THE AGES

Costumes must do more than cover the actors. They communicate information about the time and place of the play and the characters themselves. Like the set, costumes can even function symbolically. The costume designer has to keep in mind practical matters such as the budget, the sizes of the actors, costumes in stock that can be used or adapted, and colors that will work with the set. Chapter Seven addresses these concerns in detail, but at this point in the production, the costume designer should begin researching to learn about the fashions of the time and place.

Historical Accuracy

With so much information about the past available in books, magazines, television programs, and movies, audiences are quite knowledgeable about the styles of earlier times. The costume designer has to research carefully not only the time but also the specific place, since fashions varied even within a country. He or she cannot simply assume that since the company is doing a Shakespeare play, costumes should be Elizabethan. *A Midsummer Night's Dream* takes place in classical Greece, and *Julius Caesar* is set in the first century B.C. in Rome.

There are many books on historic costume to consult, and the drawings shown in this text provide a brief survey and quick reference. It's easy to see that fashion moves in cycles, repeating itself with variation. Of course, events influence fashion. During World War II, for example, a color scheme of red, white, and blue was a popular reflection of the patriotic feeling in the country.

SUMMARY

Developing a subtext for their lines can help actors better understand their roles. When choosing a performance site, remember that if your company does not have the use of a formal theatre, you can adapt a classroom or outdoor area for use as a performance space. The set designer must make sure that the setting allows for the action of the play, aids in character development, is true to the time and place of the play, helps to establish the desired mood, and reinforces the theme. Finally, both the set designer and the costume designer need to research the time and setting of the play to insure that their designs are as authentic as possible.

Classical drama virtually ceased to exist in Western civilization after the fall of Rome, but drama was reborn during the medieval period. Once again it arose out of a religious ceremony. In England in the Middle Ages the Roman Catholic Mass was celebrated in Latin. A village priest—hoping to hold the attention of his congregants, who were not well versed in Latin—inserted into the Easter Mass some dialogue in the vernacular, that is, the language spoken by the people. The technique proved popular, and it was then used in other Masses. Eventually, stories from the Bible were dramatized and, as these became more elaborate and distracted from worship, they were moved outside the church building onto the steps. From there they moved into the town square and on to nearby towns.

While the dramas were still being presented inside the churches, a series of mansions (those small platforms of individual sets) along the inside of the building made it possible to have several different scenes presented. This mansion system was also used for performances in the town squares. It was simple to mount the mansions on pageant wagons, something like horse-drawn parade floats, and pull them around the square so that the audience could stand in one spot and see the whole play.

Taking the show on the road was the next logical step, allowing people in distant towns to see the plays other towns had developed. This was "professional" theatre, as the actors and technical support people had to give up their work to travel. They would pass the hat for contributions at their performances, but they also had sponsors. Guilds (a kind of early trade union) would supply financial support as well as materials. Guilds liked to sponsor plays that had some connection with their trade, so that the shipbuilders might sponsor the story of Noah's Ark, the bakers the story of the Last Supper, and the goldsmiths, the story of the Three Magi.

Three types of religious drama developed: miracle, morality, and mystery plays. Two of the most famous, *Everyman* and *The Second Shepherd's Play,* are widely available in print and hold up well in performance even today. Once traveling theatre took over, secular or nonreligious topics began to work their way into these plays. By the fifteenth century, what had begun in the churches early in the tenth century had evolved into professional secular theatre companies, which eventually established permanent theatres.

The three types of religious drama spread quickly through continental Europe, and Pope Urban IV made the feast day of Corpus Christi the occasion for festivals of religious plays. Soon, farces commenting on society and other performances of a purely secular nature were added to the presentations of touring actors in England and continental Europe.

Design Projects

1. Rent a video of *The Wizard of Oz* and find the scene where Dorothy and her friends are lost in the woods. Invite members of the company to watch the scene with you and then discuss the symbolic scenery the movie uses at that point.

2. Choose a simple legend or fable and design a set for it that clearly establishes time and place. *Aesop's Fables* offers interesting possibilities for scene choices. For example, "The Fox and the Grapes" could take place in a woods, a vineyard, a backyard garden, or a castle orchard.

3. Choose a character from a favorite book; then design a bedroom or living room set that will show something about that person's character. Remember to make consistent decisions about colors, fabric, style of furniture, and selection of accessories.

4. Visit the paint store where your company is buying some of its supplies and examine the paint chip samples on the rack. Select and make note of the colors you would use to paint a present-day set for one of the following. If permitted, bring the paint chips to class, but if you are unable to do so, be sure to describe your color choices accurately.

    a. The nursery of a child born to wealthy parents
    b. The kitchen of a busy career woman
    c. The study of an Arctic explorer
    d. The bedroom of a teenaged boy who loves the outdoors
    e. The living room of a couple who wishes they were still living in the 1960s
    f. The library of a retired army general
    g. The dining room of an art professor
    h. The playroom of ten-year-old twins who disagree about everything

    As you can see, you will need to make decisions based on the interests, temperament, age, and economic status of the characters.

5. Sketch a series of mansion-style sets for your play. If there is a single set called for, take the various areas of action and make each a separate mansion.

6. Visit a fabric store and make a list of the different kinds of material available. You can find this information printed on labels on the ends of the bolts of fabric. Next to each fabric type on your list, jot down notes about characteristics and washability. For example, is the fabric soft or rough? sheer or opaque? stiff or flexible? heavy or light? machine- or hand-washable? expensive or moderately priced? Complete your notes by deciding which fabrics would look best for five of the costumes required in your play.

7. Choose a character from your play and sketch designs for a series of costumes that character would wear through the course of the play.

8. Research fashions in one of the following years; then sketch clothing designs for someone your age at that time. Include clothes for recreation or sports, school, work or chores, parties, and sleep.

   a. 1890
   b. 1928
   c. 1945
   d. 1968
   e. 1980

Subtext Projects

1. If you are not acting in the play, select a character and write a subtext for one of his or her longer speeches. When you have finished, if you wish, confer with the actor playing the role.

2. To see how actors use subtext to convey meaning beyond the words of their lines, watch a movie or television program with another company member. Make notes on the actor's ways of indicating subtext to the audience. Compare notes after the movie or program.

The Costume Designer

Until the middle of this century, costume design was often seen as an extension of set design and was under the set designer's jurisdiction. According to Tony Award–winning costume designer Patricia Zipprodt, if the set designer was too busy, "the producer might even send his wife or girlfriend out to shop for costumes." In fact, the Scenic Artists Guild did not offer separate costume design examinations for membership until the late 1940s.

Zipprodt, who teaches in the Master of Fine Arts program at Brandeis University in addition to her Broadway design career, was at Wellesley College when the separate costume design examination was finally offered. By the 1950s she had moved to New York, worked at a variety of jobs, and, while viewing a ballet performance, discovered what she really wanted to do. The ballet was a production of George Balanchine's *La Valse,* with costumes by Karinska. Zipprodt later told *TheaterWeek* writer Simi Horwitz, "I had never seen costumes like those. There was just something extraordinary about the layers of silk and net and beads. And the way the light hit those beads . . . . I knew, as I stared, that that's what I wanted to do for the rest of my life—just design costumes."

Growing up in the suburbs of Chicago, Zipprodt intended to be an artist. She feels it's unfortunate that people with ambitions to design costumes don't have a solid background in art, particularly in drawing and design. When she was designing costumes for the Broadway production of *Shogun,* she researched arts books and films depicting Japanese society of the fourteenth and fifteenth centuries. She wanted not only to provide the historical authenticity required, but also to interpret that history in her costume designs.

After deciding she wanted a career in costume design, Zipprodt enrolled at the Fashion Institute of Technology in New York City. After a few semesters of training, she got jobs with apparel companies and later with fashion designers in a variety of entry-level positions. Next, she applied for membership in the Scenic Artists Guild, and she passed the exam the first time. She worked as an assistant to such famous designers as William and Jean Eckhart, Irene Sharaf, and the design group Motley. Now she herself is famous, having designed the costumes for such Broadway hits as *Fiddler on the Roof, Cabaret, Sweet Charity,* and a recent production of *Cat on a Hot Tin Roof.*

Under
Construction

5

Company Meeting

At this point in the production, people are so intent on their own work that sometimes they forget to report on their progress. The company meeting serves as a reminder that the production is a group effort and every contribution is important.

PROGRESS REPORTS

The costume designer or wardrobe manager, the hairstylist, and the makeup artist are doing research, preparing rough sketches, and gathering materials. The graphic artist is readying designs for the next week. The house manager is consulting with the various technical crews. The assistant director is occupied with rehearsals. The lighting and sound people still attend rehearsals and are working on their designs. The properties manager, with the help of the company, is collecting the necessary props. This week the set designer will hand over the plans and model to the master builder and stage crew so that construction can begin.

TOPICS FOR THIS MEETING

- Memorizing Your Lines
- Voice Production
- Relaxation Techniques
- Housekeeping and Safety
- Constructing the Set
- The Load-In
- Special Situations
- The Story of Theatre: The European Renaissance
- Theatre Workshop
- Careers in the Theatre: The Set Designer

WORKING VOCABULARY

Some of the specialized vocabulary in this chapter relates to set construction. Key terms include the following: *screen, set pieces, dutching, sightlines, scrim, commedia dell'arte,* and *lazzi.*

AGENDA

At the next company meeting you'll discuss theatre games and the company spirit, publicity and public relations, and house management. Company members will also share their production progress reports.

MEMORIZING YOUR LINES

As the stage crew begins its work on the set, the actors are on their feet, moving through the blocking and trying to get off book. Thus, it's a good time to become acquainted with some of the techniques actors can use for memorization, voice production, and relaxation.

For some actors, the best way to learn lines is simply to run them with someone else, over and over again. They might close their eyes and visualize the set and the other actors, then mentally move through each scene, recalling their lines as they match the actions. Other actors hand-copy every line they have, feeling that physically tracing the shape of each word impresses it upon the memory. (Note, however, that this technique does *not* work with typing the lines). Some actors like to record their lines on tape and listen to it any chance they have, such as while riding to school, doing household chores, waiting in line, or before falling asleep at night. The lines thus become as familiar as a favorite song. But no matter which memorization technique you choose, it is very important that you do not memorize the lines merely to rattle them off when called upon. You must put emotions to the words and convey meaning and feeling with each line you say.

One way for actors to learn their lines is to go over them repeatedly with someone else.

It is also critical that you learn your lines exactly as written. Don't argue that what you've said means the same thing—that won't do. Your line is, after all, a cue to another actor. It may set up something later in the play. It may be a line that has to be echoed by someone else. It may be funny with a certain word choice but ordinary without it. Rephrasing can spoil the playwright's timing or rhythm. After all, he or she carefully chose each word. Finally, to those in the audience who know the play well, your inaccuracy will make you seem careless.

Wouldn't it be nice if your director said to you, "Whenever you can manage to be off book will be fine"? Of course, that is highly impractical. Your play has an opening date and a great deal must be accomplished by that time. Don't hold up the production by failing to be off book by the date set.

Usually the director will allow you to have the assistant director sitting on book, that is, prompting, for the first few days after the cast is due to be off book. Only the assistant director should do this prompting, however, so never feed another actor a line, and never look to another actor to feed you a line. Remember, when you need help, simply call, "Line." The "please" and "thank you" are understood; you don't take up stage time saying them. Try to stay in character and focused in the moment when calling for a line.

Similarly, don't fill in with "um" or "uh" or "you know" as you struggle to remember the line. These fillers do not provide an air of natural speech; they merely sound desperate.

Finally, don't ever say, "I'll be fine by the performance" when you do not know lines or blocking. That assurance is of no help. The rest of the cast has to work with you, and they need you to be fully prepared as the schedule requires.

VOICE PRODUCTION

An effective speaking voice is first of all *intelligible,* that is, easily understood. How can you make sure your speaking voice meets this criterion? You need to speak loudly enough, enunciate clearly, pronounce words correctly, and maintain an appropriate speaking rate. In addition, an effective speaking voice has variety; it is not a monotone. Variety is achieved by varying the rate and the pitch. An effective speaking voice also uses stress or emphasis skillfully to bring out the meaning of the words. Finally, an effective speaking voice controls the emotional quality of what is said.

Intelligibility

Loudness. Since it's not practical to move closer to your audience if they are having trouble hearing you, you must reach them by projecting your voice. This means deep breathing from the diaphragm or abdomen, not shallow breathing from the chest. Fill your lungs to capacity and then speak as you exhale, so that your breath will carry your words to the back of the theatre. Place your hand on your diaphragm, just below your rib cage. Do you feel it move as you breathe? If not, focus your mind on that area and try again.

   Enunciation. Don't be self-conscious about making an effort to speak crisply and clearly. Your audience will be grateful to hear those word endings, so they can tell *fishing* from *fission,* and to hear correct vowel sounds, so they can tell *for* from *fur* and *can* from *kin.* It does take a mental effort to keep from lazi-

Your efforts to speak clearly and crisply will pay off with audiences.

ly dropping word endings, and it does take a physical effort to open your mouth, to force your tongue to move, and to form the consonants firmly with your lips and tongue. While careless enunciation may be forgiven among friends, when you're on stage you must be easily understood.

Standards of Pronunciation. Your audience will have certain expectations about the correct pronunciation of words. You don't want to puzzle them with your own version, nor do you want them to laugh at your mistakes. And, certainly, you don't want to set them whispering, "What was that word?" Unless some sort of regional dialect is essential to the character you are playing, you need to meet the national standards of pronunciation, especially in a classic play in which the universality of the characters is emphasized. If you are in doubt about some of the words in your lines, look them up in a dictionary. The correct pronunciation will be indicated by diacritical marks, which tell how to sound out the word and where the accents fall among the syllables.

Speaking Rate. When you speak enthusiastically to friends you may jabber along as fast as 200 to 250 words per minute. Of course, your friends are right there, able to ask for clarification or repetition. Audiences don't have that opportunity, though, so when you speak to them you need to slow down to 120 to 150 words per minute. Try using a tape recorder to check your rate. If you are speaking too fast to be intelligible, make a conscious effort to slow down.

Vocal Variety. You can vary the rate at which you speak to provide vocal variety, speeding up *a little* to indicate excitement and slowing down *a little* for a more serious delivery. You can also change the pitch of your voice. *Pitch* refers to the highs and lows of your vocal tones. If you speak at the exact same pitch throughout your lines, you will be speaking in a monotone, which is very boring to the audience. Again, working with a tape recorder can help you to hear the range of your high and low tones. For practice you might want to imitate the way announcers introduce late night talk show hosts, such as Ed McMahon's famous introduction of Johnny Carson: "Heeeeeere's Johnny," with its rise up to *Job* and its fall to *nny*.

Stress or Emphasis. Where to place the emphasis in a word is a decision best left to the dictionary, but the decision about where to place the emphasis in a sentence is left to the

Delivering your lines with feeling engages the audience's attention.

actor and the director. The actor and the director should work together for the best interpretation of the material. Emphasis placed wrongly can provoke an unwanted laugh, as in "What's that in the *road,* a head?" for what should have been "What's that in the road *ahead?*"

Emotional Quality. Some people are reluctant to invest much feeling in the lines they say, but because they then appear uncaring, the audience cannot care either. Reading aloud to children is a good way to practice putting emotion into what you say. Children are a tough audience; if you're not doing a good job of reading to them, they won't stay around to listen. Because so many of the characters in children's stories are animals or monsters or supernatural creatures, it's easier to let go and be that character in all its emotions.

RELAXATION TECHNIQUES

Don't let anyone tell you that everyone must suffer through stage fright. It simply is not so. In order to manage stage fright, you need to learn to relax. First, you must develop a positive attitude about yourself and your work. You must be thoroughly prepared. You must trust your company members. Also, you must trust your audience, because they have come to have a good time and they want you to be good. After all, the better you are, the better experience they will have. You must intend to enjoy the performance and your part in it.

Don't focus on what could go wrong. Your director will have covered all those possibilities in rehearsal and will have prepared you to follow certain procedures for them. Instead, focus on the delightful bits of stage business, the lovely costumes, your big laugh in the second act, the swift scene change the crew has worked out, and the wonderful rush of excitement you will feel when you step out onstage into those lights. There is nothing quite like it!

To expend nervous energy, many actors like to do physical warm-up exercises. If that is not a company practice, you can do them on your own. You might try simple stretching; moving fingers, hands, arms, feet, or legs in a figure-eight pattern; or simply bouncing lightly on the balls of your feet.

Many actors prefer mental warm-up exercises. You might try imagining refreshing images of cool mountain streams, clear lakes, soft rain falling, or fish gliding through a pool. Or, perhaps you'll favor active, energizing images, such as clowns tumbling, bright balls being juggled, colorful laundry flapping in the breeze. The reason these images can be as relaxing as tranquil ones is that they allow you to let go of tension and to lose yourself in pleasant activity.

Other actors prefer to listen to soothing music or to quietly read or recite calming poetry. Try each method and see which one or combination best helps you to manage your stage fright by helping you relax.

HOUSEKEEPING AND SAFETY

While the actors rehearse onstage, another important group in the company gets started constructing the set in the scene shop.

This actor's warm-up stretches help her relax and focus before rehearsals and performances.

If you're involved in building the set, remember never to work in a mess! Not only is it dangerous to do so, it's tiring to the mind and it blunts creativity. Therefore, if the shop isn't clean when you arrive, put it in order before you begin work and leave it in order when you finish. Though set construction may sometimes seem to be a thankless job, your company will appreciate your efforts. Further, the discipline, good work habits, and skills you acquire, as well as the opportunities you'll have to express creativity and craftsmanship, will serve you well in the years ahead.

Power tools, paints, and lumber seem to hold the same kind of fascination for some people as do chemicals, test tubes, and Bunsen burners. Just as the latter are used in labs under strict scientific procedures, so are the former used with caution and under supervision in the scene shop.

Rules for Safe Use of Power Tools

- Always read the operating instructions before using any equipment—even if you have experience working with such a tool.
- Always wear safety glasses, and if the tool is noisy, wear ear plugs.
- Be sure all safety guards are working.
- Be sure electrical cords are in good condition.
- Be sure cutting tools are sharpened.
- Don't use extension cords with power tools.
- Don't plug in or unplug cords if your hands are wet.
- Don't play games or clown around with power tools.
- Turn off the tool before you lay it down, and pick it up before you turn it on.
- If a piece of equipment isn't working right, report it and don't use it until it has been repaired.

When you operate a power tool, always wear safety glasses.

Common sense dictates basic safety rules in set construction, but to remind yourself, meet with the other members of the crew and take turns reviewing these rules aloud.

Basic Safety in Set Construction

- Don't climb a ladder when you are working alone.
- Even when you think one bolt will hold something securely, add another bolt.
- Sweep the stage thoroughly before each rehearsal and after each work session.
- Don't handle a rope with wet hands—keep baking soda handy and dust hands with the soda before gripping rope.
- Store water next to any open flame.
- Do not use an open flame near cloth.
- Use only cloth that has been fireproofed.
- Size, that is, preshrink, any fabric before you paint it.
- Sweep up any broken glass immediately.
- Carefully sand all wood.
- Wear a mask when using a paint sprayer or when working around fumes of any kind.
- Check all furniture for sturdiness of legs, arms, and backs.
- Schedule work sessions to include breaks so that construction crew members are alert when working.
- Make certain that company members know the location of the first aid kit, fire extinguisher, and poison antidote chart at all times.
- Attend immediately to any cuts or scrapes.
- Recognize that any equipment poses danger if used incorrectly.

Make sure someone is nearby when you are climbing a ladder.

CONSTRUCTING THE SET

If the company's set construction crew is to build the set, rather than having family members, local professionals, or a wood shop class do it, by now the set design, elevations, floor plan, and model are available for guidance. Before touching a piece of lumber or fabric, however, be sure everyone has thoroughly discussed the set design and that all crew members have watched a complete rehearsal of the play to understand the flow and the requirements of the action. Although you will want use of the stage when the actors are not on it, never work without supervision by someone experienced in the kind of work you will be doing. Draft a schedule that includes not only your production deadlines but also a list of supervisors and their assigned hours.

Once the set is in place, it is the company's home until the final strike. Report or repair the slightest damage immediately and always treat your set with respect.

This text provides instruction for constructing the basic elements of scenery. If your production requires very elaborate sets, you may want to consult one of the many good books devoted to stagecraft. One of the projects suggested in Chapter

One involved compiling a list of available books on stagecraft, so that list can be of value here.

The Flat

The flat is the basic unit of stage scenery. Several flats joined together form a set. Flats are also used to mask or hide back-stage areas that could be glimpsed by the audience through a set window or door.

Consisting of a wooden frame covered with muslin or canvas, a flat is usually from 10' to 16' in height. A **screen** differs only in height; it is from 6' to 9' high. Stage scenery, in general, is not constructed with permanence in mind, although flats and screens usually last from three to five years, or even longer, depending upon care and use. Scenery is not built "solid as a rock," as one would build a home or a shop project. Scenery should be lightweight, easily moved, and adaptable to a variety of situations. A flat resembles an artist's canvas. Indeed, the historical origin of flats was in Renaissance Italy, where some of the great artists were employed for scenic painting.

Set construction should always take place under supervision.

Flats are used primarily on a proscenium arch stage, but the thrust stage can make use of such set devices as well. Even the arena stage can use them if the director chooses to sacrifice some of the seating and use a booked (v-shaped) pair of flats at some point in the circumference of the stage.

Flat sizes, particularly their height, *depend* upon the height of the proscenium opening and whether the curtain borders are adjustable up and down. Very tall flats on a small stage tend to give the illusion of a very high ceiling. Further, they tend to give an air of formality to whatever play is done. In most school situations, 10' to 12' flats give a much more intimate feeling, a desirable characteristic for most modern plays. Flat widths are more historical than practical. Flats were made 5' to 9' wide simply because that was the size of the door opening on old railway cars and also the size of the stage door. Practically speaking, a flat can be *any* width, according to its purpose. Listed is a so-called "stock" set of flats, usable for many plays and stage purposes. If your school does not have a set of flats, it is best to begin with these stock sizes. Since flats will be reused from year to year, it is important that they be a *standard* size. Flats wider than 5'9" are difficult to handle and to store on the stage.

Standard Size Flats		Recommended Screen Sizes	
Width	*Recommended* Height	Width	Height
5'9"	10'–12'	5'0"	8'–9'
4'0"	10'–12'	4'0"	8'–9'
3'6"	10'–12'	3'0"	8'–9'
3'0"	10'–12'	2'0"	8'–9'
2'6"	10'–12'	1'0"	8'–9'
2'0"	10'–12'		
1'0"	10'–12'		

Screens are recommended for schools with minimal stage facilities and a small stage area. Screens have the advantage over regular flats in that they are lighter in weight and more easily moved. Screens work better as **set pieces**—pieces of scenery designed to stand by themselves—than do regular flats. Plays produced in schools usually do not require extreme "realistic" or "naturalistic" settings, but rather only an illusion on the stage. Screens fulfill this requirement very effectively.

Selecting the Lumber

In making a flat or screen: (1) select the lumber; (2) cut the lumber; (3) assemble the flat or screen; and (4) cover the flat or screen.

Selecting lumber for the construction of flats or screens is an important task. The first decision is whether the flat or screen is to be used only for one play, or to be added to the permanent stock of scenery. Permanent flats usually are constructed with better grades of lumber than temporary scenery. Temporary, or one-show flats can be made from several common grades of lumber. Firring strips (1" × 2"), used in the home to attach paneling to walls, can be used as well as common grades of 1" × 3" and 1" × 4". Lumber is classified today as "common" and "upper." Upper is better quality and more costly than common. Within each classification are several grades; upper grades are B and Better, C, and D. Common grades are 2, 3, and 4. Nationally, the dimensions of lumber have changed in order to conserve lumber. What is called 1" × 3" in this text, and by most lumberyards, has actual dimensions of $3/4$" × $2^{1}/_{2}$"; a 2" × 4" actually measures $1^{1}/_{2}$" × $3^{1}/_{2}$". Nonetheless, people still use the *full inch* dimensions when referring to lumber.

Flats to be added to the permanent stock of scenery should be constructed from the upper grades of lumber, which are generally clearer, with fewer knots and less warp. A permanent flat, properly constructed, can serve for years and be remodeled several times for other plays. White pine is preferred to other woods because of its durability, close grain, and ease of working. If white pine is not available, or the cost is prohibitive in your area, fir is the next best choice. Two-by-fours generally are available in fir rather than pine. Fir does have a tendency to split and splinter rather easily, however.

Learning to select lumber is an experience stage crew members should have. For this reason, it is strongly recommended that they personally visit the lumber company to help select the lumber for the play. The personnel of most lumberyards have a great deal of knowledge about wood and its use. Lumber should be inspected to make certain all pieces will meet the needs of the set to be built—even the "common" grades vary considerably in knots and warp. Selection should be made to get lumber as straight as possible. Knots can frequently be worked around in the cutting process. If lumber is ordered by phone, the grade, thickness, width (in full inches), and length should be stated. It is also wise to inquire about the cost, since lumber prices are usually on the increase. Though waste should be kept to a minimum, crews and directors are apt to make mistakes in figuring, cutting, or laying out the scenery. Therefore, it is wise to order more than is absolutely essential to build the necessary units. Ordering stock in longer lengths (12' and 16') assures a sufficient supply of lumber on hand when needed. Lumber companies figure lumber in *board feet,* whereas most flats are figured in *lineal feet* or meters. To avoid board feet-lineal feet confusion, it is best to order lumber by the number of lengths (12' or 16') needed; for example: a single 5' × 10' flat requires four (4) 12' lengths, with about 4'6" left over for a toggle bar (a support piece) on another flat.

Cutting the Lumber

Figure 5.1 shows the parts of a flat. The top and bottom are called *rails;* the side pieces are called *stiles;* the center brace is called a *toggle bar.*

Each flat or screen consists of the following five pieces:

- 2 rails—the exact width of the finished flat or screen

- 2 stiles—the finished height of the flat or screen less twice the width of the lumber

- 1 toggle bar—the finished width of the flat less twice the width of the lumber

A square should be used to mark all cuts, even when using power saws with cross-cut gauges and guides. Before making any cuts it is wise to check and *double-check* all measurements. Always allow $1/16$" for saw cuts.

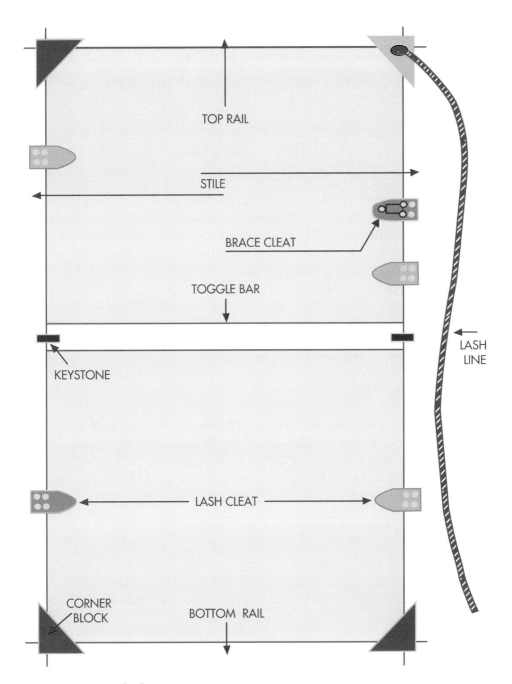

TOP RAIL

STILE

BRACE CLEAT

TOGGLE BAR

LASH
LINE

KEYSTONE

LASH CLEAT

CORNER
BLOCK

BOTTOM RAIL

Figure 5.1. Parts of a flat.

Assembly

Once the rails, stiles, and toggle bar have been cut, the assembly involves the following steps: (1) squaring the corners, (2) attaching the corner blocks, and (3) attaching the keystones.

Squaring the corners was, for a number of years, one of the major problems scenery crews had in making flats; however, today, thanks to a picture-frame miter clamp, *any* scenery crew can build square flats. Picture-frame miter clamps can be purchased at nearly all hardware stores for a reasonable price. Make certain the clamps will open to 3" because they come in various sizes. The crew hard-pressed for cash can operate with one set of clamps, although two sets are recommended for assembly-line building. The picture-frame miter clamps are attached to the top rail and stiles by sliding each piece into the clamp opening and screwing it tight. Make certain the rail and stile touch at each corner. Frequently, saw cuts will be uneven, so let the clamp square the corner! Do not force two unevenly cut pieces of wood together. The clamps should not be removed until the corner blocks have been attached.

Corner blocks are made from $1/4$" plywood cut in an $8^1/2$" × 6" triangle. (See Figure 5.2.) The grain on the top layer of plywood should run as illustrated for maximum support. If the grain runs counter to this there is danger that the block will crack, as the top layers of plywood are stronger than the inner core.

Begin by cutting the plywood sheet (4' × 8') in half (2' × 4'). This makes it much easier to handle and does not affect the number of corner blocks and keystones you can cut out of a sheet. How many corner blocks and how many keystones can you figure from a 2' × 4' piece of plywood?

There are several methods of attaching corner blocks to the flat frame. Nailing is the first method, using either *clout nails* or blue lath nails. A *clout nail* is a special soft metal, flat-sided nail designed to curl under when it strikes a hard surface, steel, or concrete. The clout nail forms a very secure bond between the corner block and the flat frame. Clout nails ($1^1/4$") are a special kind of hardware available *only* from theatre supply houses. Blue lath nails (1" or $1^1/4$") are a substitute for clout nails because they are readily available from lumberyards and hardware stores. The 1" lath nail usually does not need to be clinched (bent over on the front side of the flat); however, the $1^1/4$" does need to be clinched. When corner block or keystone nails are

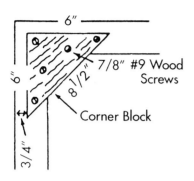

Figure 5.2.
Corner block and keystone.

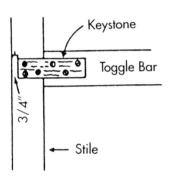

clinched on the front side of the flat, it is important that they be buried in the wood so that no sharp points are sticking up at any point where they may tear the muslin or canvas covering of the flat when it is sized. A good grade of white glue is usually applied to the down side of the corner block before it is nailed. Be certain to keep both the corner block and keystones 3/4" from the outside edge of the stile of the flat. It helps to keep a scrap of 1"× 3" to use as a template guide for this measurement.

Attaching corner blocks and keystones with screws is another method of assembly. Five holes need to be drilled through the block and part way into the stile and rail. Use a 1/8" bit in either an electric drill or hand-type push drill; this is just about the right size to take the #9, 7/8" wood screws used to attach the block. The drilling pattern seen in Figure 5.1 gives strength to the joint. Once all four corners have been attached, the toggle bar is fitted in the center of the wooden frame and attached to the right and left stiles with keystones. Keystones are $1/4$" pieces of plywood, about 5" or 6" long and $2^1/2$" or 3" wide, and are attached to the toggle bar and rail with at least five screws, as are the corner blocks. It is not necessary to use the picture-frame miter clamps on these joints. To test the squareness of the flat, stand it on all four sides; it should stand straight on each side.

Covering the Flat

Unbleached muslin is the least expensive and most readily available covering material for flats or screens. While some scenery makers advocate using canvas, it is not recommended. Canvas is bulky and difficult to work with. In addition, the cost is about twice that of unbleached muslin.

Most fabric stores handle unbleached muslin in 36" and 48" widths. While these widths are usually too narrow for 5' flats or screens, they work nicely for narrower flats. Scenic muslin, slightly heavier, comes in 72" and 78" widths and is much easier to use. Scenic muslin is cheaper when purchased in bolts of 50 to 70 yards, but it can be bought by the yard from some theatrical supply houses. Any group planning to build a new stock of flats or add a considerable number to its present stock should consider purchasing muslin in bolts rather than by the yard. Several large textile mills offer discounts on muslin at least once a year, and a school can realize a considerable savings by purchasing at these times. Narrower widths can, in an emergency, be sewn together. A seam will appear in the middle, but usually this is not too noticeable once the flat is painted, provided the seam has been closely stitched. The prime disadvantage in sewing muslin together is that the seam is the first place the flat will come apart.

Covering the flat involves the following steps: (1) laying on the unbleached muslin, (2) gluing and stapling the muslin, and (3) trimming the muslin. Using 72" muslin, unroll enough so that about 6" extends over the bottom and top rails and the left and right stiles. The flat frame should be lying face up on the stage or scene-shop floor. Face up means that the corner blocks and keystones will be resting on the floor. The muslin *should not be pulled taut* but should lie loosely on the frame and slightly off the floor. If muslin is stretched too tightly before it is sized or painted it can warp and twist the entire flat out of shape. A tack or staple should be placed in each of the four corners to hold the muslin in place.

Gluing the muslin to the frame is the next step. Three kinds of glue may be used for this purpose: any of the white glues on the market today, Elmer's or Leech glue (frequently used by art departments), or casein glue. Be certain to spread the glue on *both* sides of the muslin to be glued to the rails and stiles. Mix the casein glue with water (warm or cold) and spread it on the muslin and wood with a paint brush. Another type of glue is regular hide glue, which must be prepared in a double boiler or a glue pot. The bonding power of hide glue is greater than either the white or casein glue, but it involves more preparation (soaking and heating) and has a rather unpleasant odor.

The glue is spread along the stile first; then the muslin is pressed down on it and another application of glue is put on the muslin. Smooth out the wrinkles with a piece of scrap lumber about 3" long. *Be careful not to stretch the muslin or pull it too tightly.* Glue the entire flat first, then staple or tack. The reason for this is to avoid developing wrinkles in the muslin that could show up later. Glue the rails in the same manner as the stiles, making certain the wrinkles are smoothed out completely by pulling the muslin toward the outer edges of the rails. Finally, a row of tacks or staples about 6" apart is placed all around the frame, rails, and stiles. *Never glue or tack the toggle bar.* It is best to allow eight to twelve hours for the glue to dry properly, so it is advised that all gluing and stapling of muslin be done in one work session. Once the muslin on the rails and stiles has dried, the surplus muslin must be trimmed off 1/4" to 1/2" in from the outer edge of the flat with a trim knife or single-edge razor blade. (See Figure 5.3.) Make the first cut on the stile and gently pull the surplus as you cut, in order to keep the material taut and make the cutting easier. The pull-cutting operation takes a little practice to get the right amount of tension, but it makes a neatly finished flat. The flats are now ready for the final preparation step—sizing.

Sizing is the process of filling the weave of the muslin fibre with a glue and water mixture to make painting easier. Sizing

111

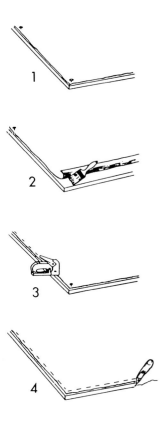

Figure 5.3.
Gluing, stapling, and trimming.

also shrinks the muslin a great deal and makes the fabric taut, like an artist's canvas. Flats that have not been sized before painting may warp, and the paint, when applied, will "bleed" through the open weave.

Size water is a mixture of glue and water. The mix is made as follows: one cup of hide glue to one gallon of water. Commercial wall sizing, available in most paint stores, will work *if it is thinned* with more water after the directions on the box have been followed. If it is applied according to directions, it is too heavy with glue and the muslin becomes hard and brittle. Add water a little at a time to the commercial wall size until your fingers just stick together. Brush sizing on just as though you were painting the flat. The stage floor, if that is where the painting is to be done, should be protected with a layer of old newspapers or plastic dropcloths. Sized flats should stand for twenty-four hours before the base coat of paint is applied.

Door and Window Flats

Building door (see Figure 5.4) and window flats is a modification of the basic flat-construction process. Door and window flats are usually 5'9" in width, and seldom less than 5'6". This is so the door flat or window flat, when used alone as a set piece, does not appear out of proportion.

The major parts of a 5'9"-wide door flat are as follows:

- 2 outer stiles
- 1 top rail
- 1 toggle bar
- 2 bottom rails
- 2 inner stiles
- 2 short toggle bars
- 6 corner blocks, 4 keystones

The top rail and the two outer stiles are assembled as in the basic flat. The long toggle bar is placed so it is exactly 3' from the top of the top rail to the bottom of the toggle bar. Inner stiles and bottom rails can be assembled as separate units, using the picture-frame miter clamps at all corners. Remember, the stile rests on the rail. The assembled inner stiles are laid in the assembled outer frame. The corner blocks used on the inner stiles need to be trimmed on one corner so they will fit properly with-

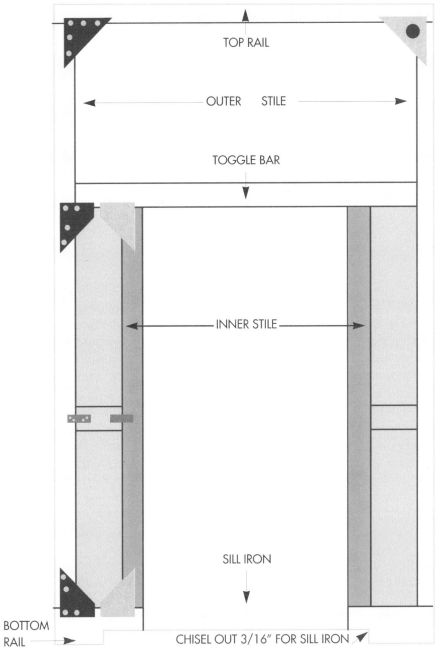

TOP RAIL

OUTER STILE

TOGGLE BAR

INNER STILE

SILL IRON

BOTTOM RAIL

CHISEL OUT 3/16" FOR SILL IRON

Figure 5.4. Door flat.

out overlapping. Remember to keep the corner blocks $^3/_4''$ from the outer edge of the flat. Corner blocks should be trimmed before they are attached to the flat frame. Note that corner blocks are used on the inside, where the inner stile and the toggle bar meet; this is for added strength. Be certain to follow the drill-hole pattern for attaching all corner blocks.

To cover door flats use three pieces of muslin. Lap them on the long toggle bar and use a single row of staples or tacks to ensure that the muslin will not pull loose. After the muslin has been applied and trimmed, as in the basic flat, a "saddle iron" is added to the bottom of the frame. Saddle irons, or "sill irons," can be purchased from commercial theatrical supply companies (be sure to give the exact size of the opening). Saddle irons can be made from $^3/_{16}'' \times ^3/_4''$ strap iron that is cut 6" shorter than the bottom rails. A sill iron of some nature is necessary to give stability to all door flats.

Window flats are constructed just as the door flat and basic flat, with the following exceptions: (1) the bottom rail is complete—5'9"; (2) the sill of the window is placed 3' up from the bottom rail; (3) the opening for the window should be 3' × 4'. Assembly of the window flat is the same as for the basic flat or door flat. Extra toggle braces are usually added to window flats at the 5' mark. A window flat can be covered with one piece or with four pieces of muslin, lapping at the bottom and top toggle bars.

It is possible to convert door flats into window flats by using a 3' × 3' plug, made of Upson board, and a wooden frame. The plug should be nailed or screwed to the inner stiles of the door flat, and a "dutchman" is used to cover the cracks. A dutchman is a 5" or 6" strip of muslin that is applied to the flat with glue to hide cracks, such as those made by the plug. This process is called **dutching.**

Standardization of door and window flats is not a necessity since scenery needs will vary from play to play, and many sizes may be used to fit any situation. What has been described here are "stock" sizes.

Door Frames and Window Frames

The door and window flats just described are not complete and ready to place on the stage. A frame to hold the door and windows is necessary for them to be functional.

The door frame (see Figure 5.5) is constructed as follows:

(2) 1" × 6" × 6'6"
(2) 1" × 6" × 6'10"
(1) 1" × 6" × 2'10"
(1) 1" × 6" × 3'

The door frame is made to be slid in the flat, from the *front,* so the frame facing rests against the flat. The jamb of the door is the depth the door goes into the flat. The jamb of the door is built by using the two 6'6" pieces and the two 2'10" pieces of 1" × 6". The frame should measure 6'6" *inside,* not outside. Place the 3' piece so it rests on top of the two long 1" × 6" pieces. Use either flat Ls or mending plates to join the pieces together. The jamb is assembled by using 1½" #9 wood screws and 90° Ls. (See Figure 5.6) The jamb is now laid on the floor and the facing frame is laid on top of it. The two units are joined in a butt joint with 1½" #9 wood screws in at least six places on the facing frame. The facing frame will be fragile, so handle it carefully when placing it on the jamb. Once the wood screws are countersunk securely, the unit can be turned over on the facing, and

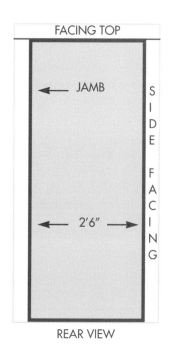

REAR VIEW

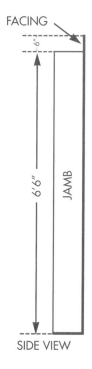

SIDE VIEW

Figure 5.5.
Door frame.

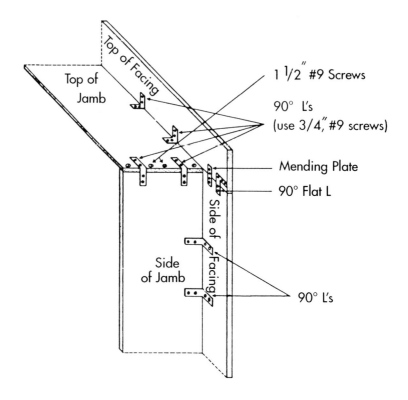

Figure 5.6. Door frame assembly detail.

more 90° Ls should be added to hold the two units together firmly. Be careful not to use too many Ls on the top, however, as they might block the easy sliding of the door frame into the door flat.

The bottom sill should be beveled with a draw knife or a plane to prevent actors from stumbling over the sill. The door attached to the frame is made the same size as the *inside* dimensions of the frame. The door is made of either Upson board or plywood. Upson board is preferable since it is lighter and easier to handle and is cheaper. The door can be as plain or ornate as desired. It is best to begin with a plain door and decorate it as needed with picture frame mouldings of various widths and thicknesses. Rope has been used to create Victorian ornate doors and thin strips of scrap lumber create interesting depth to doors. The door, without the Upson board cover, is built just as the flat frame was constructed: i.e., top rail and bottom rail are the exact same width and the stiles are shorter than the finished height.

The Upson board is then tacked or stapled to the door. The door is hinged to the door frame with loose pin hinges on the *left side* for door frames going on stage right and on the *right side* for frames going on stage left. *Doors should always open downstage* (to mask the offstage area); *doors should be hinged on the upstage side.*

Window frames are constructed in a fashion similar to the door frame, except they are made shorter to fit the window flat. The width of the unit is the same. The height is 3'8" *inside* the window proper. While some designers make windows that slide up and down, like regular home windows, small windowpanes can be designed and nailed to the jamb of the window as need dictates. Regular plaster lath or trellis material may be used to effect a variety of designs from modern to colonial windows. Door or window frames may be held in the flat by several methods. An old-fashioned 6" strap hinge can be placed at an angle on both sides of the jamb so that when it is opened it presses firmly against the flat stile. This method makes shifting the scenery very easy. Another method is to use either 1" × 3" or 2" × 4" blocks, 6" to 8" long, and screw them to the jamb once the frame is in the flat. This method is more permanent and is recommended for single-set plays only. Some stage crews use 90° Ls to fasten the frame to the flat. Door and window flats should be braced with stage braces on *both sides* of the frame. Door frames in flats add considerable weight, and such bracing is necessary to make certain the flats do not fall. Using regular house doors for stage purposes is not advised, because they are much too heavy and create more problems than they solve.

Platforms

Creating various levels on the stage is one of the most interesting effects a stage crew can produce. Platforms vary in height from 4" to several feet. In the smaller heights, 4" and 6", it is best to build a solid platform using 2" × 4"s or 2" × 6"s for the outer frame and the "stringer," a horizontal support piece. Build all platforms using a sheet of 3/4" A/D (A/D means one side good, the other side rough) plywood that is 4' × 8'. If platforms are constructed in widths of 4' × 8' and 2' × 4', it is possible to use one top for several platforms. (Sometimes the movable tops are called "lids.") The lids will interchange with the parallel platforms as well.

Tops or lids, made from 3/4" plywood and blocks, are placed on the rough side to prevent the lid from shifting once it is on the platform. Tops should be padded with old carpeting, wrong side up, or with layers of newspaper and unbleached muslin. Avoid using any "noisy" substance as a covering material for lids.

Parallel platforms usually are constructed in 12", 18", 24", 30", and 36" heights. The design of each is the same, and the leg heights and the braces just increase in size. In Figure 5.7 the side and end structures are pictured. It is best to join the parallel with more than five screws at the joints. *Remember, this structure is designed to give strength without weight.* It is constructed of a 1" × 3" of the same quality used in building flats. In Figure 5.8 the hinging process is illustrated. If this is not followed exactly, the parallel will not fold properly. Drop-pin hinges should be used.

There is a tendency for beginners to build platforms rock-solid with regular construction materials, the 2" × 4"s, 2" × 6"s, and 2" × 8"s used in home building. If you have ample storage space backstage this is not a bad practice, as platforms to hold human beings *should* be strong. However, space limitations and costs should lead stage crews to consider building with lighter materials but constructing to gain maximum strength. While parallels of 1" × 3" or 1" × 4" are strong up to a height of 3 feet, platforms over that height must be built of 2" × 4" or 2" × 6" for sufficient strength and rigidity.

Figure 5.7. Sides of the parallel platform.

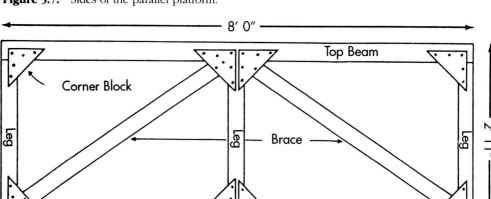

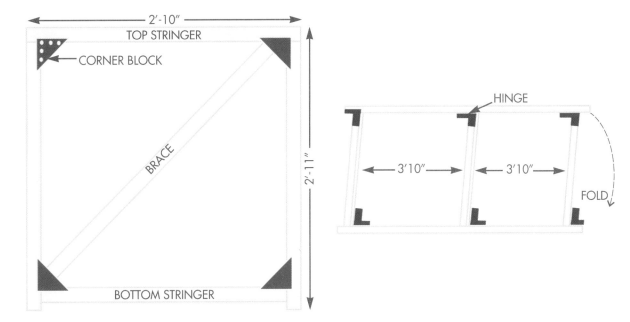

Figure 5.8. The hinging process: (Left) The ends and middle of the parallel platform; (right) placement of hinges.

Special Sizes and Shapes

Any size or shape flat, door flat, door frame, or platform can be constructed to meet special needs. Basic scenery construction methods and suggestions toward standardization in sizes have been discussed here. Many of the plays to be produced in schools today are one-set shows requiring such standard items.

Once the scenery is constructed, it is ready for painting.

Choosing Colors for the Set

Usually before set construction even begins the color scheme for the set has been chosen. The director may make the selection, or he or she may consult with the set designer. The choice of colors involves many considerations. For example, should the chosen colors be warm or cool? (See Figure 5.9.) Certainly, there are many theories about what colors say and do. Consider asking an art teacher to talk briefly to the company about color, the color wheel, and the messages various colors communicate.

One theory is that cool colors are best for serious dramas, mysteries, and classic plays, while warm colors are best for comedies, farces, and lighter dramas. Another theory is based on

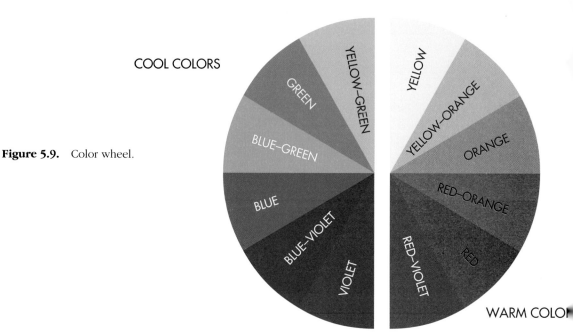

COOL COLORS

Figure 5.9. Color wheel.

WARM COLOR

some psychologists' beliefs about how colors affect us; for example, green walls are restful and reassuring, while red or purple walls are intense and provoke quarreling. Still other theories concern the symbolic use of colors in literature; blue is like the sea, vast and cool, while white connotes purity and innocence.

Finally, what purpose does the set have in the production? For example, if the set is to be symbolic or will serve merely to reinforce a theme, theories such as those mentioned previously will likely influence color choices. However, if the set is meant to represent the room of a certain character or characters in a specific time and place, then the popular decorating colors of that period and the income and personality of the characters will tend to dictate color choice.

Mixing the Paint

After the set colors are chosen, painting scenery involves the following steps: (1) mixing the base coat, (2) applying the base coat, and (3) adding texture coats.

For many years all scenery was painted with regular artists' dry colors. Indeed, they still are used by many scenic artists. Frequently, scenery or paint crews have a great deal of difficulty in mixing dry paint properly, though, so a substitute of suitable quality is desirable.

Most major paint companies produce a waterbase *casein paint* that can be mixed in almost as many shades as dry color. Mixing casein paints is much simpler than mixing dry paints. Casein comes in a very thick consistency (much like butter), and mixing a gallon of base with a gallon and a half of water produces paint of about the thickness of heavy cream, just the right painting consistency. With casein paints, *no glue need be added* to the mix. If you use white as the base for nearly all colors, it will be possible to get the exact color desired, and white is rather inexpensive compared to the intense colors of raw umber and burnt sienna. As in dry color, *a little intense color goes a long way,* so add color slowly.

Casein paints are readily available from hardware, paint stores, and lumberyards. Scenery or paint crews can mix paint easily with minimum supervision by the director once the color and proper proportions have been determined. Mixing requires three or more 10-quart plastic buckets, a strong paint paddle, warm water, the base color, and tinting colors. A plastic measuring cup (one cup or one quart) will help in determining exact measurements. In the beginning it is wise to *mix more* paint than you feel you will need. Casein paints keep a week or more if they are covered with a wet towel or rag when not in use.

A more recent development in scenic paint is a super-saturated paint that combines the advantages of casein paint and artists' dry pigments. The concentrated paints offer a rich variety of colors in a heavy paste form at a very low cost per gallon. Two quarts of the concentrate make a gallon or more of paint. Roscopaint, the manufacturer's trade name, overcomes some of the problems of casein paint: limited color range, powdering, and rather quick deterioration. In addition, the advantages over dry pigments are greater: quick mixing, exact color duplication from one pint to several gallons, and slow deterioration. The texture of the concentrated paints is a smooth, non-glare, matte surface that reflects light very well. The manufacturer offers a test kit for scenery crews and paint crews to try before purchasing larger quantities. The paint is available only from theatre supply houses or the manufacturer.

Reminders About Painting

- Do not use any form of enamel or oil-base paint on flats unless you plan to throw them away after one show. You cannot paint over oil-base paints on muslin.

- Do not use spray cans of gold, silver, or copper paint on flats. It is nearly impossible to paint over gold, silver, and copper paints.

- Avoid latex paints except for door frames and furniture. It builds up on flats, makes them sag, and gives them a shiny appearance under stage lights.

- If several people on the crew are painting flats, it is best that they work together and blend their work, since no two people paint alike.

- No one learns to paint out of a book. Practice is the only way to perfect painting techniques.

Applying the Base Coat

To apply the base coat of paint, all the flats are laid face up on the stage or the scene-shop floor. Be certain that a walkway is left between the flats so that painters can walk all the way around a flat. Using 4"—or better still, 6"—nylon-bristle brushes, apply the paint by dipping the brush into the paint and wiping the excess off on the inside edge of the paint pail. Care should be taken not to get too much paint on the brush or to dip the brush too deeply in the paint. The paint is then applied to the flat in a series of overlapping strokes, in the shape of figure 8s or Xs. (See Figure 5.10.) Do not attempt to paint too far with one brushload of paint; instead, dip the brush frequently in the paint.

Figure 5.10.
Applying the base coat.

Painting flats as they lie flat on the floor presents the possibility of puddling—of paint collecting in puddles at various points on the flat, usually near the center above and below the toggle bar. It is best to work from the center to the outer rail as you apply the base coat. Paint applied in figure 8s gives a much better texture than that applied in straight lines. The base coat should be allowed to dry at least twelve hours before any other paint is applied to the flat.

It is best to stir the paint frequently, although casein and concentrated paints settle out less than dry-color mixes. If many flats are to be painted, begin painting the flats at one end of the stage and work to the other end; in an hour or two the flats that were painted first have "set" enough that they can be leaned against the back wall of the stage and will take up much less space than if they were left lying horizontally.

Adding Texture Coats

Flats painted with a base coat are *not* complete; they lack texture and depth. To achieve a more realistic finish, the flats need another paint treatment. Various methods have been employed by scenic artists to get the proper texture desired. These include spattering, spraying, and dry brushing—a special effects technique for creating a wood-grain appearance.

Spattering

Spattering (see Figure 5.11) is one of the techniques used to add texture or to age a set, bringing depth and surface interest to the walls. Aging makes the set appear more realistic and lived in and avoids a newly painted look.

To spatter, the clean brush is dipped lightly into the paint color selected as the *first* spatter coat, and the paint is "flipped" toward the flat so that the paint lands in tiny drops. To achieve this look, the brush can be struck against a board or hit against the hand. The size of the drops will vary with the amount of

Figure 5.11. Spattering.

Figure 5.12. Dry brushing.

paint used. Be careful not to get too much paint on, though, as this will spoil the effect. It's best to try this technique on a practice flat first, if possible.

The color of the first spatter coat should be either a full shade lighter or darker than the base coat, but of the same hue. A good rule is that if the base coat is light, spatter with a darker shade first; if the base coat is dark, spatter with a lighter shade first. The second spatter coat can be applied once the first coat has dried, usually in three to four hours. The second spatter coat should be an opposite color—across the color wheel from the base coat. (See Figure 5.9.) Be particularly careful not to spatter opposite colors too heavily, because doing so will change the color of the set. A third and fourth spatter coat can be applied, depending upon the texture desired. To make flats look old, spatter with dark brown and black, especially near the top of the flat.

Spraying

Spraying is a quick method of achieving results similar to spattering. The use of hand fly-spray guns is not usually effective, however. Occasionally, one of the more expensive large-capacity models will work for a while, but eventually the nozzle will clog. Paint used in spray guns should be thinned down considerably and stirred thoroughly so that there are no lumps. Spraying should be done 10 to 18 inches from the flat, depending on the kind of gun. The large tank-type garden spray is one of the most dependable kinds of hand-operated sprayers. Although they are much more expensive to purchase, they outlast many of the inexpensive fly-spray guns. The best spray gun is the electric type, and some models now are fairly inexpensive. This gun takes practice to use properly but produces wonderful results. Needless to say, all spray guns should be cleaned completely after each spray coat. Spraying gives a much finer texture than spattering, and more colors can be used. Both spraying and spattering a set can produce some very effective texture results.

Dry Brushing

Some sets require the effect of wood grain. To achieve this look, start with a base coat that is the same tone as the finished job. Then paint on a pattern of streaks to represent the wood grain.

This calls for a dry-brushing technique, which requires that you start with a dry brush and dip it very lightly in paint several shades lighter than the base. Then drag it across the surface to be grained. (See Figure 5.12.) Next, take a different dry brush and dip it lightly in a paint several shades darker than the base, and drag it across the surface to be grained. Be sure the brush is *absolutely dry* to start and dip it very lightly into the paint. Keep in mind that you can always add more grain, but you can't erase it. To simulate the look of rough planks, paint cracks at what would be the edges of individual boards.

Special Effects

The top of the set should be darkened so it will not lead the eye of the audience upward and distract them from the action of the play. The shadow paint may be a darker version of the darkest tone already used on the walls, or it may be a mixture of burnt umber and ultramarine. You need to spatter the shadow paint thickly at the top of the set, begin thinning it out at the 11-foot level, and allow it to disappear entirely at 8 feet. Shadow the corners to a little lower than that; that way the shadowing won't be exactly even all the way around or look too mechanical.

Ceilings. If your set is to have a ceiling, remember that a light ceiling is distracting to the audience. Instead, paint the ceiling with a medium-tan base coat and then add spatters of dull blue and dull red, slightly paler than the base coat. This color scheme should blend in with a set of almost any color. Probably, though, you will not need to bother with a ceiling. Instead let the border—the short curtain running along the top of the stage—serve to mask the open area above the stage.

Wallpaper. Seldom does a set have actual wallpaper on it. Instead, you apply the pattern or design you want with a stencil, a sponge, or by freehand. Then the surface is spattered until the pattern is more subtle. Note that when the spatter still is wet, the wallpaper pattern will be more visible than when the paint has dried, so don't overdo the spattering.

Stone. To create the effect of stones, make the base coat a blend of several stonelike tones and paint mortar (the mixture that cements stones together) lines over this. Then spatter irregularly with a mixture of burnt umber and ultramarine. Use this same mix of colors to shadow each stone (draw a dark outline around what would be individual stones) and to draw cracks.

125

Brick. To create the effect of a smooth brick wall, use brick color for the base coat and a sand or grey color for the mortar. For a rough brick effect, use mortar color for the base coat and then paint in each brick separately with just two strokes of the brush. For either type of brick effect, finish by shadowing each brick and then spattering with a dark paint to give texture.

THE LOAD-IN

Once the scenery has been constructed and painted, it's ready for the load-in, or placement onstage. It is most important that no one attempt to carry a flat alone. Flats must be carried by two people, with one person positioned at each end of the flat. If you try to carry a flat alone, you risk personal injury and you can easily crack the stiles or rails of the flat or tear the muslin on other scenery.

As the flats are placed on stage they need to be attached to one another in some way. There are three methods of assembly: lashing, nailing, and hinging.

Lashing

Lashing flats together is the commonest and simplest method of putting up scenery. Each flat has a length of clothesline, called *lashline,* attached to the upper right-hand corner (as one looks at the back of the flat). To attach the lashline, drill a $7/16''$ hole through the upper right-hand corner block of the flat to the left of the right-hand edge. Pass a $1/2''$ sash cord as long as the flat is high through this hole and knot it on the inner end. (See Figure 5.1, page 107.)

Spaced at regular intervals below the lashline are *lash cleats,* over which the lashline is thrown or flipped by holding onto the lower end of the lashline and aiming for the top lash cleat with the natural loop created by the throw. Lashing requires a little practice, so crew members should not be discouraged if they miss the lash cleat a few times. Some stage managers or scenery chairpeople prefer to lash with the aid of a stepladder. The lashline is then moved from one cleat to the other. The bottom cleats on most flats are called *tie-off* cleats and are somewhat thinner than the regular lash cleat. After all cleats have been included in the lashline, a tie-off is made according to Figure 5.13. You

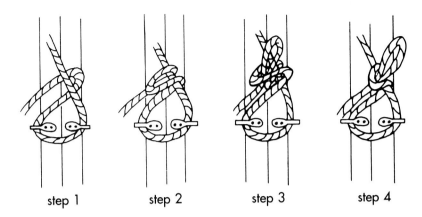

Figure 5.13.
Lashing tie-off.

step 1   step 2   step 3   step 4

should remember to keep the lashline as tight as possible during the entire process, including the tie-off. A little practice lashing and tying-off will make most members of the stage crew proficient after one play.

Nailing

Nailing scenery together is another method of assembly; however, doing so presents safety problems. Be sure to exercise caution when you use a hammer. To nail flats together in pairs it is necessary to place the flat down on the stage and to use short scraps of 1" × 3" as the joiner. It is best if the flats are joined in at least three places—top, bottom, and at the middle above the toggle bar. Occasionally two flats will meet at 90°, more or less, and you can join these by placing a six-penny nail in the stile at the top, bottom, and middle. Make certain that the nail hits the edge of the stile of flat #2 in this process. It is best not to drive the nail all the way in, but to leave just enough of the head out so that it can be removed with a claw hammer. A supply of sixpenny (2") or eightpenny (2½") double-headed nails can be kept on hand for this purpose. The nailing method of assembly should not be used if the set is to be changed during the play or if it is necessary to clear the stage for other activities before the actual production date. Since this situation occurs in most schools, it is recommended that the flats be nailed in pairs so the set can quickly be reassembled without repeating the nailing process.

Hinging

Hinging flats together is a third method of assembly. Drop-pin or loose-pin hinges are used in *all* hinging on the stage. (See Figure 5.14.) The reason for this should be quite clear. All flats must come apart for easy storage, and unless the flats are built as two- or threefolds, they cannot be folded completely. In putting hinges on the flats for assembly purposes, they must be attached at a standard distance from the top and the bottom of the flat. Flats are not always assembled in the same order for each production, and they should be interchangeable with one another.

While hinging has many apparent advantages, cost is not one of them; hinges will probably cost at least $2.50 a pair. Another disadvantage is that, no matter how hard the stage crew tries, not all flats are going to assemble with hinges alone. Matching up hinges on ten flats so that all interchange is nearly impossible; the set always assembles best the way it was done originally. Hinging works best on twofold and threefold flats, intended to be permanently hinged together. In making this assembly it is necessary to use a "jigger," a 1" × 2" strip placed between the two flats to facilitate folding. (See Figure 5.15.)

Large walls may be assembled by using a "stiffener" (a long length of 1" × 3") and a "keeper hook." The keeper hook is a piece, usually of 1/2"-wide flat-iron, bent to an S shape to slide over the toggle bar of the flat. When you are assembling three flats, it is necessary to have three keepers, one for each flat, placed in the center of the toggle bar, and the 1" × 3" stiffener is dropped in the bottom loop of the S.

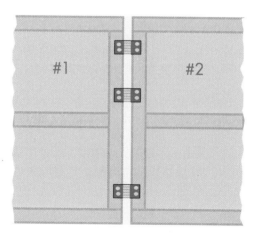

Figure 5.14.
Hinging flats.

#1   #2

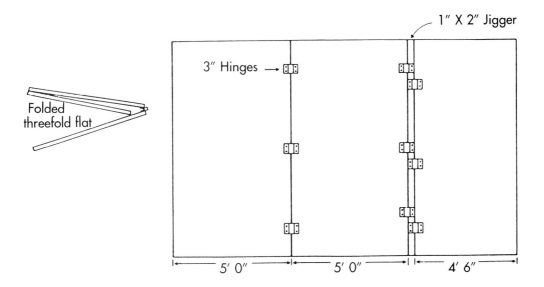

1" X 2" Jigger

3" Hinges

Folded
threefold flat

5' 0"   5' 0"   4' 6"

Figure 5.15. Threefold flats.

Large, straight walls of 3 or more flats may be assembled by
using a stiffener (a long length of 1" × 3") placed across the back
of all the flats of the wall and nailed to each individual flat in
several places with double-headed nails. Usually two stiffeners
are needed to give the wall sufficient rigidity and stability. Care
should be taken not to drive the nails through the flat, but just
far enough in to secure a bond.

Bracing the Set

At certain key points all sets need to be braced with stage braces
or homemade versions of stage braces. (See Figure 5.16.)
Entrances require bracing on both sides of the door (hinged and
opening). Long, flat walls require at least one brace, and frequently the windows need bracing. A commercial stage brace,
either of wood or aluminum, lasts for years. The hook at the top
of the brace is inserted upside down into the brace cleat on the
flat and turned 180° so that the brace rests against the flat stile
and the brace cleat. These directions are important! A misapplied
brace can ruin weeks of work by ripping through the muslin
covering with the first jar the brace gets backstage. The "rocker"
end of the stage brace is either screwed to the stage floor with a

Figure 5.16.
Adjustable stage brace.

Figure 5.17.
Non-skid floor plate.

Figure 5.18.
Scenery jack.

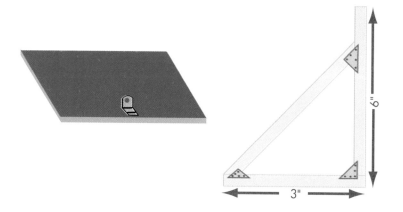

stage screw or nailed with #10 or #12 nails. The nails are then bent over. The adjustment in the center of the brace provides for making certain the flat stands straight and does not tilt backward or forward. Be certain the thumb screw is tight once the flat stands straight.

In many schools nailing into the stage floor or drilling holes for stage screws is strictly forbidden. In other schools the stage floor is made of regular hardwood flooring instead of softwood, as recommended by theatre architects. One manufacturer of stage hardware has perfected a "non-skid floor plate" for use with stage braces. (See Figure 5.17.) These are useful on hardwood or tile floors. Another method is to build a bracing strip of 2" × 4"s attached to the back and side walls of the stage so the set is braced from the top rail of the flat to the bracing strip.

Other methods of bracing are making pseudo-stage braces of 1" × 3"s in a T shape and nailing them to the flat stile edge. Set pieces may be braced with a stage brace or it may be held upright by means of scenery jacks. A scenery jack is made of 1" × 3"s in a triangle shape in varying heights, according to the height of the flat or set piece. (See Figure 5.18.) The height of the jack is usually twice that of the base, but this may vary according to backstage conditions. Jacks are attached to the flat at the toggle bar with hinges. The flat should be laid face down on the stage and the jack laid on the flat $1/2''$ from the bottom rail. The $1/2''$ provides space for the flat to rock back, and the weight of the flat is carried on the back one-third of the jack. Sometimes jacks are attached to both the right and left stiles and sandbags are used to weight them down. It is not necessary to screw scenery jacks to the stage floor.

Dutching

Often a good set is spoiled by noticeable cracks between the flats. This problem is easily solved by dutching the seams. (Recall that previously, in a discussion of door and window flats, a "dutchman"—a 5" to 6" strip of muslin—could be applied directly to the flat with paint to hide cracks.) Anyone not actively involved in the load-in can help out in some way with this. First, tear leftover long scraps of muslin into strips 4' or 5' wide. Obviously, if the strips are as long as the flats are tall, so much the better, but the strips can be pieced together. The edges of the muslin strips must be smooth, so carefully pull off any hanging threads. This takes patience, but actors can sit and run lines while they help do it.

Next, glue the strips of muslin over the cracks between flats. When they are dry, the dutchman strips of muslin can be painted to match the flats. The smooth effect achieved is worth the effort.

Shifting Scenery

Frequently, sets need to be shifted during the course of a performance, and thus nailing flats together for assembly is impractical. After all, you don't want the audience sitting in the dark, staring at a closed curtain, and listening to hammering for five minutes.

As you know, plays are divided into acts and scenes, and these divisions often indicate a change in time or place—the points at which you would be most likely to shift scenery. To give the stage crew time to shift scenery, allow for a formal intermission between acts. Indicate it in the program, sell or serve refreshments in the lobby, and play music in keeping with the time period or mood of the play over the speaker system.

Like a kind of backstage blocking, the shifting of any scenery requires detailed planning and rehearsing. Each crew member must know exactly what he or she is to do to complete the shift. A "shifting chart" can be used to record each crew member's specific task.

In the plan shown on page 133 the first set is taken down completely, starting at the two downstage sides. Once the walls are removed, the set furnishings are struck. Then the furnishings for the second set are loaded-in before the walls of the second set are loaded-in. Each flat is numbered on the back, and a unit is two flats joined together.

Shifting scenery requires practice and strict adherence to the agreed-upon plan.

SPECIAL SITUATIONS

The Arena Stage

Since an arena stage has audience on all sides, any elements of scenery must be low enough to satisfy audience sightlines. As there is no curtain, any scene changes are made in full view of the audience. Often, the crew members who make the changes dress alike in nonobtrusive clothing, such as black or grey sweatsuits. Spike marks—bits of phosphorescent tape—can be used to mark the position of all furniture and ground rows, so that even if you have to make changes in the dark or twenty percent light, you can find positions easily. This kind of scenery shifting takes at least as much practice and planning as that carried out backstage.

Sightlines

The imaginary lines from the audience to the stage are known as **sightlines.** Directors plan the blocking to accommodate the sightlines so that all members of the audience are able to see the play's action.

Set designers and builders must ensure that offstage areas are masked from every spot in the house. This is often accomplished by using masking flats. For example, if a door is opened on-

Shifting Chart

PHASE ONE
Vijay and Shannon strike Unit One
Kelly and Kendra strike Unit Seven
Roberto and Matt strike Unit Two
Casey and Shana strike Unit Six

PHASE TWO
Vijay, Shannon, Kelly, and Kendra strike Units Three-Four-
    Five intact
Roberto and Matt strike sofa
Casey and Shana strike chairs

PHASE THREE
Vijay and Shannon strike lamps
Kelly and Kendra strike table
Roberto and Matt strike bookcase and books
Casey and Shana strike coffee table and vase of flowers

PHASE FOUR
Vijay and Shannon strike carpet
Kelly and Kendra set park bench
Roberto and Matt set hedges
Casey and Shana set street lights

PHASE FIVE
Vijay and Shannon set Unit Eight
Kelly and Kendra set Unit Fourteen
Roberto and Matt set Unit Nine
Casey and Shana set Unit Thirteen

PHASE SIX
Vijay, Shannon, Kelly, and Kendra set Units Ten-Eleven-
    Twelve intact
Roberto and Matt set moon
Casey and Shana set stars

stage, instead of the audience glimpsing the wings or a theatre wall, they see a flat painted to look like a hallway or another room or the outdoors.

Scrim

A dark blue theatrical gauze sturdier than commercial gauze, a **scrim** can be hung as a drop in front of a set. With special lighting effects it can function as a set in front of the main set. To change the set, simply raise the scrim out of sight and the inner set is revealed.

Set within a Set

The set to be used first is smaller, built inside the second or outer set. (See Figure 5.19.) To shift the first set you remove a unit of the second set and strike the inner set through that opening. When the inner set has been completely struck—this includes the furnishings—you load-in the furnishings of the second or outer set and then replace the unit you used as the opening for the strike. This is a good method for scene shifting, especially if you need to go back to the first, or inner set, again later in the play.

Figure 5.19.   Set within a set.

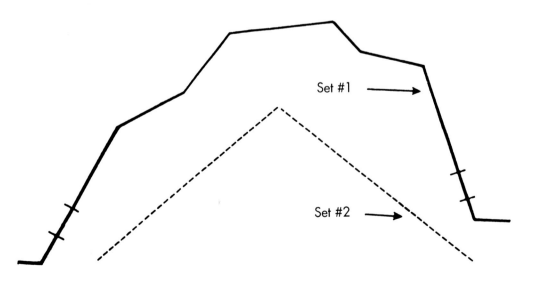

SUMMARY

There are several actor's techniques for memorization of lines, voice production, and relaxation. You should experiment with them to learn which methods work best for you. Work areas such as the scene shop must be kept clean and orderly for safety and maximum effectiveness. Constructing the set begins with building the flats, and this requires careful and deliberate selection and preparation of lumber, fabric, glue, hardware, and paint. Through painting techniques you can go on to create the effect of surfaces for your set such as brick, stone, wallpaper, and wood grain. Finally, any scene shifting must be carefully planned and rehearsed.

The European Renaissance is known for the painting and sculpture of Italy, the exploration and conquests of Spain, and the social reorganization and philosophical speculations of France. In addition, the theatre thrived during this period. Public theatre in Germany was stimulated by traveling troupes of English actors. In Spain, the theatre flourished with the plays of Cervantes and Lope. France had its court drama, which was later to affect the English Restoration. But the most important and most lasting in influence was the **commedia dell'arte** of Italy, an improvisational comedy using stock characters.

After the fall of Rome, formal drama ceased to exist for centuries, but theatre was kept alive by the vagabond troupes who traveled the countryside, usually in family groups, performing wherever and whenever they could for whatever pay—usually food and lodging—they could get. The skills and arts of juggling, acrobatics, singing, dancing, and comic routines were passed down from generation to generation. By the sixteenth century, permanent theatre structures were used, and the commedia dell'arte was established.

There are no existing scripts from commedia productions because the shows were largely improvisational. There would be a *scenario* or plot outline, and then the performers would try various jokes, tricks, or bits of stage business they called **lazzi.** The performers kept what audiences liked and used it again and again, each troupe jealously guarding its own lazzi and passing them down from parent to child. The basic scenarios were from Roman comedy, as was the cast of stock characters.

Commedia actors needed to be skilled in all the performing arts. Performers played the same character for years, maybe for an entire career. The most famous of the young lovers were Arlecchino (later Harlequin) and Columbina. Arlecchino is sometimes one of the *zanni* or clown servants, and his lazzi included turning a somersault while holding a glass of water on a tray and not spilling a drop. His costume of black and white diamond-shaped patches has been used for centuries in masquerade and design. Columbina first appeared as a pert servant girl character. Gradually she became the daughter or ward of a tyrannical father. She loved Arlecchino and eventually eloped with him, but was often presented as unhappy in love. Other commedia stock characters were Scaramouche, Scapino, Pantaloon, and Coralina.

Commedia played to all types of audiences. It was truly family entertainment, and its descendants can be seen in today's clowns and mimes. The stock characters of Roman comedy, expanded upon by commedia, are the ancestors of today's staples of situation comedy: the arrogant jock, the stuffy English butler, the outraged father of teenagers, and the saucy secretary.

THEATRE WORKSHOP

Problem-solving Projects

1. Divide the cast into small groups of four or five actors and conduct brainstorming sessions about techniques for memorizing lines. Encourage cast members to discuss *their* memorization techniques.

2. To help improve enunciation, try quickly saying aloud the following tongue-twisting phrases, repeating each several times.
   a. Spring fling
   b. Floy joy
   c. Azure zoo
   d. Toy boat
   e. Dump truck
   f. Pink skink
   g. Chimney sweep
   h. Bogs, fogs, and frogs
   i. Pack him in pickles
   j. Chunky monkey

3. To understand how placing the emphasis can change the meaning of the sentence, choose one of the following sentences and repeat it six times, each time stressing a different word. What differences in meaning or attitude are expressed?
   a. I'd like some ice cream now.
   b. Our friends are staying here tonight.
   c. Mike is buying Sandy this ring.
   d. Can I really have pepperoni pizza?

4. Decide what you should do in each of the following situations:
   a. You want to touch up the paint at the top of a flat but there is no one else around.
   b. The ceiling of the set is too white; it seems to stand out like a light.
   c. The set design calls for a door leading to the kitchen. Since there is no actual kitchen, the door merely opens onto the wing area.
   d. You are working on the flat framing and the electric sander is making a funny noise.

5. Practice breathing from the diaphragm with the following exercises. Be careful not to do this for so long that you hyperventilate.
   a. Breathe in, and then with your exhale say:
   Ah hah hah hah hah hah hah.
   b. Breathe in and then exhale a stream of air with a hissing sound. Repeat this until you can sustain the hissing sound for thirty seconds without having to inhale again.
   c. Breathe in and with your exhale count to twenty. By repeating this exercise build to a count of twenty-five and then thirty.
   d. This exercise is particularly helpful in the phrasing of long lines of poetry that must be delivered without a break. Inhale deeply and then with your exhale recite the entire passage without taking a breath.
   - When the voices of children are heard on the green
   And laughing is heard on the hill

- In Xanadu did Kubla Khan
  A stately pleasure dome decree
- From rainbow clouds there
  flow not drops so bright to see
  As thy presence showers a rain
  of melody
- When I have fears that I may
  cease to be
  Before my pen has glean'd my
  teeming brain
- Paint must never hope to
  reproduce
  The faint half-flush that dies
  along her throat
- Midwinter spring is its own
  season
  Sempiternal though sodden
  towards sundown

e. Breathe in, and then with your
exhale say:
Ah haaaaaaaaaaaaaaaaaaah
(sliding up the scale). Then say:
Ah haaaaaaaaaaaaaaaaaaah
(sliding down the scale)

6. To make yourself more conscious of
carelessly enunciated words, for each
of the following write the correct
spelling and say it aloud with proper
enunciations.

a. Probly   j. Goinn
b. Yer   k. Lotta
c. Twunny   l. Useta
d. Tuh   m. Gimme
e. Becuz   n. Cuppa
f. Sposeta   o. Pertect
g. Hafta   p. Lemme
h. Gunna   q. Getcha
i. Wanna

Construction Projects

1. Construct a miniature version of a
flat, about 4" × 6", cover it with
muslin, and paint it to create one of
the following effects.
   a. Floral wallpaper
   b. Geometric patterned wallpaper
   c. Wood paneling
   d. Brick
   e. Stone

2. Make a set model for one of the
following:
   a. A box set for an interior scene in
      a play such as *Cinderella* or
      Sleeping Beauty.
   b. An arena stage set for an outdoor
      scene in a play such as *Ethan
      Frome, The Legend of Sleepy
      Hollow*, or *Jack and the Beanstalk*.
   c. An arras set with furniture for the
      tomb scene in *Romeo and Juliet*
      or the assassination scene in *Julius
      Caesar*.

3. Design a miniature periaktos to use in
a production of *Anne of Green Gables,
The Hobbit*, or *You're a Good Man,
Charlie Brown*.

4. Devise a scene-shifting chart for your
own production. If there is only one
set, make a chart for the load-in.

The Set Designer

Adrianne Lobel, a set designer whose work ranges from operas and Broadway musicals to Hollywood films and music videos, approaches each project by sketching, sketching, and sketching until something interesting shows up.

Because her parents wrote and illustrated children's books and led rather isolated lives, Lobel decided very early that she wanted to work in a field that involved other people. She went to Art and Design High School in New York City, where she learned to letter and "things like that." At the same time, she was taking evening classes at the Brooklyn Museum School. She was quite serious about painting, and wanted to be an Impressionist. But she also felt she should be doing something more collaborative.

After high school, Lobel attended Marlboro College in Vermont for a year. Marlboro had a small theatre department, and Lobel worked in the basement, building sets and making costumes for the productions. The summer after her first year there, she received a scholarship to work as a costume assistant at a summer stock theatre in the Berkshire Mountains. She took responsibility for the props and scenery because no one else seemed interested. Impressed with Lobel's talents,

the wardrobe manager suggested she study at the Lester Polakov Studio in New York.

While at the Polakov Studio, Lobel took a mask-making class with Fred Nihda and a set model–making class from Paul Zalon. She worked for awhile as Zalon's assistant, but wanted to be a designer. She applied to Yale Drama School and was accepted, but chose to go first to California, where she worked in film rather than theatre.

After two and a half years, Lobel felt ready to attend Yale, where she studied with Tony Award–winning designer Ming Cho Lee. At Yale she met future Broadway director Peter Sellars, with whom she worked on eight productions, including *My One and Only* and *The Magic Flute*.

Some of Adrianne Lobel's other credits include the films *Five Corners* and *Ask Me Again* and music videos. She designed the sets for Michael Jackson's "Bad," Herbie Hancock's "Hard Rock," and Janet Jackson's "Let's Wait Awhile." When Ronn Smith interviewed Lobel for his book *American Set Design 2*, Lobel described her designs as having a strong logic, adding, "I also think my work is very clean and modern . . . my sets require very good, neat, solid construction."

Reaching
the Audience

6

Company Meeting

In getting a production under way, difficulties often arise. These should be brought to the company meeting to share and solve.

PROGRESS REPORTS

By this point, each technical area should have developed its own specific schedule within the master production schedule. It's helpful to the entire company to hear how each area is doing at meeting its schedule. In addition, this week house management needs the time and attention of the company in order to start the publicity campaign.

TOPICS FOR THIS MEETING

- Theatre Games and the Company Spirit
- Publicity and Public Relations
- House Management

- The Story of Theatre: The English Renaissance
- Theatre Workshop
- Careers in the Theatre: The Poster Designer

WORKING VOCABULARY

Theatre terms of special interest in this chapter include: *theatre games, centering, public service announcement, press kit, set-ups,* and *comps.*

AGENDA

At the next company meeting you'll discuss "the treasured object," special circumstances in acting, building the costumes, wardrobe fittings, fabricating the props, selecting hairstyles, and designing the makeup. This will follow discussions by company members regarding production progress.

THEATRE GAMES AND COMPANY SPIRIT

Because the members of your company are each so busy with their individual responsibilities, occasionally your director may want to use part of a company meeting to focus on the company spirit. It's a chance to look around and remind yourself of each company member's contribution and your common goal of working together to produce a good show. Your director may want to involve you in some **theatre games**—structured improvisation, designed to bring the company closer together. One such theatre game puts the assistant director in charge of an expedition of company members—some cast, some crew. They

Theatre games, such as this expedition in the woods, can bring the company closer together.

become lost in the woods and must react according to their current role in the company. For example, the set construction crew attempts to build a shelter; the actor who plays the spoiled brat in the play whines about everything; and the person with the "Pollyanna" role in the play keeps trying to cheer up everyone.

In another theatre game, each member of the company draws the name of another and makes a collage that represents that person's role in the production. A collection of old magazines, paper, glue, and scissors are useful for playing this game.

Improvising on a Scene

If some of the actors are having difficulty with a particular section of a scene, it is often helpful to forget for the moment about the actual lines of the scene. Instead, work on what is *happening* by improvising on the general situation posed in the troublesome section. Your director may ask you to sit on the set and begin **centering** yourselves. This means to concentrate, to focus on the work at hand, to stay in character and in the moment of the play. Then, instead of trying to recall the lines, you simply talk to the others in the scene about what is going on at that moment in the action and how you feel about it. For example, if you were doing the part in Thornton Wilder's *Our Town* where Emily and George are at the soda fountain, you might talk about what's in the store, what the weather is like, what happened at school, what your friends are doing, how your family is, what kind of ice cream you like, and so on. This exercise can help you to fully understand your character at that moment in the play.

PUBLICITY AND PUBLIC RELATIONS

The nightmare of every host—giving a party and no one showing up—is magnified in the plight of well-rehearsed and eager actors, standing on stage and facing an audience that numbers fewer than the cast. Who lures the audience to the theatre? Mainly it is the responsibility of the publicist. The play may be a great one and the cast members may be known to everyone in town, but without posters, fliers, radio and television **public service announcements** (called *PSAs*), newspaper articles, and clever publicity, people will not be drawn to the performance.

While the actors work to perfect their performance, the house management crew turns its attention to attracting an audience for the production. Although publicity and public relations sometimes are handled separately from house management, both areas are supervised by the house manager. The function of house management is to attend to the needs of the audience, so publicity and public relations are included in the list of responsibilities.

The first rule of publicity is that *every* word or photo sent out must first be approved by the director. Don't ever be in too much of a hurry to do this. Remember, the director takes responsibility for every aspect of production and must therefore be consulted.

Press Lists

The company should have an up-to-date list of every publication in the community: commercial newspapers, school newspapers, business newspapers, magazines, club bulletins, radio and television guides, and food market circulars. The phone book is a source to start with, but don't depend on it because it may be out of date. With a quick phone call, you can check each listing and learn the name of the contact person at the publication. Whether you mail or hand-deliver your packet of information, it's helpful to address it to a particular person. Afterward, be sure to call or write to thank the individual and the publication for the publicity they gave your show. Not only is this courteous, it is good public relations for the company.

Press Kits

The **press kit** is a folder or large envelope of information sent to publications in order to gain publicity for a show. The press kit usually includes a 5" × 7" black-and-white glossy photograph of cast members, often in costume and posed as though in a scene from the play; a cast list; and a description of the play. The photograph should be accompanied by a caption identifying the actors shown and a sentence explaining the scene pictured. If there is something particularly noteworthy about the production—for example, the twenty-fifth show by the director, an anniversary of the play, the first production in the new auditorium—include that information in the press kit as well.

Obviously, preparing and mailing press kits consumes a portion of your budget, but the expenditure pays off when it attracts a paying audience into your theatre.

Photography

Given a choice between running a story with a photo or one without, editors will tend to use the piece accompanied by a photo. Readers, too, are drawn to an illustrated article. Thus, look for another way to save money and include a good photo to bring in audiences. Students from a photography club in your school or a staff member of the school newspaper or yearbook might be asked to shoot publicity photos. If there are no student photographers to help, ask among the school faculty and families of company members for someone with photography skills to do a shoot. Even an inquiry at a local camera shop could yield a volunteer, as employees tend to have a keen interest in photography. Finally, if no volunteers step forward, then approach a professional photographer and offer a free ad in the play program in exchange for a discount on publicity photos. (Although a newspaper sometimes will send a staff photographer,

Publicity photos submitted with the press kit should stimulate the public's curiosity about the production.

more often it is preferred that you supply your own pictures.) Regardless of who does the photography, however, the company publicist should confer with the director to choose the best photos for inclusion in press kits.

Photo Call

Six to eight weeks before the play opens a photo call should be scheduled. This offers the opportunity to photograph the entire company in head shots for the houseboard, and the cast, in some semblance of costuming, for the press kits. Each member of the company should be photographed from the shoulders up. These pictures are later arranged on a piece of bristol board, usually 3' × 4'. Bristol board is heavier than poster board and available in art supply stores, craft stores, and most variety stores. The houseboard is hung in the lobby or just outside it at all performances. In professional theatres the houseboard often features only the photos of the stars of the show. In educational theatre it is more appropriate, however, to include the entire company. Although the photos can simply be arranged in rows, it is preferable to place the photos attractively in clusters around a copy of the play program. If there is no room in the theatre department to display the houseboards of all the school's shows, it is customary to present the board to the house manager at the end of the show's run.

When photographing the cast for the press kits, the costumes worn need not be exactly those to be used in the play, as long as the clothing suggests the time of the play and the characters portrayed. Whoever arranges the photo call should confer with the director regarding not only time and place, but also set-ups.

Set-ups are staged situations that will make good photos— for example, someone peeking around a door, eavesdropping; someone showing surprise or horror or shock; or people arguing or dancing or dealing with awkward props. The goal is to take photos that will intrigue the potential audience and make them want to see the play. If the set has been loaded-in, consider shooting the photos there. If necessary, arrange something elsewhere to suggest the setting of the play. The photos won't show much more background than a couch or a tree anyway.

As the photos are being shot, a publicity crew member should be making notes on the following: the names of the actors in that photo, the characters they portray, and a summary of the action in the scene. This information will be helpful later when writing captions for the photos included in the press kits.

Paid Publicity

If your budget allows it, consider placing an ad in the entertainment section of the local paper. Depending on the amount of space your company can afford, you may want to include a photo. Be certain the information you include is complete. If you give a phone number for reservations, that phone should be equipped with an answering machine, as people like to be able to call at any hour. If your school offers a journalism class, consult with the teacher about the composition of the ad. Finally, to determine the effectiveness of your ad, include a statement that anyone presenting the ad at the box office will receive a certain discount on the admission price. If almost no one presents the ad, you may want to look for another way to invest the company's advertising budget for the next production.

Public Service Announcements

Television and radio advertising is very expensive, but often stations will broadcast free public service announcements (PSA) for nonprofit organizations and schools. They will want the information a few weeks ahead of time, and they may suggest that you offer **comps,** that is, free tickets, to give away as a promotion. This benefits both your company and their organization, so don't hesitate to oblige them by providing comps at their request.

In most areas radio and television stations are required to provide public service, and broadcasting PSAs is one way to do this. Your announcement must be precise and well written, of course, and you should try to incorporate some intriguing aspect about your production, if possible. When a station receives many requests for PSAs, they probably will choose the most interesting to broadcast. Is this the first production in your new theatre? Is this a West Coast (or Midwest or Atlantic Seaboard) premiere of the play? Is it the ten thousandth performance of the play in this country? Highlight some aspect or detail that will prompt the station to choose your PSA from among all those it receives.

Posters

Since almost every place you can hang posters—store windows, community bulletin boards, school hallways—is probably already cluttered with paper, you need to make your message as attractive and conspicuous as possible. If there is no artist in your company, ask for the help of students in art classes. Perhaps you could hold a competition for the best poster design, offering a prize of tickets to the play and, if the budget allows, a gift certificate to an art supplies store. If no one at school shows interest, open the competition to a nearby college. The prize of art supplies is one any artist would appreciate, as well as the exposure gained by having the winning design appear, with a credit, on posters, fliers, and programs. Finally, if artistic talent and originality are too hard to come by, don't overlook the convenience of computer-generated graphic designs.

If your school has no print shop, take posters, fliers, and programs to a local photocopy shop for printing. If you want to economize, consider having the fliers and posters be exactly

Hang fliers and posters for your production in school hallways, shops, and other public places, but make sure you obtain permission first.

alike in design and size, but print the fliers on paper and the posters on card stock. Make sure the color selected for the publicity materials is approved by the director and matches set decor or in some way ties in with the play.

Everyone in the company should take responsibility for putting up some posters. You might want to divide up the town businesses, clubs, churches, libraries, community centers, and public buildings among the company members. The publicity crew could then check periodically and replace any posters spoiled by weather or removed. Of course, you must obtain permission before posting anything.

Fliers

Because the price per sheet for photocopying decreases for large orders, you may find the flier the best method for publicity. It can be posted indoors, mailed, and distributed at public events.

Press kits need to be mailed a month in advance of the performance so that publicity releases can be published the week before the opening. Posters can be hung two weeks before the performance, followed by fliers the week before the opening. If your company had T-shirts or sweatshirts printed with the show's logo, these should be worn whenever fliers are distributed to attract attention and to reinforce the name of the show.

Gimmicks

A gimmick is a clever means to attract attention to your show. The company T-shirt is a gimmick; another is the pin-on button. Companies such as Broadway Buttons in New York City will use your own art work, such as your poster design, or will typeset your own wording and make buttons to advertise your show. Prices start at about one dollar a button. These not only provide publicity but also make good souvenirs.

You might try asking local businesses to buy a block of tickets at the group rate. Then they can give away tickets with any purchase over a minimum amount. If customers get one ticket that way, they are apt to buy another and bring a friend to the play.

Gimmicks such as company T-shirts help advertise your show.

If your play has some brief scenes that can stand on their own out of context, you could ask the homeroom teachers for a few minutes of class time to present one. Prepare several, so that everyone in the cast will have a chance to work in these and so that every student won't see the same scene. You might also approach community organizations and churches and offer your scene as entertainment at one of their meetings. Senior citizen centers, the chamber of commerce, or scout troops in your area might welcome the chance to preview your play. Be sure to offer group rates to these organizations when you visit them.

Publicity promotes your event. Public relations maintains a courteous and pleasant relationship with the public. Any person or organization helping to publicize your play and anyone attending a performance should be thanked.

HOUSE MANAGEMENT

The members of the house management crew are the hosts of your show. They have direct contact with the audience, whose safety, comfort, and enjoyment are their primary concerns. By enhancing a patron's enjoyment, these company members build a return audience for future shows.

The Box Office

The box office for your show may be an actual ticket booth just outside the theatre or in the lobby, or it may be a folding table positioned at the door to the house. At some schools, the practice is to have the box office run by school administrators, teachers, or members of the PTA. If company members do work in the box office, they should be friendly, quick at making change, and able to remain calm when large groups of people arrive just before curtain time. If company members are only to assist in the box office, they can distribute the tickets, find and cross names off the reservation list, and, of course, make gracious comments such as "Enjoy the show," or "Thank you for coming."

Reservations and Advance Ticket Sales

More and more theatre companies are using a system of taking reservations but not actually selling any tickets in advance. That way the money is handled all at one time and no one has to worry about taking an allotment of tickets to sell and then turning back unsold tickets in time to know how many are sold for a given performance. While it's true that a few people will make a reservation and then not show up, usually there will be some walk-ins glad to have the tickets. You should inform patrons that reservations will be held at the box office until fifteen minutes before curtain (longer or shorter times if you prefer, but shorter times can mean a logjam at the box office just before curtain). After that, tickets will be released to walk-in patrons. With this method, you don't need to print any fancy tickets since the patrons will be giving them to the ushers just a few feet away. Something simple photocopied on card stock and then cut on a paper cutter will be adequate. The ticket color should match the programs, and if you print all the dates of the show's run on the

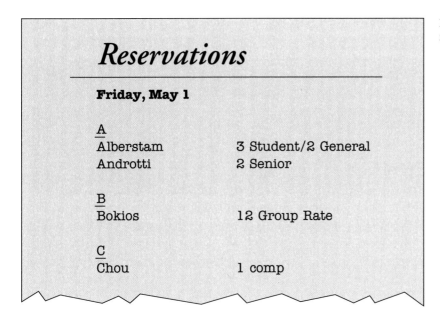

Figure 6.1.
Sample reservations list.

tickets you have only to circle the appropriate date as you hand out the ticket.

If the company policy is to sell advance tickets, they should be printed on sturdy stock that matches the color of the program, and they should contain time, date, and place information about the performance. One or two people on the house management crew should be in charge of ticket sales so that the house manager can find out quickly how many tickets are left for a given performance.

Numbered Tickets

If your theatre is large and some seats are definitely better than others, you may want to have a range of ticket prices and number the tickets to indicate the specific seat the patron must occupy. However, more and more educational and community theatres are using "festival seating," that is, first to arrive has the pick of the seats. If you do decide to use festival seating, be sure to explain that policy to all reservation makers and ticket buyers.

Reservation Lists

As the reservations come in over the phone or in person, the crew member in charge needs to make a note of them. A good system for keeping track of reservations is to have a notebook with a separate page for each night of performance. Close to the opening of the box office, which usually is forty-five minutes to half an hour before curtain, the reservation list for that performance should be typed, in alphabetical order, and given to the house manager. In Figure 6.1, there are three ticket prices: General Admission, Senior Citizen/Student, and Group Rate.

Comps

There may be a school policy about complimentary or free tickets. If not, the director may set a policy for each production, or he or she may allow the company to establish a policy for their show. Policies range from allowing no comps at all to providing comps for people who have helped the company (by giving or loaning props and costumes, or helping with set construction or publicity) to comps for all company members. Even if the company members are allowed to give out comp tickets, some rules need to be established. For example:

1. No comps for anyone who would attend anyway.
2. No more than one comp per individual or family. That way any guests they bring will be paying.
3. Don't "force" a comp on someone who isn't interested. That just wastes it.
4. Comps may be given away in a free drawing in one's homeroom, club, or church.

Box Office Statement

After each performance, the box office statement, or account of the evening's attendance and income, should be checked and signed by the house manager and then given to the director or school authority. No house manager should ever sign the statement without checking the figures thoroughly. The form for the statement can be as simple as the one shown in Figure 6.2, or it can be elaborate, showing denominations of all bills taken in, number of walk-ins versus reservations, and even a note of such circumstances as weather conditions and competing events that evening.

Figure 6.2.
Sample box office statement.

BOX OFFICE STATEMENT		
Date House Manager		
	Number	Amount
General Admission ($6)		
Senior Citizens ($5)		
Students ($5)		
Group Rate (10 or more) ($4)		
Comps		none
Total House	Total Take	

Ushers

Usually members of the house management crew act as ushers. Cast members with small parts, who don't come on until later in the play, can also act as ushers, if needed. They can wear their costumes if it doesn't give anything away or dressy attire if there is time for them to change after they have greeted the patrons and taken their tickets. If cast members wear costumes to usher, they stay in character as they usher, greeting each person, known or unknown to them, in the same manner. No private conversations are held and nothing is done to spoil the illusion. If festival seating is used, ushers need only help patrons to spot empty seats. If tickets are numbered, however, ushers will need to help patrons find their designated rows and seats. For good public relations, ushers should be pleasant and neatly dressed, so don't press a stagehand, grimy after setting up a worklight for the props manager, into ushering duties!

Ushers need to know the location of pay telephones, water fountains, restrooms, and emergency exits. Even though the information will be in the program, ushers can also expect to be asked if there is an intermission, if smoking is permitted in the lobby, if refreshments will be available, and what that warning bell means. In most theatres a warning bell is sounded or lights are blinked at three minutes before curtain and again at one minute before curtain. The ushers need to review this information so they can inform patrons.

Refreshments in the Lobby

Refreshments are a responsibility of house management, whether sold to raise funds or offered for hospitality. Keep the menu simple; people don't really need a choice of seven kinds of soft drinks and eight kinds of cookies when they attend a play. Punch bowls are heavy and awkward to handle, but pitchers are generally convenient. A cold punch or cider and hot coffee with one or two kinds of cookies should offer enough variety. If you don't want to set a price for each item, you might simply provide a basket for donations. Either way, you usually collect about the same amount. Finally, remind ushers to politely enforce a policy of no refreshments in the house itself.

Programs

A play program provides time and place information, cast names, crew credits, acknowledgments, and information about intermissions, refreshments, and theatre customs and regulations. In addition, it serves as something pleasing for the audience to look at while they wait for the play to begin.

A single standard-size page of card stock printed on both sides and folded in half makes an attractive program. Additional pages printed with advertising or cast photos can be included, as well. If your school has a print shop, ask about having the programs printed there. If not, inquire at a local photocopy shop.

SUMMARY

Theatre games and improvising on a scene are techniques for bringing a company closer together and working through a difficult portion of the play. Good publicity and public relations

Figure 6.3. Sample play program.

are essential to filling the house for your show. House management sees to the comfort, safety, and enjoyment of the audience through such means as ticket reservations, ushering, hospitality, and programs.

During the fifteenth to seventeenth centuries, England experienced a renaissance, or rebirth, of interest in the culture of classical times. Although the period is sometimes is referred to as *Elizabethan,* because so much of the writing was done during the reign of Elizabeth I, it covers a longer span of time than that. Distinguished playwrights of the period included Ben Jonson (1572–1637) and Christopher Marlowe (1564–1593).

The major figure of the English Renaissance, however, was poet and playwright William Shakespeare (1564–1616). Although there were few records of Shakespeare's early adulthood, in 1592 the dramatist Robert Greene wrote a pamphlet which indicates that by that time Shakespeare was probably already established as a playwright and actor in London. In 1593 and 1594, Shakespeare dedicated poems to the Earl of Southampton, suggesting that he was on familiar terms with the earl. In 1595, he was apparently a shareholder or part owner in the Lord Chamberlain's Men, an acting troupe for which he both performed and wrote plays. After 1599, he was part owner of the Globe Theatre.

It is believed that Shakespeare started writing in about 1590. He wrote at least thirty-seven plays, including histories, comedies, and tragedies. In addition to the plays, Shakespeare wrote many poems, notably his sonnets.

Ever since the Elizabethan era, Shakespeare has been regarded as the greatest English dramatist. One reason for his immortality is that his plays have a reality that appeals to people of all ages and thus a meaning for everyone. Even though Shakespeare often borrowed his plots and ideas from others, his presentation of characters and situations with which we can identify has made him one of the most enduring of playwrights.

By Shakespeare's time, the professional actors, playwrights, directors, and craftsmen—who had earlier taken their productions to various villages and towns—had begun to establish permanent theatre structures. The architecture of the theatres was loosely based on the barn and farmyard where the traveling troupes had so often performed.

One of the classical ideas that re-emerged in the English Renaissance was tragedy in drama. After the religious plays of medieval England, playwrights began to follow the Greek model of men who rise to a high position, only to fall from it through an error in judgment, often caused by excessive pride (*hubris*). Marlowe's *Doctor Faustus* and Shakespeare's *Macbeth* and *King Lear* are examples.

There were comedies, too, at that time. The comedies of Shakespeare range from the sunniness of *As You Like It* and *A Midsummer Night's Dream* to the darkly ironic *The Winter's Tale* and *All's Well That Ends Well*. Ben Jonson offered the comedy of humors, based on the theory of his time that humans are composed of four humors (body fluids) and that the dominance of one of them in the body determined a person's character.

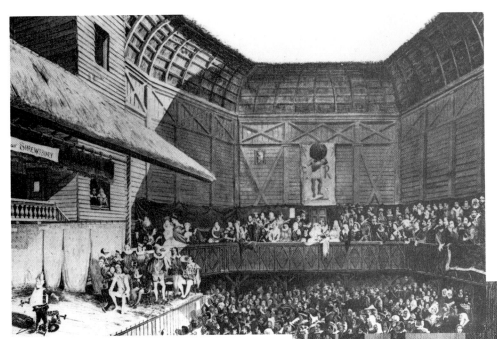

Most of Shakespeare's plays were first presented at the Globe Theatre in London. Shakespeare and other actors were part owners of the theatre.

Shakespeare himself may have performed in his own play *As You Like It*.

The casts of English Renaissance plays were men and boys, so it was a delightful jest for the audience when a playwright had a boy playing a girl who disguised "herself" as a boy! Literally thousands of plays were written and produced during this period. Hundreds have survived and are performed today, proving what a vigorous and productive time the English Renaissance was in the history of theatre.

Company Spirit Project

1. Plan a theatre game involving at least five members of the company that would build on the relationships among a specific crew or group of actors. If there is time, ask the director if you can stage the game for the company.

Design Projects

1. Design a logo either for your company or for the play you are working on. Make sure the design could be used on programs, fliers, posters, stationery, and T-shirts.
2. Locate programs used by other companies for previous shows. Choose four or five of the most appealing designs to show to the company for analysis and discussion.
3. Sketch a layout of a program for the show your company is producing.

Publicity Projects

1. Read through the book for your play and select some set-ups for a photo call.
2. Interview cast members and develop some interesting angles to use in publicity press releases about the show. For example, is any cast member the child of someone who once appeared in a play at your school?
3. Write a PSA for your show, suitable for use on local radio and television. Be thorough and precise in giving the essential information. Try to open or close with something to intrigue the potential audience.
4. Read through the book for your play and choose some bits that would work well as scenes for touring.

Hospitality Projects

1. Develop an intermission menu of refreshments. Be sure to find recipes for the foods and beverages you would serve.
2. Sketch a layout of the theatre, such as might be included in the program, with pay telephones, water fountains, restrooms, emergency exits, and smoking areas clearly marked.

The Poster Designer

You may have seen theatre posters designed by Paul Davis. His illustrations have appeared on the covers of *Time, The New Republic,* and *Rolling Stone.* His art has been collected in several books, and in August 1990, the Graphics Gallery in East Hampton, New York, held an exhibition of his works. More recently he did the poster for the Morgan Freeman/Tracey Ullman production of *The Taming of the Shrew.*

Born in 1938, Davis spent his childhood in Oklahoma, Arkansas, Montana, and Kansas. After graduating from Will Rogers High School in Tulsa, he moved to New York, where he used his National Scholastic Magazine arts scholarship to study at the School of Visual Arts.

In 1963, Davis began his freelancing career. Since then he has produced more than 500 major illustrations and has received over a dozen awards, including a Lifetime Achievement Medal from the American Institute of Graphic Arts. In the mid-1970s he turned his talents to theatre poster design, doing posters for the late producer Joseph Papp at New York's Public Theatre.

Davis's technique involves methodical research—talking to the director and the actors, reading the script carefully, and watching rehearsals. In his posters he captures not only an accurate impression of the characters, but also the philosophy and vision of the entire production.

Davis told *Theaterweek* writer Lynn Stephens, "You really want people to get excited about what you're presenting, and come and see it. That's the first function. But there's always a longer-range function as well. If they don't come to see this one, you want them to get an idea about the company, so that maybe they'll come to see the next one."

Theatre poster design has made significant advances over the last fifteen to twenty years. Truly an art form, it often is more than a decorative border around performance information. Davis advises beginning artists who would like to get into theatre poster design to find a small theatre that needs them and to stay there. Though there may be little or no pay at first, the opportunity is there to grow with the company.

161

Creating the
"Look of the Show"

7

Company Meeting

From now on, the pace of preparations increases. The company meeting is an important opportunity to take note of each exciting development.

PROGRESS REPORTS

In the midst of a busy rehearsal schedule, the actors need to schedule fittings for costumes plus makeup and hairstyling sessions. The reports this week should come mainly from wardrobe, makeup, hairstyling, and props personnel, who will need to display and explain the results of their research and designing.

TOPICS FOR THIS MEETING

- The Treasured Object
- Special Circumstances in Acting
- Finding and Building Costumes
- Acquiring and Fabricating Props
- Selecting Hairstyles
- Designing the Makeup
- The Look of the Show
- The Story of Theatre: At the French Court
- Theatre Workshop
- Careers in the Theatre: The Hairstylist

WORKING VOCABULARY

Some of the theatre terms of special interest in this chapter are *costume plot, practical props/scenery, sculpting, shaping,* and *neoclassicism.*

AGENDA

At the next company meeting you'll focus on "intensives" for rehearsals, music and sound effects, lighting instruments, the light board, and the lighting plot. Company members will discuss production progress, as well.

THE TREASURED OBJECT

Because the actors whose characters "live" on the play's set need to feel it *is* their own space, props managers often have each actor bring in a "treasured object" to place on the set for the run of the play. The object needs to be something of the actor's that suits the character he or she is portraying. For example, for a production of John M. Synge's *The Playboy of the Western World*, the actor playing Pegeen Mike brought in a tin-framed mirror, passed down to her from her grandmother, to hang in the corner of the pub where she kept her shawl. It looked old enough to suit the time period and it was believable that the character would have such a mirror hanging there.

For a production of Francis Swann's *Out of the Frying Pan,* the six actors whose characters share a New York City apartment were asked to bring in objects that represented what they brought from their small-town homes to comfort them in their struggles to break into show business. They brought a stuffed animal, a poster of a high school play, a hometown team baseball cap, a scrapbook, a framed family photograph, and a religious statue. Throughout the rehearsals and performances the actors said that their treasured objects really made them feel the set was like home.

Like Eliza Doolittle in *My Fair Lady,* actors must learn to speak clearly, even with something in their mouths.

SPECIAL CIRCUMSTANCES IN ACTING

Most plays present straightforward action, with dialogue supported by stage business and blocking. When there are special circumstances, however, don't leave them to chance. Rehearse them early and frequently.

Eating and Drinking on Stage

If you are required to eat or drink on stage, you need to rehearse the whole process carefully from the moment you are off book and have the props available. Obviously, there must be many "copies" of any consumable props in a show.

First, you need to time the moment so that you can chew and swallow before your next line. Stage eating and drinking requires taking *very* tiny bites or sips while you make it look as though you are taking large bites or full gulps. If you are required to talk through the chewing, loosely close your mouth so that you can talk as though your mouth were full.

The food supplied needs to be easily eaten, and hot beverages should actually be only tepid. A small plate makes a small serving look larger, so if you have to leave part of the food it can still look as if you have eaten a lot. If you use colored rather than clear drinking glasses, the audience cannot as easily tell that you have poured very little liquid into a glass.

In a production of Alan Ayckbourn's *The Norman Conquests,* Paula Prentiss had to eat toast while carrying on a conversation. She held the diagonally cut half piece of toast and nibbled at a point of it. As she did so she worked more and more of the slice into her hand so that soon it appeared she had eaten the entire half piece. She took up a napkin to wipe her mouth and slipped the toast into the napkin and then put it aside.

If you are called upon to chew a stick of gum, fold the piece up as though stuffing the whole thing into your mouth but in fact bite off just a bit and crumple up the rest with the foil wrapper and discard it. Here again, you close your mouth loosely as though it were full, and talk.

Kissing

If you will be embarrassed at having to kiss on stage, don't audition for a part that requires it. If you do take the part, don't put off rehearsing the kiss until dress rehearsal. Instead, rehearse it as soon as you are off book. If you truly are in character, it is not "you" doing the kissing anyway. Unless you are trying for a comic effect, don't stand apart and lean forward to kiss. For most plays, a tender, affectionate kiss is more the rule than a passionate embrace that goes on too long and causes giggles in the audience. Remember, too, when the kiss ends, continue to look affectionately at your partner—not merely relieved that it's over.

Crying

Some actors can cry on cue. Others use techniques such as recalling a sad event in their own lives. One effective trick is to cover your mouth in grief, managing to get some saliva on a finger, and then when you brush away your tears the saliva will leave a trace of moisture on your cheeks. Ideally, though, you will be so much in character that the events of the moment will bring forth the required tears. Remember not to stop crying abruptly, however, instead, continue to sniffle and dab at your eyes a bit longer.

Carrying Heavy Loads

If your suitcase is supposed to be heavy, it's best to fill it with a heavy, yet portable, weight. If that's not possible, then rehearse by carrying something heavy until you have the knack of it. Then duplicate the look of the effort in performance. If a rock is made of Styrofoam or papier-mâché, practice lifting a real rock to see just how high you can heft it and how you look when you carry it. It's helpful to check your posture and movements in a mirror for this, or, even better, to record your efforts with a video camera.

Telephoning

The usual problem in conducting a telephone conversation onstage is not allowing enough time for someone on the other end to say something. Rehearse by imagining the words of the other party; then speed up that response by about one third. If the responses from the other end are meant to be quite long, you can keep the audience interested by nodding your head and reacting to the supposed conversation with facial expressions and gestures. Don't hold the receiver mouthpiece directly over your mouth, as it muffles your own lines. Instead, keep it just below your chin.

Playing an Expert

If you are asked to play someone like a doctor or pianist or artist, you will need to request an appointment to visit such a person and observe the way he or she handles things. Watch the way the doctor holds the stethoscope, the position of the pianist's hands on the keys, the grasp the painter takes on the palette and brush. Attending to details such as these will make your portrayal more convincing.

Slapping

It is very difficult to fake a slap, especially in a small theatre. If you do the slapping, don't wear rings on the hand you slap with. Keep your hand loose and make a broad gesture that you "pull" or lessen just as it gets to the face of the other actor. If you are to be slapped, don't flinch in anticipation unless the script calls for that kind of reaction. Always stay in the same position through-out rehearsal and performance, so that when the slapper "pulls" the slap it lands just where it's supposed to. Both the slapper and the victim can use body language and facial expressions to support the impression of a strong slap.

Fights

Stage fighting requires expert instruction. It is choreographed as carefully as a dance. In general, though, it also is greatly enhanced with grunts, squeals, and panting for breath as though from exertion. If fencing is called for, the participants should take formal instruction and not try to fake fencing moves.

FINDING AND BUILDING COSTUMES

For most plays you will probably borrow costumes, pull them from stock, or rent them. Sometimes, though, company members themselves build the costumes.

Stage fighting should be choreographed as carefully as a dance.

Once the costume designer has studied the time period of the play and the requirements of the individual characters, the search is on! A call goes out to the company members and their family and friends for appropriate garments, or garments that can be easily converted to what is needed. An appeal to the community may prove to be fruitful as well. Remember, if the garments are lent they must be returned in their original condition, clean, and pressed. Any alterations that have been permitted must be reversed.

If there is money in the budget to buy costumes, start with the thrift shops. The designer should accompany any buying expedition, however, as he or she knows the desired look of the show. Keep in mind that costume shops often sell as well as rent. If the budget permits it and the costume will likely be useful in future productions, purchasing it can be a good investment.

If you are renting costumes from a local business, the actors themselves—not merely their measurements—must accompany the designer to the costume shop. There are also mail-order costume rentals such as Norcosto of Minneapolis, Minnesota, which has offices in many major cities.

Costume Building

If the costumes are to be built, seek the help of students in clothing construction classes at your school. Family members and community groups also may be willing to assist. If the responsibility falls to company members, remember that costume building is easier than ordinary dressmaking because it does not require as much finish work, that is, details that must hold up in the scrutiny of everyday wear.

Don't hesitate to use bargain fabrics; velours and upholstery remnants can look like rich velvets and brocades under stage lighting. Also, consider alterations that would allow one pattern to work for many costumes. For example, a basic high-necked bodice can be cut into a V-, a U-, a square, or a sweetheart neckline. A long sleeve can be full, bell-shaped, tapered, cuffed, or gathered on elastic at the wrist. Although commercial patterns are expensive, frequently they include a range of sizes within the single pattern envelope.

In addition to building the costumes by sewing them, you can construct by ironing. Using products such as Stitch Witchery or Wonder Under, you can join two pieces of fabric by placing the fusible substance between the two pieces and adhering them with a hot iron.

With a hot glue gun you can cover a shoe with fabric to match a costume, appliqué flowers or rhinestones onto a dress or hat, and quickly construct a purse or create a multilayered effect on a jacket or coat.

Actors, remember that the costume is your character's. Don't say you feel foolish in it, or that the color doesn't suit you, or that you would rather have someone else's costume. Keep in mind, too, since the costume is lent to you, you must handle it carefully. Report any damage or soiling immediately to the wardrobe manager. When you wear your costume at the dress parade, get comfortable in it. By performance time, you must convince the audience that the garment is as familiar to you as the clothing you will change into after the show.

Wardrobe Fittings

Sometimes it is difficult to pull the actors away from rehearsal for their costume fittings. You may have to teach them how to move about in the awkward or unfamiliar clothing so that they appear to be comfortable in it. The wardrobe people should begin by doing a selling job at a company meeting. Get the actors excited about the costumes planned for them to wear. You might show some historical background material, films or

A hot-glue gun can be used to appliqué rhinestones to a dress.

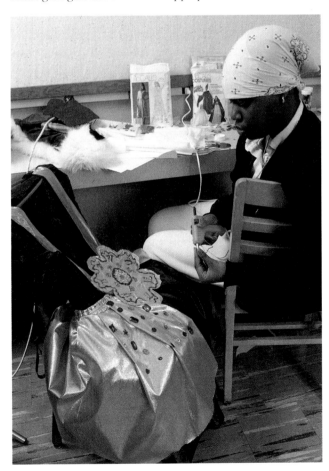

videotapes, or some photographs of famous actors in similar costumes as evidence of your research and thoughtful planning. Then, in the fitting sessions, be efficient. Suggest that the actors run lines as they are fitted so they will feel more in character.

Accessories

Accessorizing the costumes can greatly enhance their impact. A plain dark woman's suit can be made to look stylish and expensive with the addition of a fashionable hat, purse, shoes, and the replica of a jeweled lapel pin. Think of the wonderful big "picture hats" Cecil Beaton designed for the "Ascot" scene in *My Fair Lady*. Belts, sashes, muffs, parasols, necklaces, earrings, bracelets, patterned stockings, seamed stockings, spike-heeled pumps, worn and scuffed boots, badges, gold braid—all have dramatic impact and help to inform the audience about time, place, and a character's social status, economic circumstances, and personality. Never overlook the opportunity to subtly convey information through the accessories you choose to complete the wardrobe.

Costume Plot

A **costume plot** is a list of costumes and accessories, indicating when and by whom they will be worn, as well as any notes about special requirements or quick changes. Note the details included in the costume plot for Act I of a production of Norman Krasna's charming comedy *Dear Ruth*. (See Figure 7.1.)

In addition to this type of costume plot, it is helpful to keep a plot that lists every item of clothing and accessory used in the show. This functions as a checklist to ensure that everything has been acquired and either moved to the dressing room or stored in a preshow costume cabinet.

Dress Parade

When all the costumes and accessories have been acquired, the director can call for the dress parade. The parade may be called early in the rehearsal schedule, if the director chooses, but it should be held no later than two weeks before the show opens. The dress parade is a wardrobe check held onstage under stage

Act/Scene	Character	Actor	Costume	Accessories	Notes
I, 1	Dora	Jenny	Maid's uniform	White apron Black oxfords Cotton stockings	Starched
I, 1	Edith	Hollis	Quilted housecoat	Slippers	
I, 1	Miriam	Sarah	Pleated skirt Long pullover	Beret Penny loafers Ankle socks	Too large
I, 1	Harry	Felipe	Business suit White dress shirt	Pocket handkerchief Striped tie Black shoes Black socks	
I, 1	Ruth	Nikki	Black dress	White organdie collar Black shoes Small felt hat Nylon stockings Rose pinned to dress	With seams
I, 1	Bill	Tyrone	Air Corps Uniform	Uniform hat Uniform shoes	Lieutenants's insignia

Figure 7.1. Sample costume plot.

lighting, during which the actors wear their various costume changes through a kind of parade. This enables the director and costume people to check the effect of the costume colors under lighting; the fit, suitability, and movability of each costume; and its compatibility with the other costumes in the same scene.

An easy way to do this is to have the actors line up onstage while the director, accompanied by the wardrobe manager with his or her checklist, walks past each actor, observing every aspect of the costume. Then the actors walk through any portion of the action that may place demands on the costume. If there are any quick costume changes needed, the dress parade is the time to try them. Addressing all costume-related concerns at this time will also contribute to a smoother dress rehearsal.

Sometimes a question arises about a particular article used in a production. Is it wardrobe or is it a prop? Such a predicament occurred during a production of Shakespeare's *A Midsummer Night's Dream*. Was the ass's head that Bottom wears for two scenes costume or prop? It was decided that since the properties crew had constructed the head, it would be considered a prop and placed under their jurisdiction.

ACQUIRING AND FABRICATING PROPS

As with the costumes, props are acquired for a play by buying, borrowing, pulling from company stock—the collection from previous plays—or renting them. Sometimes props fabrication, that is, making the props needed, is the only way to obtain them, however.

Once the props manager has determined what is needed, he or she sends out a call to the company and sometimes the community for loans or donations of the required suit of armor, bird cage, steamer trunk, or hat rack. Of course, any articles obtained must be returned in their original condition. If you think it would be an appreciative gesture to return the item in *better* than its original condition, be sure to check with the lender first. For a production of Douglas Parkhirst's *Early Frost,* the props manager borrowed a large trunk from the local community theatre. To show their appreciation, company members painted the trunk to look like new, only to learn that the community theatre was to use the trunk in a future production and needed it to look old and worn!

Renting props can be expensive, but if the prop is featured prominently in the play, if important references are made to it in the dialogue, if purchasing it is beyond the budget, if no one offers to lend it, or if it's too difficult or costly to fabricate, then renting is the only alternative remaining. Inquire whether the rental company will give a discount for an acknowledgment in the play program.

Many props used in this scene were likely borrowed or purchased. Which might have been fabricated by the company?

For a play with a short properties plot—the list of all props used in the play—you might be able to acquire everything you need by borrowing, pulling from stock, or buying small consumable items. Most productions, however, require the fabrication of at least some of the props, and that's where the fun begins!

The Props Plot

To begin, the props manager consults the props plot at the back of the playbook, or, if none is given, develops one for the company. This begins as a list of all the props required for the production. Many props managers prepare an additional plot that designates the props that are on the stage and those that are brought on during the course of the play, including the name of the character who uses them. Two props plots for Act I of John van Druten's sparkling romantic comedy *Bell, Book and Candle* are shown in Figure 7.2.

Figure 7.2.
Two versions of a prop-
erties plot.

Act I: Complete Listing

Modern sculptures (six)
Witch sculpture
Christmas tree (decorated)
Witch bowl
Records (two, in Christmas wrapping)
Shawl (in Christmas wrapping)
Vials (two, in Christmas wrapping)
Witches' manual
Telephone
Scissors
Books (two, Christmas-wrapped, with "Redlitch" photo)
Large serving tray
Wine bottles (one red, one white)
Wine glasses (six)
Rental lease
Fountain pen
Wall mirror (antique style)
Sectional couch (semicircular arrangement)
Coffee table
Desk
Desk chair
Book/Display case
Vase (tall, with arrangement of dried reeds)
Small pillows (three, on couch)

Act I: On Stage at Opening

Modern sculptures (six, on display shelves)
Witch sculpture (on coffee table)
Christmas tree (decorated, upstage center)
Witch bowl (on display shelf)
Witches' manual (in desk, right drawer)
Telephone (on desk, top left side)
Scissors (in desk, top left drawer)
Serving tray (on desk, right side)
Wine bottles (two, on tray)
Wine glasses (six, on tray)

Rental lease (in desk, top left drawer)
Fountain pen (in desk, top left drawer)
Mirror (on wall above desk, left side)
Sectional couch (down center stage)
Coffee table (center stage down of couch)
Desk (stage right, 2/3 up)
Chair (at desk)
Book/Display case (stage right, down of desk)
Vase with reeds (on floor, stage left down of door)
Pillows (three, on couch)
Christmas-wrapped records (under Christmas tree)
Christmas-wrapped shawl (under Christmas tree)

Act I: Brought On

Christmas-wrapped vials (Nicky)
Christmas-wrapped books (Aunt Queenie)

Basic Materials

If the scene shop has a section reserved for props fabrication, there already may be some basic supplies stored there. Look for things like

- aviary wire, which is finer than chicken wire and can be used for papier-mâché frames
- casting resin, a polyester resin for casting solid objects
- dulling wax, to dull shiny objects so that the lighting won't cause a glare on the stage
- epoxy putty, which is hard-drying and suitable for small items that are to be treated roughly
- erosion cloth, an open weave, oil-treated, texturing fabric for creating foliage
- fuller's earth, a fine powder used as smoke or dust
- Pellon, a nonwoven fabric that can be cut without regard to grain, and which leaves a smooth edge with no need for hemming

- plaster of paris, a fast-setting plaster used for small statues
- plasticine, an oil-based modeling clay used for medium-sized items
- urethane foam, available in rigid logs for sculpting, or in sheets.

Check existing stock carefully before purchasing additional materials.

Some Basic Fabrication Methods

If your production calls for blood, stage blood is easily and inexpensively made. Pour a sixteen-ounce bottle of white corn syrup into a large mixing bowl or clear glass bottle that holds more than sixteen ounces. Add about one tablespoon of red food coloring (be sure it is food coloring, not dye, because, in small amounts, food coloring will not stain). Add one-fourth cup clear liquid detergent. This keeps the "blood" from drying out during the performance and aids in washing it out later. Last, adjust to a true blood color by carefully adding, drop by drop, two or three drops of blue food coloring. Store in a bottle and shake well before using.

The corn syrup will give the "blood" a heavy consistency, so be careful in pouring out the blood onto the person or object to be bloodied. And, though the detergent ingredient aids in cleanup, always be sure to wash the bloodied garment in cold water immediately after the performance.

Mystery plays often are favorites of audience and cast. Occasionally, they call for a knife to protrude from the body of the murder victim. To fabricate such a prop, purchase a twelve- to fifteen-inch knife at a rummage sale or thrift store. An instructor should cut three to four inches from the tip of the knife with a grinding wheel, then remove the cutting edge. Next, make a loop of thirty inches of lightweight, flexible wire and affix the wire to the blunt tip of the knife with epoxy. When dry, paint the epoxy a blood-red color. (See Figure 7.3.)

To use the prop, slip the wire around the neck of the "victim" and settle the knife on the actor's chest or back. The wire holds the knife in place and the painted epoxy gives the effect of a bloody wound.

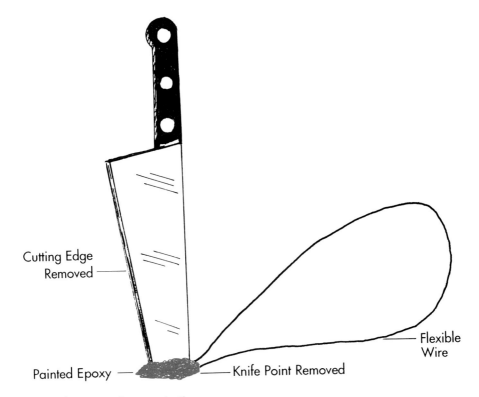

Cutting Edge
Removed

Painted Epoxy

Flexible
Wire

Knife Point Removed

Figure 7.3. Fabrication of a stage knife.

To create a cover (dust jacket) for a book that is supposed to have been written by a character in the play, you need a black-and-white photograph of the actor playing the character; a small color drawing or design, clipped from a magazine or drawn by someone in the company; and print copy for the book cover, which you can clip from various magazines or print on a computer. Cut paper to the book cover size and arrange the design, print copy, and photograph in their proper places on the cover paper. (The author's photograph always goes on the back cover.) Secure each item with rubber cement or double-faced cellophane tape. Take the layout to a copy shop that has a color copier and make reproductions of the cover. The dust jacket is now ready to use. Note that you should have a "protection copy" (a spare) in case of any damage to the prop cover.

Practical props, like **practical scenery,** must be able to work. If a practical bookcase, that is, one holding real books that can be removed and read, is too heavy, awkward, or expensive for your show, make a flat or one side of a periaktos of nonpractical bookshelves. To do this, cut a sheet of plywood to the dimensions needed. Paint on lines to represent each shelf. Prepare "books" and use hot glue to position them on each "shelf." To prepare the "books," buy books at a rummage sale, garage sale, or library sale where the books are offered at a small price per bagful, or ask for donations from the community and library. With an X-acto knife, cut the spine (the portion that shows on a shelf) from the book and glue it in place on your shelf. When the bookcase is filled according to your requirements, you may want to lightly coat the book spines with shellac to seal them, or you may choose to dull some volumes and brighten others at random. If you need to obscure the titles because many of the books are the same, simply muddy the title with a little thin paint.

Food Prop Fabrication

Many plays include eating scenes in which food props are required. If the props are not actually consumed onstage, you can choose from a variety of techniques for fabrication.

Sculpting an item of food starts with the real thing or a good picture for reference. Don't just trust your memory! Use a block of urethane foam slightly larger than the item you want to create. The foam is soft and can almost be worked by hand, so don't apply too much pressure. Using a wood rasp, gently shape the foam to the desired form, then cover the item with a thin coat of spackling compound. When dry, add a second thin coat of spackling compound. Carefully sand to achieve the desired surface texture, then paint the finished product with carefully blended paint. Don't simply brush on a solid brown color for a turkey or a tan shade for a loaf of bread. Look at the original or the picture you used and reproduce the highlights and shadows with color shading.

Fabricating an item of food from papier-mâché also begins with the real thing or a good picture of it for inspiration. First, shape aviary wire into the desired form. Then, tear a porous paper such as tissue, paper towels, or newsprint, into two-inch strips and dampen them in water. Dip these paper strips into a binder such as wheat paste and strong glue sizing. Gently squeeze excess moisture from the paper and apply the strips to the wire frame, laying the strips horizontally and then vertically, building up the layers until the wire frame is completely covered. Note that you must allow each layer to dry before adding another, or the papier-mâché may turn moldy. When the entire form is completely covered and dry, paint the item to resemble your reference model. As with the sculpted foam form, be sure to highlight and shadow with paints to make the prop look realistic.

Shaping the food item from plasticine, an oil-based modeling clay, is a third method of fabrication. Plasticine is not suitable for very large objects, and the resulting form will be soft, but it is a quick means of producing a prop that can be placed on a serving plate and then not handled. Again, it is important to paint carefully to reproduce the colors of your model.

Edible Food Props

There are a few problems to address when using edible food props: maintaining hygiene, keeping the food fresh, and keeping company members from eating it backstage! It's best if one person takes charge of all the edible food props. That person needs to understand the importance of handling the food with just-washed hands. (Foil packets of moist towelettes are useful in these circumstances and should be available in the props cupboard.) In addition, waxed paper or plastic wrap should be used to pick up the food. Finally, just as important, the dishes and utensils used for the stage meal must be thoroughly clean.

Since the food needs to be fresh for every performance, it must either be appropriately stored or renewed for each performance. Many food items, especially crackers, cookies, and candy, seem to tempt cast and crew, so the props manager may have to be very strict about forbidding any unauthorized tasting. Sometimes the best deterrent is to impose a fine on anyone who eats a food prop backstage.

The items of edible food need not be what they represent—especially if the item called for requires a lot of chewing or is crumbly in a way that presents a choking hazard. Nothing should be hot, only tepid, and if you need the effect of a steaming hot plate of food, a hidden lump of dry ice can provide the look of steam.

White bread and mashed potatoes lend themselves to a variety of forms. For example, small squares of white bread dusted with cocoa become fudge brownies, and scoops of mashed potatoes become ice cream. Cold tea can be used for rum, bread toasted and cut into thin strips for french fries, and an apricot half on a circle of white bread for a fried egg.

As with other types of props, actors should begin rehearsing with edible food props as soon as they are off book. Use rehearsal props for the more fragile, expensive, or valuable props, but be sure the actors see and hold the performance props occasionally during the rehearsal schedule. Finally, be certain a sufficient supply of consumable props (used up in performance) is on hand.

Props Table and Storage

Once all the props have been acquired, prepare the backstage props table. Use a long narrow table or tables covered with clean, plain paper such as butcher paper or unprinted newspaper available in large rolls. Secure the paper to the table. Then take each prop in the order it is brought onto the stage, place it on the table, and trace its outline onto the covering paper. Remove the prop and label inside its outline the name of the prop, the act and scene in which it is used, and the character who brings it onstage. Between rehearsals and performances the props should be kept in a designated prop cupboard that can be locked. The director has a key, and the props manager either has a copy or must request the key from the director each time the cupboard is used.

Each outline on the backstage props table should be labeled with the name of the prop, the act and scene in which it is used, and the character who brings it onstage.

SELECTING HAIRSTYLES

If wigs must be used, natural-hair wigs are the only wigs worth using in a production. Anything else loudly proclaims that it is artificial. If these cannot be borrowed they may have to be rented, as usually they are too expensive to buy for a single production. Your company may have some stock of wigs, and if so, be sure to clean the wigs before using them. (A commercial product is available from beauty supply stores or shops that sell wigs.) Although a wig usually will hold its style through the run of the play, it still must be checked at each performance both before and after the actor wears it.

Most of the time, however, the actors will not be wearing wigs and will need to have a hairstyle designed for them. Their hair must be dressed for the dress parade and dress rehearsal, as well as for each performance. Generally, once cast, no actor

Check each wig before and after every performance to make sure it has held its style.

should have his or her hair cut, permed, or colored without permission of the director and notification of the hairstylist.

Like the other technical specialties, hairstyling requires research of the time period and place represented in the play. There are many books devoted to hairstyling, but old movies, magazines, and mail-order catalogs can also give the designer a good idea of popular hairstyles in a given era. Movies on videotape are especially helpful because you can stop the tape to study the hairstyle. Also, through the course of the movie you can see the hairstyle from all angles. The best hairstyles for the production are those that are as scrupulously authentic as possible so they will support the costumes and the feel of the show.

Hairstyles denote social class or economic status as well as time period. A character who cannot afford to visit a beauty salon or who has a job requiring manual labor would not have an elaborate, high-maintenance hairstyle such as long ringlets. Further, in an era in which hats were in vogue, a character would not have a hairstyle that a hat would crush or dishevel.

Hairstyles can make strong statements. For humorous effect, braids can be wired to stand straight out from the head of the character. A cowlick can add mischief and long bangs can make a character look like an eager terrier.

Hairstyles can be used to change the shape of a face as well. Generally, long hair makes a face look longer. Ear-length or chin-length hair breaks up the long line of a face, while hair fluffed out on the sides can minimize a broad face. To emphasize the roundness of a face, hair can be tightly pulled back.

If the hairstyles are fairly close to the actors' own, they can dress their own hair once they have been shown how to do so. Before each performance, however, the hairstylist must check each actor in the makeup room. When the styles are quite different from the actors' own, the stylist needs a crew to help dress the cast's hair. All hairstyles need to be secured with pins, clips, ribbons, barrettes, elastic bands, or hairspray. While the latter is usually necessary, constant spraying can create a breathing hazard in the dressing room, so ventilate the area well.

If an actor's hair must be colored, there are wash-in/wash-out rinses and temporary sprays. Often, stage makeup is used to gray hair, but it must be used sparingly and in small areas, such as gray at the temples.

DESIGNING THE MAKEUP

Stage makeup is of two types: straight makeup and character makeup. Straight makeup enhances the actor's natural features and intensifies his or her coloring so that it will not be washed out under the stage lighting. Most actors can apply their own straight makeup once they have been shown how to do so.

Character makeup requires an initial design and, generally, help in application. It is never a simple process, so do not be tempted to take shortcuts. The application of black lines across an actor's forehead to suggest aging seldom looks like anything but a striped forehead.

Equipment and Materials

If you do not have a formal makeup room, set up an area as near to the dressing room as possible. You will need good incan-

Most actors can apply their own straight makeup once they have been shown how it should be done.

descent lighting, mirrors, chairs, and a counter or table. The mirrors should be placed so that the person applying the makeup and standing next to the actor always has a good view of the actor's face in reflection.

You will need a large supply of small makeup sponges for applying the basic color, a stippling sponge for effects such as five-o'clock shadow or blotchy complexion, fine brushes of sable hair to use for shadowing or highlighting, powder puffs, a powder brush for brushing excess powder from the face, and the makeup itself. Collect these items in a standard makeup case, a fishing tackle box, or a sewing basket with divided lift-out trays.

Regarding the makeup itself, there are two basic types: greasepaint, which covers smoothly and blends easily but is harsh on the complexion, and water-based makeup, which is more difficult to blend but does not need powdering and is kinder to the skin. Suppliers of theatrical makeup generally offer a basic kit for student actors that will be adequate for most makeup needs. Materials for special effects can be purchased separately.

Other supplies you may need are dermatographic pencils, which produce soft, easily smudged lines and are available in colors from black and brown to red, white, and green; powder in a transparent, neutral shade; mastic adhesive for beards and mustaches; crepe, or false, hair for building beards and mustaches a few hairs at a time; nose putty, which is also used for creating warts and scars; tooth varnish for blackening a tooth; makeup remover; acetone to remove mastic adhesive; and soap for washing, as well as for building up eyebrows.

Basic instructions for applying the makeup base will be furnished with the materials, but in general you begin by applying the greasepaint or the water-based makeup with a slightly damp sponge. Use a light brushing motion starting at the center of the face and sweeping toward the sides. Apply sparingly, as you can always add more. Be sure to blend the makeup into the hairline so that there is no visible border. Continue the base down onto the neck and as far as the costume reveals flesh.

Use colors to create the desired highlights and shadows and be sure the colors are appropriate to the coloring of the actor, unless you are trying to achieve an obvious makeup effect. If you are using greasepaint, finish off with the transparent powder.

Makeup should be blended into the hairline so that no color difference is visible on the forehead.

With water-based makeup, the powder is not necessary. Carefully brush away any excess. The eyes are an important and expressive feature, so shape and color the eyebrows carefully and finish the effect with eye shadow color and mascara. Outline the lips in the desired shape with lip liner and then fill in with lip color. Apply rouge according to the time period you are representing. In the 1920s, for example, a round spot of rouge on each cheek was the fashion.

Make sure that the actors take time to remove their makeup carefully and to wash their faces before they leave the makeup room. They should not spoil the illusion of the performance by greeting audience members in full or even partial makeup. Also, leaving the makeup on longer than needed is not good for their skin. Finally, be sure that the makeup room is clean and organized before you leave and that soiled applicators are disposed of so they aren't used again.

THE LOOK OF THE SHOW

Audiences come to a show willing to suspend their disbelief and enter into the spirit of what they are offered, abiding by theatrical convention. This convention is the unwritten and unspoken but implicit contract between audience and company that for the length of the performance, the audience will accept as real whatever is presented to them. However, no company should try the patience of the audience with attitudes like "They'll never know the difference between 1920s hairstyles and 1930s hairstyles," or "It's only a school play after all, and the audience members are our friends."

The costumes, props, hairstyles, and makeup not only help make the play real for the audience, they help make it real for the actors. It's hard to walk in a relaxed, loose stride while wearing a boned corset, floor-length gown, and high-buttoned shoes. Indeed, the costume dictates movement for the actor just as it did for the Victorian woman who originally wore it. Likewise, pouring tea from a silver tea service promotes an elegance of manner. Spit curls, bee-stung lips, and rouged circles re-create the roaring twenties.

While it's true you don't want the audience to leave the show talking only about the great costumes or the clever makeup, you don't want them to comment, "Those dresses just struck such a wrong note that I was distracted from enjoying the play." Make the look of the show as authentic as possible—it will add to the audience's enjoyment as well as your own.

SUMMARY

Using a treasured object on the set can help actors to feel at home in the space. Special circumstances in acting, such as eating and drinking, kissing, or crying require careful planning and thorough rehearsing. Costumes not acquired by purchases, loans, or rental can be built using sewing, ironing, or gluing techniques. Props not acquired by purchases, loans, or rentals can be fabricated by assembling, sculpting, or shaping. Hygiene and freshness are important concerns when using edible food props. Hairstyles and makeup must be carefully researched and then developed according to the play's time, place, and action.

*I*n England the theatre of the Renaissance degenerated into the excesses of Jacobean revenge tragedy. The intention of many productions was to see how many different ways could be used to kill off most of the characters.

When the Puritan party under Oliver Cromwell took control of the government, authorities closed the theatres and forbade dramatic performances. King Charles I was executed and the future King Charles II fled to France where, in the court of King Louis XIV, he saw the brilliant comedies of Molière and the exquisite verse tragedies of Racine. The Renaissance was late in coming to France, but when it did arrive, **neoclassicism**—the revival of the classical forms of ancient Greece and Rome—became the dominant mode of the seventeenth and eighteenth centuries.

Neoclassicism followed these basic principles: verisimilitude, or the appearance of truth; purity of dramatic types, with no mixing of forms; the five-act play structure; decorum, or truthfulness to time, place, and character; didacticism, or drama for the purpose of teaching moral lessons; and strict adherence to the unities of time, place, and action.

Acting troupes in the French Renaissance included women, who had equal rights with the men. When Charles II returned to England, some of these women returned with him to act in English companies, and since then women have taken their place on the stage.

King Louis XIV not only encouraged theatre in France, he even sponsored performances at various royal buildings such as the Louvre, the Tuileries, and Versailles. Another popular performance space was the quickly converted tennis court. Because the tennis court is a long, narrow structure, the theatres built on that foundation had difficult sightlines; most of the audience was a long way from the stage. This necessitated the development of a declamatory style of acting, complete with broad gestures and exaggerated facial expressions intended to reach the distant audience.

No one better typifies the French court theatre than Molière. His witty comedies *Tartuffe, The Misanthrope, The Miser,* and *The Doctor in Spite of Himself* are standard repertoire for theatre companies all over the world to this day.

French neoclassical theatre also had two great writers of tragedy, Corneille and Racine. Corneille emphasized the triumph of the human will, while Racine's protagonists fall helplessly into evil and bring about their own destruction. New translations of Corneille's plays, such as *Le Cid,* have become successes again in this century, while Racine's tragedies—written in verse difficult to translate into contemporary English—are less frequently performed on the English-language stage.

In 1680 the Comedie-Française united the repertoires of Molière, Racine, and Corneille and dedicated itself to preserving the heritage of French drama. More than three centuries later, the Comedie-Française is still in existence.

Construction Projects

1. Borrowing a doll or buying an inexpensive one at a garage sale, design and build a costume for one of the characters in your current production. Most fabric stores sell remnants—small amounts of fabric left on a bolt—at a greatly reduced price, or you can cut up a garment from a thrift store. If you do not have any decorative trims, ask friends or relatives who sew for scraps of ribbon and lace, or return to the remnant table at the fabric store. After the company has seen the doll dressed in your costume design, use the doll to help decorate the lobby while the play is running. If several of you choose this project, the results could make a cute publicity gimmick for the newspapers.

2. Buy a garment from a thrift store or rummage sale and modify it to fit another time period. Later it can serve you as a Halloween costume.

3. Try the following in a group of three students. Assume your play calls for a roast chicken that is never carved or eaten. One student should sculpt a chicken from a rigid log of urethane foam; another student should fabricate a chicken of papier-mâché; and the third student should shape a chicken from plasticine. All three should paint their chickens. Display the three props for the company and have members decide which works best on stage.

4. Fabricate one of the following standard props. If it cannot be used in the current production, keep it in stock for the future.
   a. Stage blood
   b. A book cover featuring you as the author
   c. A knife to protrude from the chest of a corpse
   d. A shelf of nonpractical books

Design Projects

1. Read carefully through your playbook and write a properties plot.
2. Read carefully through your playbook and develop a costume plot.
3. Design makeup for one of the following:
   a. A teen going to the governor's inaugural ball
   b. A clown
   c. A lion
   d. An elderly man or woman
4. Design a hairstyle for another company member (not necessarily an actor) from the time period of your play. If the play is contemporary, try a style from another decade, such as the 1930s or 1940s.

Investigation Project

1. Help out the whole company by conferring with actors and wardrobe people about their schedules. Then develop a schedule for costume fittings.

The Hairstylist

Bobby H. Grayson came to New York City as a performer in musical comedy and stayed to become "the hair doctor." Grayson grew up in Corsicana, Texas, and performed at Six Flags over Texas and with the Dallas Summer Musicals. When he came to New York he did two shows at Radio City Music Hall and then toured with the national company of *Oklahoma!* in 1980–81.

When the *Oklahoma!* troupe arrived in Boston, a local hairdresser took the wigs away for cleaning, thinking the opening was two days away. It actually was the next night and the wigs were not ready. Grayson had occasionally done the *Oklahoma!* girls' hair for fun and so he was pressed into service. He was offered the job of hairstylist for the rest of the show.

When the *Oklahoma!* tour ended, Grayson returned to New York and did hair maintenance on the Bob Fosse show *Dancin'*. Deciding to get his hairstylist's license, he attended Wilfred Beauty Academy. To become a member of Local 798 Broadway Makeup and Hairdressers Union, he needed to have a cosmetology license and to be certified. The certification process included a four-hour written exam and a demonstration of hairdressing, permanent wave, and hair coloring techniques.

When Grayson got the call to do Robert Harling's *Steel Magnolias,* it was a chance not only to design the hairstyles, but also to teach the actors in the play how to do the professional hairdressing that is an essential part of the play's action. In fact, Grayson helped select the cast, decisions based partially on each performer's ability to style hair.

In *Steel Magnolias* Grayson's principal concern was to keep the actors' hair in good condition because one of them had to have her hair washed, rolled, and set eight times a week and two of the others also had their hair washed or styled in each performance.

Although he misses performing and would like to be able to sing professionally again, Grayson is in demand for his expertise both in Broadway productions and with a private clientele.

Adding Light and Sound

8

Company Meeting

As the actors fine-tune their performance skills, the lighting and sound technicians come into prominence in the rehearsal schedule.

PROGRESS REPORTS

Although the cast is in the throes of rehearsal and the technicians concerned with sets, costumes, props, hairstyles, and makeup have completed their preperformance work, there may be last-minute changes to report or tasks to assign to the company.

TOPICS FOR THIS MEETING

- Intensives for Rehearsals
- Music Effects
- Sound Effects
- Amplification
- Stage Lighting

- The Story of Theatre: The English Restoration
- Theatre Workshop
- Careers in the Theatre: The Lighting Designer

WORKING VOCABULARY

Some of the theatre terms of special interest in this chapter are *fade, crash box, lighting instrument, gel, gobo, cyclorama, catwalk, blackout,* and *flies.*

AGENDA

At the next company meeting you'll discuss the countdown to performance, the technical rehearsal, dress rehearsal, the curtain call, understudy takeover, and last-minute publicity. You'll also hear reports on production progress.

INTENSIVES FOR REHEARSALS

Intensives involve isolating small portions of the play that are proving difficult and rehearsing them over and over outside the context of the play. Some helpful methods for participating in this kind of intensive work are role reversal, the untrained observer, the silent scene, the interview, sense memory, emotion memory, and obstacles.

In role reversal, two actors in a scene trade parts and read through the scene. This helps one actor better understand the other's character by experiencing the action from that character's point of view.

To use the untrained observer rehearsal technique, invite someone from outside the company to watch a scene that's proving difficult. After the scene ask the untrained observer what was happening, that is, what he or she understood from the scene. Remember, you are not asking the observer to offer suggestions for improvement, nor are you asking the observer to criticize the actors. Instead, you are hearing the reactions of someone with a fresh perspective who is new to the material being rehearsed.

In the silent scene rehearsal, actors convey as much meaning as possible through facial expression, gesture, and body language.

The silent scene requires the actors to move through the scene without speaking, but to convey as much meaning as possible through facial expression, gestures, and body language. Nothing should be exaggerated, but the actors should focus on the visual aspect of their characterizations.

For the interview technique, one actor in the scene assumes the role of an interviewer who wants to know why the other actor's character behaves as he or she does in the scene. This forces the actor being interviewed to examine all his or her motivations in the scene. Then the actors change positions and the second interview is conducted for the same reason.

Sense memory and emotion memory exercises ask the actors to recall previous experiences that parallel incidents in the play under rehearsal. Though the theatre is warm, perhaps your character has to convince the audience that the room you are in is cold and drafty. You remember a time when you were cold—perhaps you were caught in a chilly rain and nothing seemed to warm you. Or perhaps your character swallows some bitter medicine. Actually, the prop is cold cider, but you must make a face to indicate the bitterness. You recall the time you tasted what you thought was lemonade, only to find that the sugar hadn't been added yet.

Suppose your character must be furious with another character. The actor playing that other character is your best friend and you cannot imagine being angry with him or her. You recall a time you were very angry; perhaps you witnessed an act of cruelty to someone. Remember how you felt; how your mouth shaped in anger; how your stomach seemed to churn; how there seemed to be an acidic taste in your mouth. Use all those remembered sensations to be furious when the scene requires it.

An obstacle is anything that stands in the way of a character's intention in a scene. Often, the obstacle is not a physical one, but if you can find a physical equivalent you can work to overcome it on stage. For example, if another character's selfishness prevents your character from sharing in an inheritance, you can physicalize the conflict this way: Each of you wants to work on an art project. There is only one worktable in the room. Do you divide it in half and each use half the space? Do you each try to work, constantly pushing the other's materials out of the way? Do you work out a schedule with equal time at the table for each? In working out a compromise, you learn how to overcome obstacles to your intentions.

MUSIC EFFECTS

Music is one of the most important mood creators in a theatre. Once the house is open there should be music playing over the speaker system to begin setting the time, place, and emotion of the play to follow. It would confuse an audience to hear the latest in rap music played just before the curtain opens on a Victorian play, or the sounds of country-western music when the play takes place in New York City.

The sound technician must choose house music to prepare for the play, and the mood must carry through the music selected for intermission and any brief interludes between scenes. Just as the technicians concerned with the look of the show carefully research the play's time and place, so must the sound designer investigate the music appropriate to the play.

If the sound technician is a music lover, this task is a most pleasant one. If musical knowledge is not a strong point, there are sure to be others in the company eager to offer advice. The school music teacher can be helpful, as well, not only in matters of selection. He or she may also have access to records, compact discs, and tapes that can be used in the show.

Record one cassette for house and intermission music and a separate one for each piece of scene interlude music.

For a production of Shakespeare's *A Midsummer Night's Dream,* the music Felix Mendelssohn wrote for the play will provide beautiful house and interlude music. There are many classical compositions that capture the flavor of much earlier civilizations, and for modern times there are songs available from every decade.

It is best to record the various pieces on one cassette for house and intermission music and to have a separate cassette for each bit of scene interlude music. Most sound-light booths still contain cassette tape players. If yours has a compact disc player, it may be possible to go to a professional recording studio to record all the music cues on one disc and to program the player for each cut as needed.

Remember, no music cue should start or stop abruptly. Rather, each should **fade** in and out, that is, the volume should be increased or decreased gradually.

SOUND EFFECTS

Often abbreviated to *FX*, sound effects can be taped and broadcast from the sound booth in some cases, but in others must be created live from the wings or backstage. Whatever the sound needs of a show, be sure to provide the effects at rehearsal as soon as they are ready—certainly no later than the eighth week.

The sound effects that are to broadcast from the booth must be pretaped and carefully timed to the action on stage. A late effect provokes an unwanted laugh and spoils the moment, so the sound engineer needs to be attentive at rehearsals and to have the sound cues clearly marked in his or her copy of the book. Many sounds do not reproduce accurately on tape, but there are commercial tapes that successfully reproduce the sounds of a thunderstorm, a windstorm, a train chugging along, or ocean surf. Another sound effect that can be prerecorded and broadcast from the booth is the voice-over—the voice of God or a character speaking his or her thoughts.

Always be sure to rewind completely all tapes used in the performance. Don't plan to do it before the next performance. As the props manager is storing the props and the actors are removing their makeup, you should be restoring your work area to preperformance condition.

Live Sound Effects

Some sound effects work better if done live from the wings or backstage. Even if your show's FX are all on tape, you should know how some of the standard live effects are produced.

Thunder. Use a thunder sheet, a piece of heavy sheet metal about 2' × 6' hung from a rope where it does not touch anything solid. When shaken it produces the sound of a roll of thunder. (See Figure 8.1a.)

Wind. Use a wind machine, a wooden drum about three feet in diameter made of slats and covered with muslin. When turned by means of a handle it makes a noise like a howling wind.

Tolling bells. Use a set of metal pipes hung from a rope attached to a hole drilled in the top of each pipe. Some kinds of wind chimes will also create the pleasant sound of bells tolling.

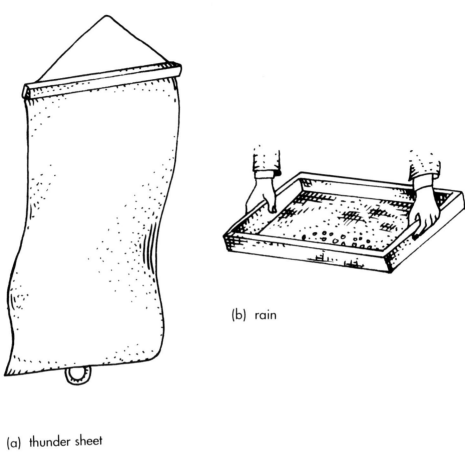

(b) rain

(a) thunder sheet

(c) horse hoofbeats

Figure 8.1.   Sound effects

Rainstorm. Use a drum of wire mesh containing bird shot. Turn the drum by means of a handle and create the effect of falling rain. Or, place some bird shot in a high-sided tray covered on the bottom with wire mesh. Hold the tray at each end and gently shake it. (See Figure 8.1b.)

Horse hoofbeats. The old standard of early radio—halves of hollowed coconut shells—still works well for creating the sound of horse hoofbeats. Watch a horse running or a film of one to practice the gait. Then, holding a shell in each hand, cut side down, recreate the rhythm for your sound effect. (See Figure 8.1c.)

Door slams. Place a full door in a frame just offstage and slam on cue. A door slammed on the set tends to shake the set, so be sure your sound effect door is not attached to the set at any point.

Gunshot. With a strong, wide rubber band attach two stacked pieces of wood about 2" thick and measuring about 4" × 6". When you lift the top piece of wood and allow it to snap back into place quickly it will create the sharp crack of a gunshot.

Breaking dishes. First build a **crash box**—a narrow, high-sided wooden box with a metal weight at the bottom and a firmly attached lid. Then acquire a stock of old plates—cracks and chips don't matter—at a thrift shop or rummage sale. Usually you can get them for a dime apiece. Place the crash box just offstage, and when the sound effect is required, place the plates in the box, attach the lid firmly, then shake vigorously or drop the box. A most satisfying crash will be heard! A very thin plate will often work for the sound of shattering glass.

Buzzer Board

A buzzer board can provide many sound effects: doorbell, door chime, telephone bell (old-fashioned or modern), and warning beep—such as from a smoke alarm or a rocket system.

To construct one, take a piece of half-inch plywood. (The dimensions depend on the number of buzzer effects you want to mount on the board.) First, mount the buzzer effect (doorbell, etc.) and a switch on the plywood. Then, with electrical cord (such as lamp cord) hook the one side of the switch and the buzzer together. Hook the other side of the switch with electrical cord and run the free end of the cord to the power source (either battery or AC). For each buzzer effect you will need a separate switch and power source on the board.

AMPLIFICATION

School productions do not usually use amplified sound for performers. Student actors are expected to project to all members of the audience and to that end, acoustics experts are consulted in the designing of any theatre. Even though the found space involved no such planning, it generally is small enough to enable the actors to be heard in the back row.

However, many students see professional productions that have been "miked" and they may want to imitate what they saw. There are two ways to provide amplified sound: the first is the use of wireless or radio microphones. These are frequently placed in an actor's wig and a thin flesh-colored wire runs to a battery pack–radio transmitter worn by the actor in some inconspicuous place. The radio signal is transmitted to a receiver on the sound-mixing panel. Such mikes are called *wireless* because they do not require wires leading from the actor to the mixing panel.

The second type of amplification is provided by mounting microphones among the footlights or by hanging them from the **flies** (the area above the stage, hidden by drapery). These are wired into the mixing panel.

STAGE LIGHTING

Stage lighting serves many purposes. Of course, it provides visibility. Even if the setting is an attic and the time is midnight, the audience needs to see the set and the actors. Lighting can help to establish time and place. By its color and intensity it suggests the hour of the day, the season of the year, and whether the action is taking place indoors or outdoors.

The lighting assists in creating the desired mood, in keeping with the set and the costumes. It can focus on and draw attention to a specific area of the stage or a specific character. Further, the type of lighting used to indicate scene interludes can establish a rhythm for the play. Slow fades, that is, gradual dim-

In addition to providing visibility, stage lighting helps establish mood.

ming of the lighting, establish a leisurely rhythm, while **blackouts**—the immediate cessation of all stage lighting—establish a fast-moving rhythm.

The Lighting Designer

The lighting designer needs a creative visual imagination as well as technical knowledge of the lighting instruments and the light board. He or she must know the play well and must watch rehearsals to determine the intensity and placing of the lighting for each moment of the play. Of course, the lighting designer must confer with the costume and set designers and with the director through the process of developing the lighting plot.

Lighting Instruments

The **lighting instrument** is composed of four parts: the lamp, the actual source of the light; the reflector, or the shade around the lamp; the lens, which shapes the light beam; and the housing, the metal shell that surrounds the system and provides a convenient attachment for hanging the instrument. The housing also holds the gels that are used to color the light beam.

Reflectors commonly come in three types: the *flood* or *scoop* gives a general, soft lighting that does not cast hard shadows; the *sphere* is used for single direction; and the *ellipsoidal* produces a sharply defined beam.

There are two principal lens types now commonly used. The *plano-convex,* which has one flat side and one convex side, gives a sharply defined beam. The *Fresnel* lens is stepped in concentric rings and provides a wider, softer beam.

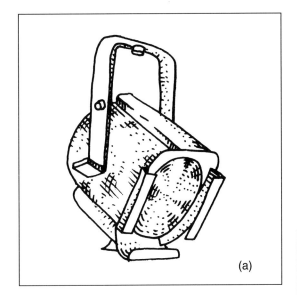

(a)

Figure 8.2.
(a) Fresnel spotlight; (b) ellipsoidal spotlight.

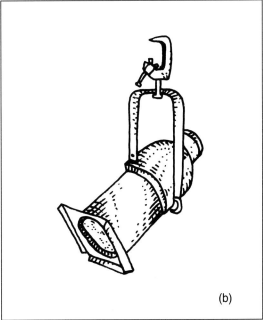

(b)

A **gel** is a very thin sheet of gelatin (available in a wide range of colors) set in a frame and mounted in front of a lighting instrument in order to color the beam directed onto the set. The sheets of colored plastic now coming into use are still called *gels*.

A **gobo,** also called a "cookie," is a disc of heat-resistant material into which a pattern—circles, stars, tree branches—has been cut. When the gobo is placed over the lens of an ellipsoidal spotlight, the pattern is projected onto a backdrop, set wall, or **cyclorama** (a fabric drape hung to create a semicircular backdrop). The gobo is a handy device for creating the effect of background woods or a city skyline.

In addition to the floodlights which bathe the area with light and the spotlights which pinpoint the light beam, there are strip or border lights and follow spots. The strip or border is mounted above the stage and serves to cast a whole area in light. The follow spot, whether in the lighting booth or stationed on an outside platform, is operated by a crew member, who uses it to illuminate and follow an actor moving across the stage.

If your lighting system is not adequate for the present production, you can rent lighting instruments from companies such as Premier Lighting and Production Company in North Hollywood, California.

The Light Board

Also called the control board or the dimmer board, the light board is used to operate and control the stage lighting. Each hanging position for an instrument is numbered and the number corresponds to a numbered switch on the control panel. Each instrument can be controlled independently, or all the instruments can be faded or even blacked out at once.

The control levers on the board move up to increase the intensity of the light and move down to dim it, hence the expressions "Bring up the lights" or "Take down the lights." There also should be a master switch that allows you to black out all the lighting in the show at once.

The newer computerized boards permit you to program all the lighting cues for the show into the board in advance. Always check the lighting program before each show in case the information has been accidentally erased.

Each switch on the light board corresponds to a hanging position for a lighting instrument.

The Lighting Plot

The lighting plot is a detailed plan by the lighting designer that includes a floor plan of the set with a longitudinal section—called an elevation—showing the height of the set, a lighting instruments schedule, and a lighting control board cue sheet. The floor plan and longitudinal section show the location of each lighting instrument and the area lit by each. The longitudinal section also shows the vertical angles of the beams of light.

The instrument schedule shows the type, wattage, outlet, dimmer, and color of each instrument. The cue sheet shows the dimmer readings for each instrument—a range from 100 percent for full to 10 percent for very dim. The lighting technician uses the plot when running the lighting for a show.

The Qualities of Light

Before you develop the lighting plot you need to consider the qualities of light in order to use them for maximum effect. The qualities to consider include intensity, color, distribution, and movement.

Intensity. The intensity or brightness of the lighting is controlled by the lighting or dimmer board. It may vary from little illumination, to suggest the break of day, to brilliant illumination, to suggest high noon.

Color. A skillful use of gels either singly or in combination—that is, having light beams colored by two different gels crossing at a position on the stage—can wash the set in anything from a sunny glow to a spooky haze.

Distribution. The distribution of light can range from a flood over the entire area to a pencil-thin ray concentrated on an actor's hand as he reaches for a weapon.

Movement. With the use of various dimmers on the control board, you can shift the focus of the light from one area to another on stage.

Once you have studied the play, watched rehearsals, conferred with the director and the other designers, learned the working of the lighting control board, and developed your lighting plot, you are ready to hang the lighting instruments.

Hanging the Instruments

Hanging the lighting instruments takes a crew of at least four: one person at the board in the light booth, one on the ladder or scaffold, and two to steady the ladder or help move it and to act as subjects on which to focus. Even if you have a **catwalk** to the lights—a metal bridge in the flies near the roof of the stage—you still need a crew to ensure the safety of all and swift completion of the work.

The work of the crew is to hang each lighting instrument from the battens or bars arranged across the top of the theatre and directed toward the stage. Once in place, the instruments are then angled in the required direction and focused onto the area to be lit. Last, they are circuited, that is, plugged into the sockets in the hanging battens. This puts the lights under the control of the lighting board.

No matter how carefully you have worked, there still will need to be minor adjustments during the **technical rehearsal,** which is devoted to practice of scene changes, sound and lighting effects, and so on. You can keep those adjustments to a min-

Even after careful planning, you will need to make adjustments in the lighting during the technical rehearsal.

imum however, by hanging and adjusting the instruments carefully according to the lighting plot and by running a test of them before you end the work session.

Lighting Safety Tips

If you're working on the lighting crew, remember:

- Always have the safety covers on the lighting instruments.
- Always wear gloves when handling the lighting instruments.
- Never work below a ladder or catwalk when somone is working above you.

Lighting Effects

You may believe that you need some practical lighting for your show. This lighting comes from working sources such as candles, lamps, fireplaces, or lanterns on the stage. Remember the drawbacks of such lighting, however. For example, candles will have to be lit by the actor on the first attempt or he or she will provoke unwanted laughter. Lamp cords can trip an actor and lamp bulbs can burn out, quite inconveniently, in the middle of a scene. Fireplaces generally use a lightbulb in the grate, covered with crumpled pieces of amber gel. But if an actor pokes at the fire, he or she must be careful not to break the bulb. Finally, a lantern must be lit by an actor, and the fumes can be unpleasant, even noxious. Indeed, practical lighting from such sources on the stage is often more trouble than it is worth, since stage lighting, controlled from the booth, can provide almost any desired effect.

Just as the artist paints a canvas with brushes dipped in color, the lighting technician paints a stage with lights of varying intensity and hue. The most beautiful set, if poorly lit, will only frustrate audience members as they strain to see it. The most beautiful costumes, if bathed in gels that muddy the fabric colors, will only disappoint.

The lighting and sound technicians, although often remote in a booth at the back of the house, are an integral part of any stage performance. Clearly, lighting and sound help to set the scene—the time, the place, the mood—and prepare the audience for the action of the play.

SUMMARY

Intensives are rehearsals of small portions of the play. Music should be used to introduce the play and to carry the audience through intermissions and scene interludes. Sound effects can be pretaped and then played from the booth on cue in the performance, or they can be created live backstage as needed. Stage lighting not only illuminates the stage, but also provides information and sets the mood or the tempo of the play. The light board controls the lighting instruments, and the lighting plot details the placement of those instruments, as well as all lighting cues.

Once Oliver Cromwell and the Puritan party were defeated and the monarchy restored in England, the theatres were allowed to open and resume performances. The former Prince Charles, now King Charles II of England, returned from the French court, bringing with him new ideas for the theatre. While Charles ruled only from 1660 to 1685, the Restoration period in the history of drama is considered to be from 1660 to 1700.

Although heroic and neoclassical tragedies were produced during that time, the period is known especially for the comedy of manners. These plays mocked the pretender, the fop (someone overly concerned with and excessively vain about his appearance), the old man who takes a young wife, or the old woman trying to be young.

The playhouses chartered by King Charles II were like the French theatres he had attended in his exile in the court of Louis XIV. In fact, the first two theatres were actually tennis courts converted in the French manner. However, the English version featured a seating area where the standing-room-only pit had been. The new pit and the stage were both raked, or slanted. Often an apron or forestage projected into the house, providing a small acting area that gave the illusion of intimacy.

The doors opened early to allow patrons to buy refreshments and socialize before the play began, and the addition of women to the acting company promoted a social atmosphere backstage, as well. The aristocracy—even the king—were frequent backstage visitors.

The fashions of the rich were elaborate, and such splendor of design, detail, and fabric was reflected in the lavish costumes seen onstage. It was an era of satins, silks, and laces; of high-heeled shoes for men and women; and of towering curled and powdered wigs called *perukes.* Some women attended the theatre in masks so that both offstage and onstage there was a general air of artifice and striving for effect.

The most respected playwright of the Restoration was poet and critic John Dryden, who wrote some thirty plays, among them the verse tragedy *All for Love,* based on Shakespeare's *Antony and Cleopatra.* Among the writers of witty, elegant comedy were William Wycherley, William Congreve, George Etherege, and George Farquhar.

One of the humorous devices employed in Restoration comedy was naming the characters in a way that described them—Fainall, Wilfull Witwound, Petulant, Waitwell, and Foible in Congreve's *The Way of the World;* Pinchwife in Wycherley's *The Country Wife;* and Sir Fopling Flutter in Etherege's *The Man of Mode.*

Toward the end of the seventeenth century the rise of the middle class—people who felt no kinship with the characters in the comedy of manners—and the resurgence of Puritan disapproval of the theatre led to changes in the subject matter and spirit of English drama.

Acting Projects

1. To utilize the technique of sense memory, go through your play or another play with which you are familiar and make a list of any place where the character must react to some sensory experience: sight, hearing, touch, taste, or smell. Then find some common life experience that could provide a sense memory for the actor to use in each of those places.
2. To further understand the process of overcoming obstacles, develop some improvisational premises (situations) that must be solved by some degree of compromise.

Music and Sound Projects

1. Analyze the mood of your play and decide on some selections appropriate for house music, intermission, and scene interludes. Play your choices at the next company meeting.
2. Using a tape recorder, create sound effects for the following:
   a. A shower running
   b. A car starting up and driving away
   c. Birds chirping or singing
   d. A crowd at a sports event
   e. Any sound required for your play
3. Create a "live" effect to be used for the following:
   a. Dishes breaking
   b. Rain

   c. A rifle shot
   d. A telephone ringing
   e. Any sound required for your play

Lighting Projects

1. Using an aluminum pie plate, make a gobo for one of the following effects:
   a. A starry night
   b. A tree branch
   c. Bars on a window
   d. A cobweb
   e. Any effect needed in your play
2. Read through your playbook and note places where gels should be used for a certain effect. Then go through the stock of gels and decide which colors would work best for the effects you want to achieve. Make a list of effects desired and gel colors to achieve them.
3. Learn how to operate the light control board and demonstrate your new knowledge by teaching the operation to someone else. Be sure the lighting technician checks out your work.
4. Inventory your stock of lighting instruments, taking care to note the type and condition of each. Don't overlook any strip lighting or follow spots.
5. Go through your playbook and note each scene ending. Decide whether a slow fade or a blackout would work best for the tempo of the play at that point.

The Lighting Designer

In the New York theatre, today's lighting designers are predominantly women, and premier among them is Tharon Musser, who has designed the lighting for more than one hundred Broadway shows. She has three Tony Awards and, in fact, is responsible for establishing lighting design as a category in the Tonys. In 1970, when Musser was asked to buy an ad in the Tony Awards ceremony program, she protested that lighting designers weren't even being recognized by the Tonys. Chuck Bowden, then producer of the ceremonies, called her a few days later to report not only that there would be a lighting design category in the awards, but also that she had been nominated for her work on Betty Comden and Adoph Green's *Applause.*

Earlier in the century the purpose of stage lighting was visibility, and it was considered part of the scenery designer's job. There were no shadings, shadows, or variations; there was no "painting with lights." The electricians hung the lighting instruments and moved them around, often in response to the star's request.

Although lighting still is one of the last things an audience appreciates about a play, in some shows it plays a major role, such as in *A Chorus Line* and *Dreamgirls*—two shows for which Musser won Tonys. Early in her career she felt she was being typecast as a designer for serious plays, but she managed to make a transition to musicals with *Shinbone Alley.*

Other musicals—*Mame, Applause, A Little Night Music,* and *Hallelujah Baby!*—followed.

In an interview with *TheatreWeek* writer Simi Horwitz, Musser commented that the big difference between designing a straight play and a musical is the quantity of lights required for a musical. So lighting does play an important role in the musical, tipping off the audience to the big numbers.

Musser was an early supporter of the computerized lighting board, the "memory board" that can provide such smoothness and consistency. To those who would find that too mechanical, Musser points out that use of the board frees the designer from concerns about an electrician who decides to change things or who forgets a cue.

Throughout her English and philosophy studies at Berea College in Kentucky, Musser did sets and lighting for college productions. Later, at Yale University she decided to specialize in lighting, even though she studied set and costume design as well.

Color is the key ingredient in Musser's designs. She studies the play first. Then, after conferring with the set and costume designers and the director, she decides on the colors that best evoke the desired mood. She explains, "The end result has to look like the creation of one set of eyes, not three. [Lighting design] is a collaborative art."

211

Countdown to Performance

9

Company Meeting

All too often this time is a low point in the production schedule. "Will we ever be ready?" "Will anyone come to the play?" The members of the company become overwhelmed. It is at times such as these that the assistant director and the stage manager need to step forward to encourage the company members, regardless of what remains to be done. Of course, the director must continue to polish and fine-tune each aspect of the production. Use this company meeting to rally enthusiasm among all members.

PROGRESS REPORTS

By now, most of the reports given should be of work completed. Everyone should express proper appreciation to fellow company members for their efforts. Address any last-minute problems with calm and orderly consideration, not panic, to seek a solution.

TOPICS FOR THIS MEETING

- Countdown to Performance
- The Technical Rehearsal
- The Dress Rehearsal
- Understudy Takeover
- Last-Minute Publicity
- The Story of Theatre: The Eighteenth Century
- Theatre Workshop
- Careers in the Theatre: The Stage Manager

WORKING VOCABULARY

Theatre terms of special interest in this chapter include *notes, call,* and *curtain call.*

AGENDA

At the next company meeting you'll discuss opening night, waiting to go on stage, maintaining the illusion, hospitality, the box office, after-performance duties, closing night, and the strike. You'll also be updated on production progress.

COUNTDOWN TO PERFORMANCE

As you approach opening night, the production schedule changes from a week-by-week to a day-by-day orientation. As carefully as you may have planned every detail, there always will be last-minute glitches to address, as well as those tasks that can't be done until just before opening. For example, in a production of Shakespeare's *As You Like It,* the set design called for topiary trees (trees with foliage sculpted into stylized shapes such as globes or pyramids). The wooden frames and the aviary wire globes were built weeks ahead of time, but the crew had to wait until the afternoon of the dress rehearsal to insert the real foliage into the wire. It was hectic, but the effect achieved was well worth it.

To spare the company some frantic moments, be sure that everything that *can* be done in advance *is* done. Then follow up by ensuring that an adequate number of technicians are both available and well instructed to handle the inevitable final details.

THE TECHNICAL REHEARSAL

The technical rehearsal has a well-deserved reputation for being long and tedious. It is absolutely necessary, however, so make up your mind to participate enthusiastically. Such an attitude will not only promote good working relationships, but also help move the rehearsal along more efficiently.

The purpose of the technical rehearsal is to coordinate the actors' performances with all the technical aspects of the production. It may be that your lighting and sound cues, your props and costumes, and your complete set changes have been ready and incorporated into rehearsals long before now. In this case, you may have two dress rehearsals instead of a technical and a dress, or you may be content to have only one dress rehearsal the night or day before opening night. However, if you share the performance space with other companies or events, you may have had to wait to hang your lights. Now you must make certain that all the lighting cues are well integrated into the performance.

At the technical rehearsal the stage manager is backstage running things, while the assistant director is in the house

215

At the technical rehearsal, the assistant director prepares a list of comments and observations that will be shared with the company afterward.

preparing **notes,** that is, the director's comments. If a problem with the lighting develops, the actors should be permitted to sit down and quietly run lines while the technicians attend to the difficulty. There is no need to keep the cast standing around on stage while lights are moved or refocused. Likewise, the actors must make a mental note about their own lighting in this rehearsal. If necessary, they can make minor adjustments in their position on stage during a performance when they feel they are out of their light.

After the technical rehearsal the assistant director and director present their notes (comments on what was good and what still needs work). The actors should ask questions and jot down any of the notes that apply specifically to them.

If the props and costumes were ready on time, the load-in took place on schedule, and the lighting instruments were hung and focused, then the technical rehearsal should progress smoothly.

THE DRESS REHEARSAL

The dress rehearsal is *exactly* like a performance, minus the audience. There can be no stopping for anything. In other words, any problems must be solved right then and there onstage and in full view of the would-be audience.

The **call**—the time established for arrival at your station in the theatre—should be the same as it will be for the performance. Sign in at the sign-in board, if there is one then go to your station, whether backstage or the dressing room. If there is no sign-in board, report to the stage manager when you arrive at the theatre. Be prompt for the call time, and don't grant yourself any exceptions. In a production of *Two on an Island* the actor playing John decided that with such a large cast, the makeup room would be too crowded. He decided to do his own make-up at home and go to the theatre at 7:30 in the evening, rather than at 7:00. Imagine the alarm of the entire company when the stage manager had to announce that the actor playing John still had not arrived. The understudy was already in costume when the actor finally appeared, half an hour late for the call.

All the technical crews should set up and operate in their areas just as they will for each performance. The props manager puts out all the props that are on the set as the play opens and

Before dress rehearsal, prop and costume crews must make sure that all necessary items are in place.

then lays out the other props on the props table. The stage manager goes through the list with the props manager as a final check. Never skip this procedure.

The wardrobe manager makes sure all costumes are ready and helps the actors to dress. He or she needs to check each actor for accessories and buttoned buttons, snapped snaps, and zipped zippers. The makeup artist and hairstylist step in next to help the actors prepare. Then, once again, the actors are checked to see that every detail is complete. It's best if the actors don't wear perfume or aftershave unless it's called for in the lines of the play. Too many scents mingling can be unpleasant, even gagging. Because of the excitement and the heat of the lights, actors need to be reminded that a fresh application of deodorant is essential! The stage crew should walk over the entire set, checking supports, paint, and any practical elements. If there is to be a set change, they need to see that all units are ready for the shift.

The lighting and sound engineers should be in the booth ready for the cues. The house music should start at the moment the house would open for a performance, usually half an hour before curtain. While the sound engineer waits for the house to open, he or she must check out the equipment and make sure

Lighting and sound technicians check their controls and equipment before the house opens for dress rehearsal.

each sound cue is at its proper setting on the tape. At the same time the lighting engineer tests the control board, the settings, and the lighting instruments. Never take for granted that equipment will be as you left it when you were last in the booth.

If your performance space has no curtain, no one can go onstage once the house music has started and the house is open. All your checking must be done prior to that. If your theatre does have a curtain, resist the temptation to peek through it at the house. *Any* movement of that curtain is seen by the audience.

At ten minutes to curtain the cast should assemble in the greenroom, a room backstage or immediately adjacent to backstage, set aside for the actors. The room should have seating for everyone and, if possible, a television monitor showing the stage area. If your performance space has no formal greenroom, the stage manager should set up an area backstage, out of the way of technicians. Once again the stage manager needs to make sure everyone is present and ready. Actors leaving the stage to await their next entrance should wait in the greenroom unless there is a costume change or their next entrance is immediate. The stage manager has enough to monitor without having to call roll constantly.

The rehearsal itself should begin at the scheduled curtain time and take full intermissions and scene interludes. If an actor forgets a line, the play must continue. Actors who are truly in character will find a way to proceed without calling attention to the momentary lapse.

After the rehearsal the cast should quickly get out of costume and makeup and assemble with the crew in the greenroom to hear the director's notes, which will incorporate the assistant director's observations. Although this is an emotional time, listen carefully to the notes and resolve to make the improvements or adjustments required. No director is going to introduce new business or major changes at this point unless absolutely necessary, but there may be small adjustments to make to ensure a better performance.

Perhaps you have heard the old saying that a bad dress rehearsal means a good opening night. Of course, that is not the case. Why would it be true? It may be that an individual who has been lagging will suddenly realize that he or she needs to give a lot more effort, but a play is not going to come together overnight if weeks of rehearsals have yielded poor results. Your best and most sincere effort is required at all times.

When dress rehearsal has ended, listen to the director's notes carefully and resolve to make any changes asked of you.

The Curtain Call

The dress rehearsal should include a **curtain call**—when the cast bows to the audience—even though there is no audience present to applaud. You may have been rehearsing a curtain call all along, or the director may have waited until now to decide on which type to use. Curtain calls may be a line of the entire cast across the stage, all bowing in unison. In a small cast, the curtain call may bring the actors out one by one until they are all onstage together. The director may choose to bring the cast out in groups. In a production of Shakespeare's *Twelfth Night* the groups were "the outsiders," Olivia's household, and Orsino's household.

Another type of curtain call is the gimmick—something that carries on the spirit of the play or comments on it. For a production of John Van Druten's *Bell, Book, and Candle,* the director had the character of Queenie, the would-be witch, cast a spell. To Queenie's evident delight, she managed to summon forth the other characters to take a bow.

Whichever type of curtain call you use, don't milk the applause until it becomes half-hearted. You want to close the curtain on a still enthusiastic audience. Also, don't bring out technicians or the director for a curtain call. Properly, only the actors take a bow. Although curtain calls for professional performances generally start with the minor roles and work up to the leads, the company spirit would dictate that in educational theatre such distinctions not be maintained. Finally, remember that the curtain call is an acknowledgment of the audience's applause and attention. Do not use it as an opportunity for actors to hug or applaud each other.

UNDERSTUDY TAKEOVER

The takeover of a role by an understudy is usually a last-minute event brought on by an emergency. When an understudy steps into a role the quality of the production should not suffer, so understudies must be chosen with care, rehearsed regularly, and fitted with costumes.

The audience must be made aware of the substitution by a sign in the lobby and a slip of paper included in the program. Thanks to speedy photocopying this is not difficult. Some theatres announce the substitution over the speaker system, but the vocal disappointment of some thoughtless audience members can discourage an already anxious understudy.

If the understudy has had a small role in the play, someone must take over that small role when the understudy steps in for someone else. Perhaps another actor with a small role may be able to double in both small roles without difficulty. If that is not possible, then someone else must read the small role. The assistant director or stage manager both know the play and all the blocking well and are thus obvious candidates to step in.

If an understudy must read the part in performance, then the announcement should be worded "reading the part of" rather than "taking over the part of." Once the announcement has been posted in the lobby and on a slip of paper in the program there need not be any tricks such as hiding the book or planting pages of it all over the set. The audience knows an understudy has taken over and someone else is reading the role the understudy had.

If the understudy had no acting role previously, then he or she can simply get into costume and makeup and, time permitting, run lines with the cast. An understudy should be able to step onstage confident that the company will support him or her in every possible way. This is an opportunity for an understudy to shine and for the company to rally around.

If your company has only one male understudy and one female understudy for all the roles in the play, the understudies will have been taking over in rehearsal for any absent actor, but they probably will not know all the lines of all the actors they understudy. There are exceptions to this, of course, as some understudies manage to know the whole play by curtain time.

Confident of the full company's support, the understudy can take full advantage of this opportunity to shine.

LAST-MINUTE PUBLICITY

House management and publicity may have saved some ideas for a final campaign the week before opening. Set these into motion now. If all plans for publicity have been carried out and the ticket sales or reservations still are sparse, you will want to develop some new tactics quickly.

A paid ad may help. Or, obtain permission to attend some public events in costume to pass out fliers. Consider setting up a table in front of the school library or cafeteria and offering free raffle tickets to everyone. At the end of the week have a drawing during lunch period for tickets to the play. Give singles, not pairs of tickets, so the winners will be encouraged to bring a paying guest. If you have an assembly period, arrange to present a scene from the play and then distribute fliers. It's important to continue with publicity efforts until the last performance of the play.

SUMMARY

As company members count down the days to opening night, they need to make sure everything that can be done in advance is completed. The technical rehearsal can run efficiently if everyone remains alert and enthusiastic. The dress rehearsal is carried out exactly like a performance for the public. The curtain call acknowledges the audience's applause and is not the place for company affection. If an understudy must take over a role at the last minute, the audience is notified and the company supports the understudy in every way. Last-minute publicity strategies can be employed to increase ticket sales.

*E*arly in the eighteenth century, writer Charles Gildon collected the thoughts on acting of Thomas Betterton, a famous Restoration actor. The book Gildon published, *The Life of Mr. Thomas Betterton, The Late Tragedian,* was the first book in English on the subject of acting. It advised actors that "When you speak of yourself, the Right not the Left hand must be apply'd to the Bosom." Betterton had dominated the English stage from 1670 to 1710, excelling in tragic and heroic parts. His elocutionary style—his manner of delivering his lines—became the model for many actors who followed him.

In the eighteenth century, though, it was David Garrick who exerted the most influence upon the acting profession with his natural style. By today's standards Garrick's acting would be considered too stylized—too obviously acting—but in his time it was a refreshing change from the posturing and declamatory style fostered by the French tennis court theatres.

Another major figure of the British theatre was Edmund Kean (1787–1833). Though he was snubbed by some critics for being uneducated and lacking the good looks and pleasing voice of popular actors, he was acknowledged to have a powerful emotional effect on his audiences. His most famous roles were in Shakespeare's tragedies, but he also played in some of Ben Jonson's comedies.

For the first time in the history of drama, the actors as well as the plays were prominent and memorable. This trend was to continue into the nineteenth century, when the actors actually became more important than the playwrights.

In the eighteenth century the dominant types of drama were the sentimental comedy and the domestic tragedy. Richard Steele is regarded as the leading writer of sentimental comedy, which was a reaction to the immorality expressed in Restoration comedy. His plays include *The Tender Husband* and *The Conscious Lovers.* Sentimental comedy lacked humor, reality, and a light touch. The characters were all-good or all-bad, becoming caricatures, and the plots were contrived to have virtue always triumph.

Domestic tragedy dealt with the domestic lives of ordinary people, as opposed to classical tragedy, which had dealt with the lives of kings or noblemen who fell from power or grace. George Lillo's *The London Merchant* first popularized this type of drama. Its title alludes to the growing merchant class, which was a potential theatre audience.

In North America, audiences were seeing touring British companies. This so influenced new American companies that it wasn't until the nineteenth century that the U.S. developed a truly native tradition in the theatre.

French drama moved further away from neoclassical standards as the eighteenth century progressed. Sentimental comedy and domestic tragedy gained popularity. A prominent French playwright of the century was Beaumarchais,

who wrote *The Barber of Seville* and *The Marriage of Figaro*. These comedies are well known today as operas by Rossini (*Barber*) and Mozart (*Figaro*).

At that time Italy was preoccupied with opera—both grand opera and the newly developing comic opera, which used domestic and rural scenes to advantage. Interest continued in the commedia dell'arte, and Carlo Goldoni, in an attempt to "reform" commedia, used traditional characters such as Arlecchino. He sentimentalized them, however, and removed what he considered indecent *lazzi* (the bits of stage business the commedia clown characters developed).

In the eighteenth century European and American drama moved away from the neoclassical ideals of the previous century and closer to the romanticism that would dominate drama for much of the nineteenth century.

Beaumarchais's comedy *The Marriage of Figaro* was first performed in 1784. Two years later, Mozart wrote an opera based on the play.

Publicity Projects

1. Research the history of your play, its previous performances, and the lives of your cast to find a story for some last-minute publicity.
2. Check on all the posters and fliers that were previously distributed. Replace any that are missing, torn, or defaced and put more up at additional sites.
3. Using a checklist, call the local radio and television stations to follow up on your public service announcement. If they have broadcast it, thank them; if they have not, offer to provide another copy of the PSA and try courteously to persuade them to air it.
4. Begin writing thank-you notes to all those who have helped in some way with the production or who have given the show publicity. This note also will serve to remind them that the play is opening soon.
5. Develop a system for ticket giveaways through a radio station, library, restaurant, or public event.

Acting Projects

1. Organize a cast activity such as a huddle, circle, or other formation to offer encouragement to each other just before curtain.
2. Develop some focusing techniques, such as imaging or listening to music, for individual actors to use before curtain.
3. Write a brief note of encouragement to each cast member and place it with the actor's costume(s).
4. If your local newspaper offers inexpensive "happy ads" in the personals column, place a "break a leg" ad to appear opening night and post it in the greenroom to inspire the cast. (The custom of saying "break a leg" to an actor about to go onstage stems from the belief that it would be tempting fate to wish an actor good luck. So instead we use reverse psychology and say "break a leg.")

Backstage Project

1. If your company has a call board—the board backstage where company correspondence, notices, and newspaper clippings are posted—add a "break a leg" message for the cast. If there is no call board, establish one for the run of the play.

The Stage Manager

Sarahjane Allison, who is the theatre manager and executive stage manager for the Interact Theatre at Cuesta College in San Luis Obispo, California, is a strong believer in education. She says it is the base from which theatre can grow, adding, "It doesn't matter if you want to work in a tech, acting, or directing job; for any job in theatre you need a strong base to grow from." She also encourages people interested in theatre to take any class they can, to try every different job. "You have to know a little bit about everything when you work in a company."

Allison herself has a bachelor of arts degree from Western Washington University, where her major was theatre, with an emphasis in technical and stage management. Her collegiate production experience includes acting as props supervisor at Essex Community College, scene technician at the Porthouse Summer Theatre, lighting technician at the Harford Opera Theatre in Baltimore, Maryland, lighting designer for the Bellingham Theatre Guild, and stage manager at the regionals of the American College Theatre Festival and for Full Circle Tour, a university group that toured high schools and community colleges in the state of Washington. Her collegiate career certainly bears out her belief in the value of having experience in as many areas of theatre as possible.

Beginning her professional career as a lighting technician with the Vancouver Symphony, Allison went on to work as stage manager for Prince George's Civic Opera Company and then for the Great American Melodrama and Vaudeville in Bakersfield, California. She spent several years touring with Ringling Brothers and Barnum and Bailey Circus, first as lighting director and sound technician, then as assistant performance director, and finally as performance director of the Blue Unit of the circus. When asked what the most difficult aspect of the job was, Allison answered that communication was the most difficult part because there were eighteen different languages spoken in the company. She explained, "Rehearsal would be in English, and then a Chinese interpreter would translate for the Chinese, a Russian interpreter for the Russians, a Spanish interpreter for the Spaniards, and so on. With all the different languages, it was almost impossible to communicate with each other."

Now, Allison manages the Interact Theatre and acts as executive stage manager to the professional company in residence and the three student companies that share the performance space. She is especially helpful and encouraging to the fledgling student stage managers and finds great satisfaction in seeing them learn and succeed.

Curtain Up,
Curtain Down

10

Company Meeting

Electricity seems to be in the air as you approach opening night. The company meeting is a chance to be among "family," discussing the topic most important to all of you at this time—the show.

PROGRESS REPORTS

Sometimes people are misled into thinking that they will have to work through the night to finish up just before the show opens. Fortunately, this is a myth. In fact, everything should have been ready for the dress rehearsal so you can get a good night's sleep before the show. There is nothing thrilling or glamorous about throwing things together at the last minute. You owe the audience, the company, and yourself more than that. So, make sure that your progress reports accurately describe all that you have accomplished. A desperate plea for last-minute help is not what your company needs from you now.

TOPICS FOR THIS MEETING

- Opening Night
- Waiting To Go Onstage
- Maintaining the Illusion
- Hospitality
- The Box Office
- After-Performance Duties
- Closing Night
- The Strike
- The Story of Theatre: The Rise of the "Isms"
- Theatre Workshop
- Careers in the Theatre: The Actor

WORKING VOCABULARY

A theatre term focused on in this chapter is *tribute*.

AGENDA

At the next company meeting you'll discuss evaluating the performance, expressing gratitude, and recommendations for the next production. Also, rather than progress reports, you'll hear wrap-up reports from each area of responsibility.

OPENING NIGHT

Performing is what theatre is all about. The actors perform onstage and the technicians perform behind the scenes. Exciting as the dress rehearsal was, it pales as you anticipate the first audience reaction to your show. The house lights dim, the stage lights come up on your set, the house music fades, and the opening line is spoken. The audience leans forward a little, already drawn into the magical experience of watching live theatre.

Enjoy every minute. Don't lose any of this exhilaration to nervousness or stage fright. You are eager and filled with energy, so channel your enthusiasm to make this performance sparkle.

Checklist

Follow the schedule you established for your dress rehearsal:

- Everyone checks in at the announced call time.
- Everyone reads the notices on the call board.
- Each person reports to area of responsibility.
- The actors get into costume with the help, as needed, of the wardrobe manager.
- The lighting and sound personnel check all the settings for the lighting and the sound cues. The house music begins as soon as the house is open.
- The makeup assistant and hairstylist help the costumed actors to complete their preparations.
- The props manager sets out all the props, both onstage and on the backstage props table. The stage manager goes through a final check with the props manager.
- The stage crew walks the set to see that all is ready. If there is a scene shift, the crew also checks that all units are ready for the shift.

WAITING TO GO ONSTAGE

When the actors have assembled in the greenroom, the director makes a few encouraging remarks and reminders, then usually leaves to sit in the house to view the performance. The stage manager is then in charge and should also be as encouraging and cheerful as possible. If there is a need for reminders, they should be given in an upbeat tone. Although cast members may want to chatter, this should be a time for concentrating and centering oneself in the moment of the play.

If the greenroom isn't a separate room but, instead, a designated area backstage, it is even more important that there be silence. Don't bring food or beverages into the greenroom or backstage area. The only exception is a personal water bottle—the kind with the built-in straw. You don't want the rattle of soft drink cans, the danger of hot coffee, or the possibility of water stains on the costumes.

Actors who return to the greenroom between appearances on the stage should avoid saying, "This is a tough audience," "They aren't laughing at anything," "There's hardly anyone out there," or "Let's throw in some gags to wake them up." Just do your best and let all your hard work pay off in a performance you are proud of.

The greenroom is not the place to criticize someone who made a mistake onstage. The director will have notes for the

Before going out into the house to watch the performance, the director gives some encouragement to the actors assembled in the greenroom.

company after the performance. Instead, briefly take the opportunity to praise each other and offer positive reinforcement.

If your greenroom is separate from the backstage area, it is an appropriate place for any centering or imaging exercises the company has agreed on. If people in the greenroom are audible to the audience, however, then the dressing room is the place for the company exercises. The final minutes before curtain should be given only to the play. No one should eat, drink, write, or read, but instead should focus all thoughts on the show. Although it might seem that a little joking around helps to relieve tension, in fact it only detracts from the moment. The theatre is an ancient and respected place in which self-discipline is very important.

MAINTAINING THE ILLUSION

Once in costume and makeup an actor never mingles with the audience before, during (intermission), or after a performance. In fact, when you are in costume and makeup you *are* the character; you belong to the play and must put aside your private life for the show. Beforehand, tell friends that you will meet them after the show. Then, following the curtain call, assemble in the greenroom or dressing room to hear the director's notes. Afterward, quickly change out of costume and makeup and then

Make your costume change immediately after you exit the stage, even if your next entrance seems hours away.

leave to meet your friends. While it is true that in the profession-al theatre actors often have friends in their dressing rooms after the performance, educational theatre does not have the luxury of individual dressing rooms. Indeed, there already is enough con-gestion and confusion when the cast is large, and adding visitors would only increase the chaos.

If you have an intercom system between backstage and light-ing booth or backstage and dressing room, only designated per-sonnel should use it, and then only if absolutely necessary. If audience members seated near the wings or lighting booth should overhear the intercom being used for personal conversa-tions, the illusion created by the performance would be spoiled for those patrons.

Finally, if you have a costume change at a time other than intermission, you should make that change as soon as you exit the stage—even if you are not due back on for some time. Make the change immediately and then settle down to await your next entrance cue.

HOSPITALITY

The house management crew is responsible for the comfort and safety of the audience. This responsibility begins at the box office and continues throughout the time the audience is at the theatre. The impression you make and the hospitality you extend not only enhance this performance, but also bring the patron back again.

If the house manager is not in the box office, he or she should be in the lobby to greet the audience. If the assistant director can leave the backstage area, he or she should join or stand in for the house manager in this pleasant task. Clothing should either be dressy or something in the period of the play. As patrons hand over their tickets they should be greeted, given a program, and directed to the appropriate seating area.

If you're serving or selling refreshments before the show as well as during intermission, you might direct the patrons first to the refreshment table. Along with the simple snacks and drinks you're offering, you might consider a gimmick. For example, at a performance of C. S. Lewis's *The Lion, the Witch, and the Ward-robe,* house management sold small packages of Turkish delight, a candy that figured prominently in the story. At a performance of Molly Newman and Barbara Damashek's *Quilters,* house management handed out tickets for a drawing to give away a hand-made quilt. See if there is some aspect of your show that lends itself to a tie-in such as this that patrons would enjoy.

Serious theatregoers are prompt, but patrons who attend plays infrequently may not take the stated curtain time seriously. While it is unfair to those who are on time to delay the curtain until all latecomers are seated, it's impractical to start the play while people are still arriving and finding their seats. Signal with blinking of house and lobby lights that the show is due to begin. If you use a warning chime as well, strike it when the lights are blinked. Some theatres prefer an announcement over the speaker system: "Two minutes to curtain." "One minute to curtain." "Curtain going up." Then abide by this timetable. Most theatres have printed on tickets, programs, and lobby signs that latecomers will not be seated until there is an appropriate break in the performance. As much as possible, keep from disturbing or inconveniencing those who are on time with the disruption of latecomers. Remember, too, to give the same curtain warnings at the end of any intermission.

Be sure you know how to direct patrons to restrooms, water fountains, public telephones, and anything else they may require. Be prepared to escort any patron with special needs—wheelchair access, guide dog, aisle seat because of crutches or walker—to the area designated.

THE BOX OFFICE

The box office is the first contact patrons make as they attend a performance, so make the greeting more than routine. If the house manager is on duty in the box office, he or she has the responsibility for the reservation list, the tickets, and the money collected. The list must be checked off accurately as patrons arrive to claim their tickets. If there are different prices or assigned seats, pay particular attention when handing out tickets.

After the performance the box office statement (see Chapter 6), which is a record of ticket sales and money received, should first be reviewed and signed by the house manager. Next, the evening's receipts (money taken in) must be turned over to the director or school authority. If a parent group, teacher, or school authority runs the box office, the company still will want to obtain a copy of the box office statement for its records.

The responsibility of the house management crew begins at the box office and continues until the last patron has left the theatre.

AFTER-PERFORMANCE DUTIES

"All the effort was worth it!" is the sentiment of actors and technicians the world over as the curtain falls or the lights dim on the opening night performance. Lines of dialogue rehearsed so often that you no longer found them funny made your audience chuckle; the pathos of the lovers' parting moved patrons to tears. You have probably been struck by the power of the words, of the actions, of the theatre!

Take a moment to enjoy the exhilaration, then focus on the director's notes so you can improve on this first triumph. Afterward, actors remove costumes and makeup while the technicians work to restore the theatre to preperformance readiness. House management attends to the box office and other house areas. The stage crew strikes what must be struck until the next performance. If no one else will be using the space until your next performance, leave the stage set. If you share the space, however, you will have arranged to strike all but the set walls. Props and set components

After the opening night performance, take a moment to enjoy the exhilaration!

must be stored carefully and left secure. A complete strike dismantles the entire set and reduces it to its basic elements. To strike props means to remove them from the set.

Even if the next performance is tomorrow night, the props and costumes must be collected, examined for damage, repaired if necessary, and stored in the assigned places. Makeup and hair supplies must be put away and work areas cleaned. Don't allow actors to wear home any barrettes, ribbons, or other accessories they wear in the show.

If there is no custodial help assigned to the area for the nights of your performances, house management takes responsibility for collecting discarded programs, paper cups, and any other litter left behind by patrons. Refreshment supplies must be wrapped and stored in a clean, secured place. The stage crew sweeps the stage and backstage areas. Finally, the stage manager should accompany the director on a tour of the facilities before locking up for the night.

237

CLOSING NIGHT

All too soon it seems the run of the show is over and it's closing night. Often, it's a blaze of flashing cameras as company members take pictures of each other to keep as mementos. A souvenir program with the autograph of every company member is another favored keepsake.

It is customary to present a **tribute,** that is, a gift in gratitude and admiration, to the director and the assistant director. Company members contribute to pay for the gifts, which need not be expensive or elaborate. A single rose with ferns or a small bouquet of garden flowers is ideal. Certainly, flowers are an appropriate tribute for both men and women. If your company would prefer to give something more lasting, however, consider a memento such as the show's program laminated to a wooden plaque. House management and the stage crew could work together to create the plaques.

There often is a temptation to present tributes at the curtain call. However, to do so spoils the illusion of the performance by bringing people out from backstage or up from the audience. Most often the tribute is presented when the company assembles for the call prior to the final performance.

Often, there are no director's notes on the last night of the show. Play production is an ongoing process, however, and you learn from each thing you do. With this in mind, the director may want to comment on the production as a whole.

THE STRIKE

The play is over when the curtain falls or the lights dim on the last performance, but the production is not complete until the strike is finished. Although the actors are expected to help, it is the technicians who take over the stage now. The strike must be as carefully planned as the load-in. Again, the stage manager, under instruction from the director, is in charge. The sample plan shown on page 239 works well whether or not you share the performance space with other companies or events.

Sample Strike Plan

1. All personal belongings and anything lent for the production must be removed from the area. Items may be stored in students' lockers or sent home with their families.

2. Actors return all costume items and props to proper areas. Anything damaged or soiled should be reported and then arrangements made for repair, replacement, or cleaning.

3. The stage crew begins striking the set.

   A. Reduce the set to its basic elements and then store these in the scene shop.

   B. Sweep the stage floor and then repaint it. (Actors help with this as needed.)

   C. Return all tools and supplies to their proper places.

4. The props manager strikes all props from the set.

   A. Be sure loaners are returned to company members or set aside in the director's office for return to community members.

   B. Discard all consumables, disposables, or props damaged beyond repair.

   C. Repair or set aside for repair any slightly damaged props.

   D. Store all other props in stock.

5. The house management restores order to all house areas.

6. Lighting crews tidy the lighting booth. Lighting technicians strike lights as necessary. Return to storage the lighting instruments and any gels that still are usable.

7. Actors restore the greenroom to order and prepare for the strike party.

8. The sound engineer restores all equipment to original positions and settings. Either store tapes for future use or, if instructed, erase them for their next use.

9. Wardrobe personnel must check in all costumes. Examine each garment for damage and soiling. Return all loaners to owners. Sort remaining garments for mending, pressing, washing, or cleaning and store them in the costume shop. If your school has laundry facilities and if there is time to do a load of wash and dry it, then get a start on that. Pressing and minor repairs can be accomplished while the rest of the strike is carried out. Return any ready garment to stock.

10. Makeup assistants and hairstylists should inventory remaining supplies, noting anything to be reordered. Dispose of all soiled materials and return others to stock. Clean and organize the work areas.

11. When the strike is complete all company members report to the greenroom for the strike party.

The stage crew's strike plan includes returning all tools and supplies to their proper places.

The Strike Party

The strike party should follow immediately after the strike and include *all* the company. It should not be an open house or a party at someone's home that includes only selected company members. If you have no formal greenroom, don't use the backstage area. Instead, obtain permission to use the cafeteria or a classroom. Of course, any area used must be returned to order at the party's end.

For the food, consider a potluck meal, take-out pizza, sandwiches and snacks, or a decorated ice-cream cake. Add music from the play, or current tunes, and enjoy yourselves. This is a time for the company to gather for a little while to celebrate what they have accomplished, from the introductions at the first company meeting to the final strike.

SUMMARY

Enjoy the excitement of opening night and each subsequent performance, but don't allow yourself to be distracted from your purpose in the company. In order to maintain the illusion created by a theatrical performance, actors should change out of costume and makeup before greeting friends and family. Dressing rooms and backstage areas should be for the company only. The house management crew is responsible for the comfort and safety of the audience. After each performance, equipment should be restored to readiness for the next use. At the conclusion of the final performance, the strike should return the performance space to preproduction condition. The strike party is for all members of the company and is an opportunity to rejoice together at all you have accomplished.

The nineteenth century saw the rise of several theatre "isms": romanticism, naturalism, realism, and symbolism. Melodrama emerged as the most popular dramatic form, and touring companies brought live theatre to people all over the Western world.

With the coming of romanticism in the first half of the nineteenth century, neo-classical ideals were abandoned. Where neoclassicism sought to exclude from plays anything that could not happen in real life, romanticism tended to emphasize the supernatural and mysterious. So, romantic dramas were filled with ghosts, witches, curses, prophecies, spells, far-fetched coincidences, and mysterious strangers. Plots included material from medieval tales, national or local legends, and folk heroes. Themes emphasized people's attempts to achieve freedom or to uncover the mysteries of the universe. Johann Wolfgang von Goethe's retelling of the Faust legend, in which a man sells his soul to the devil in order to learn the secrets of life, is the epitome of romantic drama.

A logical development of the romantic in drama, but one that far outlived the romantic era, is the form called melodrama. It is a form that relies heavily on sensationalism and sentimentality. While melodrama may follow the structure of tragedy, it tends to feature action more than motivation, stock characters, and a strict black-and-white view of morality—that is, virtue rewarded and evil punished.

The typical pattern of such plays involves provocation, pangs, and penalty. Provocation is the incident, often caused by the jealously or greed of the villain, that sets the plot in motion. For example, a banker who holds the mortgage on the heroine's home will evict her if she does not yield to his lustful demands. Pangs are the suffering of the good and innocent characters. A clerk is accused of stealing when actually the banker, who is jealous of the clerk, has taken the money himself. The penalty is a last-minute reversal of the situation. The clerk is cleared of the charges and rushes to the rescue of the homeless heroine.

Melodrama often is participatory theatre; the audience is encouraged to hiss the villain and cheer the hero. A perennially popular melodrama has been *The Drunkard,* credited to P. T. Barnum (of circus fame) and others. Recently Rupert Holmes's *The Mystery of Edwin Drood* and Stephen Sondheim's *Sweeney Todd* have been presented as melodramas to great success. The term *melodramatic* is applied to plays that are farfetched and presented in an exaggerated acting style.

By the 1870s theatre was moving in the new direction of naturalism and realism. In opposition to romanticism, naturalism dispensed with theatrical conventions in order to present what playwrights called "a slice of life." The playwrights attempted to present life with complete detachment. There was great attention to detail in stage design and costuming. Underlying naturalistic drama was pes-

simistic determinism—the notion that environment determines human fate. Two plays that express this philosophical point of view are Maksim Gorky's *The Lower Depths* and August Strindberg's *Miss Julie.*

Realism, which followed naturalism and eventually absorbed it, was also an attempt in theatre to represent everyday life and people as they appear to be, through careful attention to detail in motivation of characters, costuming, setting, and dialogue. However, unlike naturalism, realism need not adhere to a philosophy of pessimistic determinism.

In the theatre, realism spread rapidly and demanded a new type of acting to interpret the plays. This led to the development of the famed Stanislavsky Method of actors' training. Created by Konstantin Stanislavsky for the Moscow Art Theatre early in the twentieth century, the Method was an introspective kind of training that required the actor to look inside himself or herself to find the motivation needed to portray a character accurately. Using sense memory exercises is one element of the Method.

Probably the most important name in realism in drama is Henrik Ibsen, whose plays *A Doll's House, Hedda Gabler, The Wild Duck, An Enemy of the People, The Master Builder,* and *Ghosts* are an essential part of standard theatre repertoire today.

A minor revolt against naturalism and realism began in 1880, but was largely dead by 1900. It was called symbolism or neoromanticism, a highly nonrealistic form of drama that took its subjects from the romantic past or the realms of fancy. It tended toward the mysterious, making no attempt to deal with social problems of its day. Maurice Maeterlinck's *Pelleas and Melisande* is considered the best of the symbolist dramas.

In England, toward the end of the nineteenth century, George Bernard Shaw created a kind of comic realism that has made his plays popular to this day. His play *Pygmalion* was adapted into one of the most popular musicals of all time, *My Fair Lady.* And Oscar Wilde resurrected the comedy of manners with his farce *The Importance of Being Earnest.*

Realism continued into the twentieth century and brought forth other theatre "isms," but the comedy of manners survived. With both old and emerging forms, theatre in the twentieth century is highly eclectic.

Opening Night Projects

1. Find a tie-in with your show that would work well as a hospitality or refreshment gimmick.
2. Design a sign for the lobby stating that latecomers will not be seated until an appropriate break in the action. Word the message in a courteous, but firm, tone.
3. Arrange for some type of lobby decor. Could the art department prepare an exhibition to coincide with the play? Are there theatre memorabilia that could be put on display? Are costumed dolls ready from the project suggested in Chapter Seven?
4. Research some theatre superstitions and legends and share them with company members.
5. To help house management greet patrons, develop a list of various gracious ways to welcome members of the audience as they arrive at the theatre.

Closing Night Projects

1. Develop a clear, specific plan of action for the strike. Be sure to involve everyone. Submit it to the stage manager for consideration.
2. Devise a menu or several alternative menus for the strike party. Determine which one the company prefers.
3. Take responsibility for the music to be played at the strike party.
4. Write a speech of tribute to express the gratitude of the company to the director and assistant director.
5. Volunteer to make and hang some simple decorations in the greenroom for the strike party. Consider adding mock headlines praising the show or writing and displaying some of the company jokes that evolved during production.

The Actor

One of the bright new actors taking her place in the theatre today is Leslie Baldwin, who has a Master of Fine Arts degree from California Institute of the Arts. As to why she chose to continue her academic career all the way through graduate school, Leslie explains, "I realize that the majority of people believe that with the 'right look' and a good personality anyone can get on television. And in a way they're right. . . . But I'm not really interested in a 'flash in the pan' career. I believe that talent and tenacity are the keys to a long-lasting and exciting theatrical career. When the only instruments an actor possesses are her voice and body, good training becomes essential."

Certainly Baldwin's training at Cal Arts was rigorous, as it included voice, speech, dance, t'ai chi ch'uan, mask work, film and television work, fencing, stage combat, analysis of text, and a variety of classes focusing on specific acting styles. From all this Leslie has gained the flexibility she needs to pick up anything from a Shakespearean text to a soap opera script and be able to read it well within a couple of minutes. Further, her training has given her the flexibility to play a myriad of exciting roles in which she might otherwise not be cast. Baldwin's résumé (see below) demonstrates her versatility as an actor.

Baldwin believes that training (formal or informal) is a lifelong process and does not end once you have your degree. She explains, "The body and voice and mind are comprised of muscles. They must be exercised to stay in shape."

LESLIE BALDWIN

Height: 5'4"
Weight: 118

Eyes: Blue
Hair: Blonde

Representative Roles

Role	Show	Director	Company
Glory	TRAVELER IN THE DARK	Dawn McAndrews	Santa Clarita Rep.
L. Capulet	ROMEO AND JULIET	Pascal Marcotte	Santa Clarita Rep.
Ensemble	LUNATIC, LOVER, & THE POET	James Loren	Santa Clarita Rep.
Marina	PERICLES	Ralph Elias	CalArts
Volanges	LES LIAISONS DANGEREUSES	Joe DeGuglielmo	CalArts
Amanda	THE GLASS MENAGERIE	Haldor Laxness	CalArts
Hippolyta	A MIDSUMMER NIGHT'S DREAM	Bob Ellenstein	CalArts
Cordelia	KING LEAR	Alan David (R.S.C.)	CSUF
Ruth	THE EFFECT OF GAMMA RAYS . . .	Dell Yount	CSUF
Kate	SHAKESPEARE'S WOMEN	Libby Appel	CalArts
Mrs. Grigson	THE SHADOW OF A GUNMAN	Lew Palter	CalArts
Dragons	TALKING WITH . . .	Don Finn	CSUF
Girl	TWO STARS EVENLY PLACED	Jonniepat Mobley	San Luis Obispo Summer Art Fest

Education

California Institute of the Arts—M.F.A. in Acting 1991
California State University, Fullerton—B.A. in Theatre Arts 1988

Special Skills

Technical Rock Climbing (5.6), Playing the Flute,
Certified Stage Combatant (S.A.F.D.), Irish Dialect,
and American Regionalisms

Looking Back and Looking Ahead

11

Company Meeting

It is natural in the privacy of the dressing room to talk about the things that went wrong. However, once the play's run is over and the set has been struck, use the next company meeting for more general and positive observations.

WRAP-UP REPORTS

After hearing initial reactions to the whole play experience, there should be a call for wrap-up reports from each group involved, actors as well as technicians. This serves as a summary of the entire play production assignment, as an opportunity to note experiences for the next production, and, often, as a chance to hear about some unknown or previously unacknowledged work. For example, someone from house management might say, "Since our photocopying machine doesn't have folding capability, I was the one who hand-folded all four thousand programs."

TOPICS FOR THIS MEETING
- Evaluating the Performance
- Expressing Gratitude
- Tributes
- Recommendations for the Next Production
- The Story of Theatre: The Eclectic Twentieth Century
- Theatre Workshop
- Careers in the Theatre: The Critic

WORKING VOCABULARY

Terms of special interest in this chapter are *critic, reviewer,* and *notices.*

AGENDA

At the next company meeting you'll discuss another kind of production, musical theatre. Topics will include origins of musical theatre in opera and minstrel shows, choosing the musical play, auditioning for a musical, rehearsing the principals, rehearsing the chorus, and attending and evaluating a professional or community theatre performance.

EVALUATING THE PERFORMANCE

Outside evaluation of a production is done by two types of writers, the critic and the reviewer. In general, the work of the former is more enduring. It is most often found in magazines such as *The New Yorker, American Theatre,* and *TheaterWeek,* or in collections of essays published in books. The intention of the **critic** is to evaluate and analyze the play according to accepted aesthetic principles. Respected drama critics through the years include Aristotle, John Dryden, William Archer, John Gassner, Walter Kerr, Brooks Atkinson, Brendan Gill, and, more recently, Edith Oliver and Mimi Kramer.

Criticism is intended to inform and instruct. The play is measured against absolute standards and then suggestions are made for its improvement. Do not assume that criticism is always negative, despite the popular use of the word to mean "finding fault with something." Criticism also praises whatever is praiseworthy. Carefully considered criticism also looks for themes, for patterns, for parallels with other works of the same genre or dramatic type, or for parallels with the other works of the same playwright.

The **reviewer,** on the other hand, writes quickly, often for a next-day deadline, and the resulting review is published in a newspaper or broadcast on radio or television. In general, the play under review either is praised or disparaged according to the reviewer's personal taste. Many times a review does not even offer an opinion, but simply gives the time, place, and dates of performance, the cast names, and a brief plot summary. If the review is given right after the opening night, it can provide additional publicity for subsequent performances.

Sometimes a review will have a headline, such as "Crimson Oak Players Sparkle in *George Washington Slept Here,*" that can be quoted in paid advertisements or on posters. Sometimes a review will single out an actor or two for special praise: "Heidi Smeltzer's Annabelle was a delight from the opening line to the final curtain." When this happens it is said that the actor has **notices** (usually used in the plural). Actors save such notices and include them in their résumés.

It is unlikely that an educational production would be the subject of criticism, but such productions sometimes are reviewed. Some directors of high-school and community college productions have a no-review policy, as they feel beginning actors should not be subjected to such scrutiny. Other directors welcome any kind of public attention. If your production is reviewed, enjoy whatever praise is given and, if disapproval is expressed in the review, examine it for accuracy and objectivity and then profit by the attention you've been given. Ultimately, though, the director has the final say on how things should be done in a performance.

Self-Evaluation

The helpful process of self-evaluation can be anything from an open forum, where everyone in the company has a say and the discussion is summarized by the assistant director, to a written form to be completed by each company member. If the open forum method is chosen, it's best to give everyone a chance to say whatever is on his or her mind first. Then settle down to a more organized discussion, with the director or assistant director posing questions. If a written form is used instead or in addition, short-answer questions should be provided, as well as opportunities for essay opinions. (See page 251.)

A group discussion, or open forum, gives everyone in the company the chance to comment on the production.

Play Title _____

What were your production responsibilities? _____
_____

How well did you carry out your responsibilities? _____
_____
_____

Discuss anything that prevented the completion of any responsibility.
_____
_____
_____

For you personally, what was the most satisfying aspect of the production?
_____
_____

What was the least satisfying aspect? _____
_____

What could have been done to improve the situation cited above?
_____
_____

List your suggestions for the next production. _____
_____
_____
_____

Discuss what this production experience has meant to you.
_____
_____
_____
_____

Figure 11.1. Sample evaluation form.

EXPRESSING GRATITUDE

It's important to thank all the people outside the company who helped in any way with the production. You may have thanked some people already by giving them comps to the show. You may have thanked others with an acknowledgment in the program. Anyone else who helped should receive written thanks. In this age of the fax, the photocopier, and the computerized letter, a handwritten note is especially appreciated. It shows that you regard the recipient as an individual whose contribution— whether it was publicity, lending props, helping to build the set, or sewing a costume—was much appreciated by the entire company.

The job of writing thank-you notes usually falls to the house management–publicity crew, but if there are a lot of notes to be written, anyone with good handwriting should help. Thank-you notes may be hand-delivered or mailed. Even if you have phoned your thanks immediately after the help was given, follow it up with a thank-you note. If the company has some stationery bearing the company logo or play title, it would be appropriate for the thank-you notes.

TRIBUTES

The company may want to pay tribute to members who did outstanding work in the production. The acknowledgments can take the form of speeches of tribute delivered at this meeting, or the company may decide to give awards.

If you choose to present awards at the company meeting, a company party, or a schoolwide awards program, you will need to decide whether you want an audience ballot or strictly a company ballot. In the case of an audience ballot, there may be objections that a lot of Lupe's friends came to the performance, or that the audience cannot possibly be expected to know that Sari *is* her part, while Roxanne is nothing like her part and therefore gave the better performance, or that the audience won't understand some of the backstage work done for the play. If, despite these objections, you choose audience ballots, they should be distributed with the program and collected after the final curtain—not just by having ballot boxes at the exits, but by having the ushers specifically request the completed ballots. Some companies offer the incentive of a complimentary cookie given in the lobby in exchange for the completed ballot.

Figure 11.2.
Sample audience ballot.

PLEASE TAKE A MOMENT TO FILL OUT THIS FORM. THANK YOU!

1. Best Actor in a Major Role

    _____

2. Best Actor in a Minor Role

    _____

3. Best Technical Contribution to the Production

    _____

Audience ballots should be kept simple—perhaps just as short as the one shown in Figure 11.2 above. The second item may be eliminated if the parts are fairly equal in size. Audience responses to the first item will be a mixture of actors' names and character names, but those are easily sorted and tabulated. It is the third item that presents the most difficulty. It is widely remarked in the theatre that if the technicians are doing their jobs, the audience is completely unaware of them. It makes for a lengthy, complicated ballot to list each technical area, and the longer the ballot, the less likely it is that people will take the time to complete it. On the other hand, if the ballot doesn't list the technical areas, only the obvious ones—costumes, set, and props—will be acknowledged.

The alternative to the audience ballot is the company ballot. If the voting is conducted after the wrap-up reports are given, there is no danger of anyone in the company being overlooked. The award itself can be a certificate suitable for framing; a medallion, perhaps of the comedy and tragedy masks; a plaque; or a statuette. Although it is the gesture that counts, do make the award as nice as the budget allows.

RECOMMENDATIONS FOR THE NEXT PRODUCTION

Ask for recommendations for the future both at the open forum company evaluation of the production just finished and on the self-evaluation form. If your company will be staying together for another production, then the recommendations are of immediate value. If, on the other hand, you are making recommendations for next year's company, then your suggestions should reflect your desire to be helpful by offering the next company the benefit of your own experiences.

If, in the course of your Theatre Workshop projects or through audience surveys, you compiled a list of plays that would appeal to your patrons, include those titles in your recommendations. Provide lists of sources for materials, names of helpful people, updated press lists, and inventories of costume and props stock as well. In addition, detail the problems you encountered and your solutions. Theatre people are famous for their generosity, so share anything that can help in the next production.

SUMMARY

Outside evaluations of a performance either are in the form of criticism, which is a serious work meant to inform and teach, or in the form of a review, which is written quickly to serve as a guide to potential theatre patrons. When an actor is singled out for mention in a review, he or she is said to have notices, which can be included in an actor's résumé. After a production, the company should evaluate itself either by holding an open forum discussion, by writing individual self-evaluations, or both. People outside the production who have helped in some way should be given written thanks, while tributes to people inside the company can be expressed in a speech or in the presentation of some award. Recommendations for the next production should be as thorough and helpful as possible in light of what you have learned through your own production.

*B*ecause the theatrical past is so much a part of the present, this century has drawn from every era to produce an exciting mix of many dramatic forms. In the course of a season of plays in New York City or London, you could see a Greek tragedy, a medieval morality play, a Shakespearean comedy, a Molière or Ibsen or Chekhov or Shaw revival (or all four), a turn-of-the-century melodrama, a musical adapted from a Dickens novel, a mixed media verse drama, or a comedy of contemporary manners. Clearly, actors today need the versatility to play many styles, many genres.

By the twentieth century the American theatre had truly come into its own. No longer did audiences depend on British and European playwrights to set the standard for drama. To the illustrious list of Russia's Anton Chekhov, Ireland's George Bernard Shaw, John Millington Synge, and Sean O'Casey; England's Noël Coward, Terence Rattigan, Harold Pinter, Arnold Wesker, and Alan Ayckbourn; Germany's Bertolt Brecht; and France's Jean Anouilh, Jean Cocteau, and Jean Giraudoux can be added American playwrights Eugene O'Neill, Arthur Miller, Edward Albee, Tennessee Williams, August Wilson, and Tina Howe.

Realism has remained the predominant theatrical "ism" in this century, but the theatre of the absurd—as exemplified in the works of Samuel Beckett (*Waiting for Godot*) and Tom Stoppard (*Rosencrantz and Guildenstern Are Dead*)— explores the human condition with irony and a bizarre humor. And Brecht's theatre of alienation sought to keep reminding the audience that what was taking place on stage was *not* real.

After World War II the spiraling costs of mounting a Broadway production stimulated the "off-Broadway" and even "off-off-Broadway" movement of small theatres, avant garde companies, and highly experimental productions. The avant garde, literally the *advance guard,* are those on the cutting edge of what's new in the arts. In the theatre this might mean guerrilla theatre—a highly political form in which the actors, in a parallel to guerrilla warfare, seize opportunities of public meetings and events to stage short, hard-hitting skits on controversial issues or to call attention to a specific social problem.

The avant garde might mean a mixed media "happening," where elements of script, structured theatre games, music, and dance are used in what appears to be an almost spontaneous combination. Or the avant garde might be the presentation of a site-specific piece, that is, something written to be performed in a specific place: a garden, a library, a haunted house. Or it might be participatory theatre such as *Tamara,* in which spectators join the D'Annunzio family and guests at their villa and choose which cast members to follow through various rooms and various plot twists.

Evaluation Projects

1. Pretend you write for the entertainment section of your local newspaper. Write a review of your show, giving some of the actors notices.
2. In the role of a serious theatre critic, write an essay of criticism of your recent production.
3. Recall what your personal goals were in the production; then determine how well you achieved those goals. If some goals were not achieved, decide what you might do differently next time.
4. Draft a list of discussion topics and questions for the assistant director to use in leading the open forum company evaluation of the production.

Gratitude and Tribute Projects

1. Design a plaque or certificate suitable for presentation to the outstanding actors and technicians in your recent production.
2. Design a ballot to determine who should win the awards to be presented by your company. With the director's permission, conduct the voting for the awards.

3. Write a list of all the people outside the company who helped in some way with the production. You might want to divide the list into categories such as publicity, set construction, costume building, refreshment donations, and so on. Keep the list for future reference for your company or to pass along to the next production.
4. Draft several versions of a personal thank-you letter so that the acknowledgments you send are somewhat varied and aren't simply handwritten form letters.

Recommendation Projects

1. With what you have learned from your recent production experience, make a list of plays you recommend for production next season.
2. Ask everyone in the company to contribute a paragraph to a letter for the next production company. Suggest that they write encouragement and also share some important tips for a successful show.

The Critic

Brendan Gill, a longtime theatre critic for *The New Yorker* magazine, once explained two principles he followed: There is often little to be said about a very bad piece of work except that it is to be avoided, and there is often little to be said about a very good piece of work except that it is to be embraced. He once "avoided" *Dear Oscar* by dismissing it in a brief paragraph, calling it "a sad wisp of a musical which closed after five performances at the Playhouse. It succeeded in making Wilde the prince of bores—a remarkable feat, though unworthy of celebration." And he "embraced" Brian Friel's *Lovers* by observing, "His plays, like his short stories, are modest, gentle, and winning; they take us by the hand instead of by the throat . . ." That wit, that turn of phrase, is a hallmark of Gill's style.

Gill was born in Hartford, Connecticut, and attended school there. In school he not only wrote stories and poems for the literary magazine, he also drew the illustrations, took the copy to the printer, corrected galley proofs, and, in general, assumed responsibility. As a student at Yale he wrote for the university literary magazine and was elected editor in his junior year. Around that time he began sending poems and stories to *The New Yorker,* which promptly rejected them.

At Yale, Gill met the Nobel Prize–winning novelist Sinclair Lewis, and upon graduation Gill was asked to be the famous author's secretary. Instead, Gill, who graduated magna cum laude and was elected to Phi Beta Kappa, decided to marry and begin his literary career. After several weeks of flooding *The New Yorker* with carefully revised poems and having them rejected, Gill dashed off a short piece describing a fictional meeting between Sinclair Lewis and a Dr. McGrady, and the magazine accepted it. That success was followed by another story and then several others. Within a year he had moved on to writing "Reporter at Large" pieces. Soon he was invited to New York and offered a job in the magazine's "Talk of the Town" department. Later, he wrote movie reviews. In 1967, Gill became the drama editor.

Although he says he received little mail, in his book *Here at the New Yorker* he does tell of an occasional exchange of ideas with playwrights such as Edward Albee. In summing up his professional career, Gill explained, "I started at the place where I most wanted to be—*The New Yorker* magazine—and with much pleasure . . . I have remained there ever since."

Musical
Theatre

12

Company Meeting

Suppose your company has decided to produce a musical. If this is the first meeting for the company, follow the practice of any initial company meeting by taking time to get acquainted with each other and to establish some goals. After you select a play, plan the production schedule and assign major technical responsibilities. Auditions may be included in this meeting, or you may choose instead to announce the times for auditioning and describe the auditioning process.

REPORTS

It is possible that the director and others with technical responsibilities have been working at preproduction activities already. If so, everyone should be brought up-to-date on plans or accomplishments. People giving reports should allow for questions from the company, and members should not hesitate to ask about anything that seems confusing or unclear. From the beginning it's important to share information with and to involve every company member.

TOPICS FOR THIS MEETING

- Choosing the Musical Play
- Auditioning for the Musical
- Rehearsing the Principals
- Rehearsing the Chorus
- Evaluating a Professional or Community Performance
- The Story of Theatre: The American Musical
- Theatre Workshop
- Careers in the Theatre: The Choreographer

WORKING VOCABULARY

Some terms of special interest in this chapter are *book show, revue, extravaganza, principal, ingenue, juvenile, soubrette, sidekick, chorus, dance captain, ballad opera, minstrel show,* and *burlesque.*

AGENDA

At the next company meeting you'll discuss other types of productions: original work, the festival of scenes, readers' theatre, and the program of one-acts. You'll consider competitive play festivals, as well.

CHOOSING THE MUSICAL PLAY

In educational theatre a musical may be a joint venture with the music department and with the physical education department as well. Your drama teacher serves as director for the acted portions of the show, the music teacher directs the chorus and perhaps the school orchestra, and the physical education teacher acts as choreographer, directing the dance. The result is a delightful blend of students' talents in a form that America fell in love with long ago.

In choosing which musical play to perform there always is a temptation to do some show currently running on Broadway because many students have the cassette tape or CD and know the songs by heart. The trouble is that your audience also is likely to know those songs, and it would be unfair to your cast to be compared with the professional cast in the recordings. Also, a more practical consideration is that current musicals usually have very high royalties. Given this, it's best to look to the past. With a century of wonderful musicals to consider, your company is sure to choose well.

In choosing a musical for your company to perform, consider such factors as budget, performance space, and company size.

Types of Musicals

The **book show** is a type of musical that has a "book" or plot and some spoken dialogue between the musical numbers. Some of the most famous and enduring of these are Victor Herbert's operettas *Babes in Toyland* and *Naughty Marietta;* George M. Cohan's *Little Johnny Jones* and *Little Nelly Kelly;* Rudolf Friml's *Rose-Marie;* Sigmund Romberg's *The Student Prince* and *The Desert Song;* Jerome Kern's *Leave It to Jane* and *Showboat;* Irving Berlin's *Annie Get Your Gun;* George Gershwin's *Funny Face* and *Girl Crazy;* Richard Rodgers and Lorenz Hart's *Babes in Arms* and *The Boys from Syracuse* (based on Shakespeare's *A Comedy of Errors*); Cole Porter's *Kiss Me Kate* (based on Shakespeare's *The Taming of the Shrew*); Richard Rodgers and Oscar Hammerstein's *Oklahoma!* and *Carousel;* Alan Jay Lerner and Frederick Loewe's *Brigadoon* and *My Fair Lady;* Frank Loesser's *Where's Charley?* (based on Brandon Thomas's *Charley's Aunt*); and Meredith Willson's *The Music Man.*

Of course, these are just a few of the book shows among which you can choose. You must consider such factors as budget, performance space, and number of company members, however, in determining which play is best for your company.

Perhaps your company is more interested in doing a **revue,** that is, a production featuring a collection of songs, dances, and sketches. Some revues have a narrative thread, such as Elaine Kendall, Elaine Moe, and Dennis Poore's *American Cantata;* Micki Grant's *Don't Bother Me, I Can't Cope;* and Charles Gaynor's *Lend an Ear.* Other revues have songs and other material that share a common theme; for example, *Diamonds* features songs having to do with baseball. Another theme-based musical revue is Judith Martin's *Everybody, Everybody* with music by Donald Ashwander. The show provides a kids'-eye view of various aspects of American life.

A third type of revue features the songs of a particular writer from several of his or her shows, such as *By Strouse,* with the songs of Charles Strouse, composer of the musical *Annie* and various lyrics. *Jerry's Girls* includes many of the songs Jerry Herman wrote for the women in his Broadway hit shows like *Hello Dolly!* and *Mame.*

In selecting your own show, be sure to consider musical adaptations of favorite books; Margery Williams's *The Velveteen*

Rabbit, A. A. Milne's *Winnie-the-Pooh,* C. S. Lewis's *The Chronicles of Narnia,* and Lewis Carroll's *Alice in Wonderland* are among many that have been adapted into musical form.

A third type of musical production is the **extravaganza,** an elaborate, lavish, spectacular musical production with a large cast, expensive costumes, and grand sets. It is intended solely for entertainment. Although it is unlikely that your company has the resources to produce an extravaganza, it is a type of musical, and no discussion of the genre would be complete without mentioning such famous extravaganzas as *The Ziegfeld Follies* and Earl Carroll's *Vanities.*

Finally, in making a choice the company must consider the basic issues of budget, performance space, expectations of your audience, and the abilities of your company members. Better the modest success than the overly ambitious failure!

AUDITIONING FOR THE MUSICAL

What can you expect at a musical audition? A group of hopeful performers will act, sing, and dance for a director, who must choose the people who will best fill the parts in the proposed production. Remember, no matter how talented you are and how dazzling you are at the audition, you must also fit the image of the character the director has in mind. So, give your best performance, but do not feel rejected if you are not cast. Instead, share in the excitement of the production by serving as a technician in an area that interests you.

When you are notified of an audition, pay careful attention to all the instructions given. If you have questions, ask them. Once you have all the available information, begin your preparations. If you are asked to present a prepared monologue, have two ready—one comedic and one serious, or one modern and one classical. Be sure the monologues showcase your capabilities and versatility. You will find some monologues at the end of this book.

If you are asked to give a prepared reading from the playbook, become familiar with the entire play, not just the section you intend to present. If there are to be cold readings, practice reading various kinds of material aloud with clarity and feeling.

Make every effort to find the right song for your audition; then rehearse it until you can sing it confidently and with style.

At a musical audition you will be asked to sing, of course. If the instructions have been to prepare a song from the proposed production, then choose a song by the character for which you will audition. If his or her songs are not suitable for your voice, then consider auditioning for one of the other characters whose songs better suit you. Sometimes, however, you are not asked to prepare a song from the show. In that case, select a song that really demonstrates your ability. You might be surprised how many people audition with material that is very popular or difficult or showy, but does not exhibit their talent well. Do some research to develop a repertoire. Listen to tapes, view videos of shows, and talk to a music teacher or local performer. Do all you can to find the right song for you, then rehearse until you can sing it confidently and with style.

Most auditions for a musical show today do not require you to present a solo dance. Instead, the choreographer will pull aside small groups of auditioners and teach them a dance step combination. Pay close attention so you can demonstrate your ability to focus and to learn quickly.

REHEARSING THE PRINCIPALS

· ·

The **principals** of a musical production are those who sing the leading roles. Many companies use the standard titles of **ingenue** for the young female romantic lead and **juvenile** for her partner, the young male romantic lead. In *Oklahoma!* Laurey and Curly are the ingenue and juvenile roles, respectively. The ingenue often has a confidante—a young or youngish woman who is more comical than romantic, though she, too, may have a romance. She is called the **soubrette,** and her type dates back to the pert servant girls of commedia dell'arte. The juvenile often has a comic foil or **sidekick,** whose type can be traced to the confidant of the hero in Renaissance drama. The soubrette and the sidekick may share a romance as well, as do Ado Annie and Will Parker in *Oklahoma!* Thus, the ingenue, the juvenile, the soubrette, and the sidekick are the principals, though in a large production there may be other principals as well, including char-

The ingenue and the juvenile are the female and male romantic leads in a musical.

acter parts such as Eliza's father in *My Fair Lady* and Cap'n Andy in *Showboat*.

Those cast members holding the principal roles in a musical must schedule extra rehearsal time. Expect to arrive early and stay late. There will be times when the director and choreographer will need you to work after the rest of the company has been dismissed so that your solos, dances, and lines of dialogue can receive extra attention and direction.

REHEARSING THE CHORUS

The **chorus** in today's musicals sings and dances together in the larger musical numbers, often called "production numbers" because of the amount of production or work needed to ensure unison singing and dancing. Indeed, the chorus fills the stage with the sound, movement, and color that audiences expect

Chorus members spend much of their rehearsal time polishing ensemble numbers.

from a musical. Members of the chorus spend much of their rehearsal time on ensemble or group numbers until they are polished. Each note and every step are important. Then the chorus joins the principals to rehearse the entire show.

An important member of the chorus is the **dance captain.** This position is roughly equivalent to that of concertmaster in an orchestra. The dance captain works with the choreographer to learn all the dances, then helps teach them to the dancers. Often, the dance captain will work separately with a small group or an individual needing additional instruction. The dance captain may also be considered the leader of the chorus.

Over time, some interesting theatrical traditions have developed concerning chorus members. Often, they are affectionately called "gypsies" because the life of professional chorus performers requires them to travel from show to show, or with a show from town to town. There is a "gypsy robe" that is passed among the Broadway professionals. It travels from show to show, and on opening night it is presented to the senior member of the chorus, who adds a memento to it.

If you're in the chorus you're part of a tradition that dates back to the oldest recognized theatre, that of ancient Greece. Take pride in your work and carry on the respected tradition.

EVALUATING A PROFESSIONAL OR COMMUNITY PERFORMANCE

Both actors and technicians should take advantage of some of the many opportunities to see live theatre. If there is a professional company or community theatre in your area, try to attend their performances. Once there, don't find fault with everything, or you will miss the pleasure of seeing the performance. On the other hand, you won't gain from the experience if you are simply a passive viewer. If possible, attend the theatre with others who share your interest and can thoroughly discuss specific aspects of the performance afterward.

As you evaluate the production you saw, consider the choice of play. Apply the same criteria your own company does: Based on your impressions of set and costumes, did the group have a sufficient budget to successfully present the play they chose? Was the piece suitable for the performance space? Was it the sort

Attending a professional or community performance can reinforce your understanding and increase your enjoyment of the theatre.

of material the audience expected from such a company and from the publicity circulated? Were the abilities of the cast adequate for the challenge of the material?

Now consider the work of the director. Was the tempo or pace of the play appropriate for the material? Was the interpretation credible and consistent? Did the blocking arise logically out of the action of the play, or was it merely movement for the sake of movement? Were all the audience sightlines taken into consideration in the blocking? Was the full stage used, or did actors seem huddled in corners?

Next, examine the technical aspects of the production: Did the set design contribute to the look of the show? Did it establish time and place and the economic circumstances of the characters? Did the costumes satisfy the same needs? Were the props convincing? Did the lighting set the mood as well as illuminate the actors? If there was incidental music, did it contribute to the overall effect of the show or did it distract from it? Were the sound cues well timed and authentic sounding?

Consider the casting: Did the actors seem appropriately cast in their parts? Did they project so that you could hear and understand every word? Did they sound as if they knew and believed in what they were saying? If the show was a musical, were the singing voices able to meet the demands of the songs? Were the dances choreographed and danced well?

Finally, turn your attention to the house management: Were reservations and ticket sales handled efficiently? Was the play program attractive and informative? Were the ushers welcoming? Were the premises clean and the exits clearly marked?

In summary, if the company is a professional one, expect a professional performance. If it is a community group, expect a performance that has been carefully planned and well rehearsed. While you don't want to judge so harshly that you cannot enjoy yourself, do apply your knowledge and your production experience to reinforce your understanding and increase your enjoyment of the theatre.

SUMMARY

In choosing a musical play for performance the company needs to consider the standard criteria of budget, performance space, audience expectations, and performers' abilities. In addition, the company will not want to choose a play that is so popular currently that comparisons with the Broadway cast will be discouraging. To audition for a musical, one must be prepared to sing as well as act and to quickly learn dance steps from the choreographer. In a rehearsal schedule the principals often have separate rehearsals from the chorus because they need to work on different things before rehearsing together as a cast. Attending and evaluating a professional or community production is an important and enjoyable learning experience for anyone involved in educational theatre.

The musical is the United States' greatest contribution to world theatre. While the form has undergone many changes in its evolution, the American musical remains the active, tuneful entertainment of choice for the theatregoing public.

Musical theatre fuses elements of ballad opera, the minstrel show, and early burlesque. **Ballad opera** consisted of spoken dialogue on topical subjects and songs that had new lyrics set to older, already popular and instantly recognizable tunes.

The **minstrel show,** popular following the Civil War and well into this century, originated from African American humorous story-songs, called patter songs. Minstrel shows were popularized by T. D. Rice and other White entertainers who performed in blackface makeup. Eventually African American performers began to put on their own shows. No longer performed because so many consider it demeaning to African Americans, the minstrel show was one of the ancestors of modern musical comedy.

The third element inherent in musical theatre is early **burlesque,** which bears no similarity to later striptease shows. Rather, it consisted primarily of musical parodies or satires of well-known plays or other entertainments, much like the material of *Beach Blanket Babylon* and *Forbidden Broadway* today.

The uniting of ballad opera, the minstrel show, and early burlesque produced a new form—the musical comedy—that remains popular in America. *The Black Crook,* produced in 1866, often is cited as the first American musical comedy. It was a rather ridiculous melodrama loosely based on the Faust legend. Most critics date the birth of the true American musical, however, to early in the twentieth century and the works of George M. Cohan (immortalized by actor James Cagney in the Warner Brothers film *Yankee Doodle Dandy*). Cohan's musicals were noted for their exuberance and their distinctive American flavor.

Early in this century, the musical was a popular entertainment featuring pretty chorus girls who danced and sang, musical numbers, soloists, and stand-up comedians. The plot might be the least important element, often serving only as an excuse for lavish settings and catchy tunes. However, by the 1920s more attention was being given to the plot and to the motivations of the characters. Elaborate production numbers still dazzled the audience, but the songs more often grew from the plot, expressing the characters' feelings more eloquently than spoken dialogue.

For the first five decades of this century the term "musical" meant musical *comedy.* Whether amused by a stand-up comedian, an exchange of clever comments, physical (slapstick) humor, or witty song lyrics, the audience laughed a great deal in the course of the show. The major composers of those years are justly famous and their greatest works often are seen in revival: George and Ira Gershwin, Jerome Kern, Cole Porter, Irving Berlin, Richard Rodgers and Lorenz Hart, and,

later, Richard Rodgers writing with Oscar Hammerstein II.

The second half of this century has brought many musicals which are not comedies at all. There may be occasional elements of humor in some of the songs or situations, but more often the overall message is serious. For example, *Dreamgirls,* by Tom Eyen and Henry Krieger, details the betrayals and heartbreaks endured by a trio of African American pop singers as they strive for success. Stephen Sondheim has written a vast repertoire of musicals that touch on very serious themes: *Sweeney Todd, Follies, Company, Assassins,* and *Sunday in the Park with George.* Even the fairy-tale–based *Into the Woods* has a dark-spirited second act showing that all does not end "happily ever after." And despite the merriment in

Joseph Stein's *Fiddler on the Roof,* it, too, ends on a somber note.

Over the years the musical genre has served as a vehicle for all kinds of themes and songs. The charmingly simple *Best Foot Forward,* by Rodgers and Hart, features a young military school cadet who must both convince his best girl that he invited another girl to the prom by mistake and lead his team to victory on the football field—all in one hectic weekend. In sharp contrast is the complex *Pacific Overtures,* in which Sondheim uses elements of Kabuki, haiku poetry, and masks to recount Commander Perry's opening of Japan to trade with America.

Indeed, the modern American musical is a skillful blend of song and story. There seems to be unlimited room for innovation and experimentation with this genre . . . as long as the music is good.

Many critics date the birth of the American musical to the works of George M. Cohan. The composer-playwright is shown here, performing in his 1906 show *George Washington, Jr.*

B 683

Preparation Projects

1. Prepare a song for auditioning. Be sure it showcases your musical talent.
2. Propose three musical plays for your next production. Be sure the plays are feasible for your company's budget, performance space, audience, and talent.
3. Develop an evaluation form that could be used when attending a professional or community production.

Research Projects

1. Research local newspaper files to determine what musical shows have been performed in the last five years by professional, community, college, and high school companies in your area. This information will help the company narrow its selection of plays to consider.
2. Contact an arts-oriented television station to learn what musical plays will be showing in the near future. Select one or two to watch and identify the ingenue, the juvenile, the soubrette, and the sidekick characters in the production. If there are additional principals, list those characters as well.
3. Check your school and public libraries for a list of Broadway musical cast recordings they have in their collections. Your company can borrow some recordings to listen to before choosing a show to produce. In addition, the recordings may be useful for selecting audition material.

Activity Projects

1. Organize a field trip to visit backstage at a local theatre. See if you can also arrange for small groups from your company to watch part of a rehearsal of a musical.
2. Organize a trip to a local professional or community theatre performance. (Request a group rate for your tickets, if applicable.) After the show, discuss and evaluate what you saw.
3. Obtain a videotape of a professional musical production that interests your company, and organize a group viewing and follow-up discussion.

The Choreographer

In 1991 Tommy Tune won his seventh and eighth Tony Awards. He was named Best Director of a Musical and Best Choreographer for *The Will Rogers Follies*. Because he was on tour as Albert in *Bye Bye Birdie,* he had to accept the awards via satellite.

This practice of taking Broadway shows on the road so that people all over the country can see first-rate casts is one to which Tune feels strongly committed. In fact, when asked why there had been no Tune-directed or -choreographed show on Broadway between *My One and Only* in 1983 and *Grand Hotel* in 1990, Tune pointed out that he had been on the road with *My One and Only* for most of that time. He told writer Ken Mandelbaum that he felt a moral responsibility to stay with the show on tour because the role had been created for him.

Describing himself as "a guy who puts on shows," Tune traces his involvement in performing and directing back to the "patio revues" he organized at the age of five in his Houston, Texas, neighborhood. He continued staging shows through elementary school, high school, and summer stock. By 1974 he had won his first Tony Award, for Best Supporting Actor in a musical (Cy Coleman and Dorothy Fields's *Seesaw*). In all, Tune has won Tonys in four categories: Best Supporting Actor in a Musical, Best Actor in a Musical, Best Choreographer, and Best Director of a Musical.

According to Karen Akers, who played Raffaella in Tune's production *Grand Hotel* and who published a journal of her experiences when the company was workshopping (that is, continuing to work on a play that's already in production), Tommy Tune worked closely with his associates, always willing to collaborate (see Chapter 1). He is positive in addressing the company, commenting on the good work at the end of a rehearsal. Walter Willson, who played Gustafsson in the same show and who wrote an article about life backstage, mentioned the sense of "company" present in a Tune show. From the yoga breathing exercises at the beginning of each rehearsal day to the hand-holding "circle" formed at half-hour to curtain, the performers connect their energies.

As for his choreography, it has always been imaginative and energetic. He seems eager to take an adventurous leap both mentally and physically in designing the steps of his dances. His own elegant line as he dances is captured in the routines he creates for others, and his own exuberance is passed along in the choreography to those who do his shows.

Tommy Tune's early work with the late Michael Bennett, famed choreographer of *A Chorus Line,* has left him with lasting admiration for Bennett's work, but Tune is his own person—innovatively making his mark on the development of choreography in the American musical.

273

Other Types
of Productions

Company Meeting

If your production is complete before the end of the school term, your company may undertake another smaller type of production in the time remaining. Consider performing original work by company members, a festival of scenes, a reader's theatre presentation, or a program of one-act plays. Also, you may have the opportunity to take the company's **mainstage production,** that is, the major production of the school term, to a competition. Discuss the options at the company meeting.

REPORTS

Perhaps some members already have researched and given thought to the next step for the company. If so, this is the time to offer the information and share the opinions. Also, present any remaining final reports—financial, for example— from the mainstage production.

TOPICS FOR THIS MEETING

- Original Work
- The Festival of Scenes
- Reader's Theatre
- The Program of One-Act Plays
- Competitive Play Festivals
- Touring Scenes
- The Story of Theatre: What the Future Holds
- Theatre Workshop
- Careers in the Theatre: The Playwright

WORKING VOCABULARY

Terms of special interest in this chapter are *mainstage production, staged reading, static character,* and *dynamic character.*

ORIGINAL WORK

The term "original work" in this context means a play, scene, or exchange of dialogue written by a company member or members, or even the entire company. The work might have been written previously, or it could be material composed specifically for production by the company. If your school offers a creative writing class, the writing of those students is another body of original work the company might draw upon.

If you have already presented a mainstage production, you may want an invited audience of those who attended the production to view your presentation of original work. Or, you may want to perform the original work at a school assembly or for another class.

First, before the company even calls for original material, company members must decide as a group whether this production is to be a collaborative one. In other words, will the writer be able to take an active part? If yes, the writer will work with the company, making changes to the material as needed and having a say both in the casting and the direction of the piece. The alternative to collaboration is to have it clearly understood from the beginning that once the author gives the material to the company for consideration, he or she no longer has any say about how it is produced. Whatever the decision, once the company reaches an agreement on this issue, its members can move on to the choice of original work.

In selecting original work to present, the company must make an objective evaluation: Is the material well written? Is the dialogue interesting? Are the characters believable? Does the play or scene say something worth hearing? The author must be willing to have his or her work scrutinized and must accept the decision of the company regarding selection.

When performing an original work the company should bear in mind that not everything that reads well on paper transfers well to the stage. So, although it can be extremely rewarding to tackle original material, don't be hesitant to move on to something else if the material simply doesn't work out.

THE FESTIVAL OF SCENES

The festival of scenes often is very satisfying to company and audience alike. There are so many plays that are difficult for an educational company to produce—because of time, money, space, or ability—yet *scenes* from these plays frequently work well in performance. Actors get to try at least a bit of such material, and audiences can see portions of plays that are seldom performed.

A festival of scenes generally works best if the scenes are tied together by a common thread. This might be a theme, such as "An Actor's Life," which could be composed of scenes from plays about successful or still-struggling actors. Plays included could be Walter Kerr's *Stardust,* Francis Swann's *Out of the Frying Pan,* Elmer Rice's *Two on an Island,* Edna Ferber's *Stage Door,* and Moss Hart's *Light Up the Sky.* Alternately, the common thread could be the playwright. You might do scenes from Shakespeare or from Neil Simon's many comedies. Still another common thread is place—for example, all the scenes occur in a park or a haunted house. Finally, consider the common thread of characters, that is, scenes by different playwrights, but about the same character or characters—Joan of Arc (George Bernard Shaw's *Saint Joan,* Jean Anouilh's *The Lark,* Sidney Michaels's *Goodtime Charley*) or Sherlock Holmes (Arthur Conan Doyle and William Gillette's *Sherlock Holmes,* Paul Giovanni's *The Crucifer of Blood,* Tim Kelly and Jack Sharkey's *Sherlock Holmes and the Giant Rat of Sumatra*), for example.

No matter what unifying device you use for your festival of scenes, make sure that any scene you choose can stand on its own, without the context of the rest of the play.

READER'S THEATRE

Reader's theatre is a great favorite with actors who have trouble learning lines, because they can have the book in their hands. Actually, although the actor does hold the book and read from it, the book itself must be carefully prepared for the reading, and the actor must rehearse so that he or she is not totally dependent on the book, but can look up frequently.

To prepare your book, either make enlargements of the purchased script, or, if copyright laws forbid that practice, use the same means as for preparing the blocking plot (see Chapter 3)

Actors in reader's theatre learn their lines well enough so that they can look up from their books frequently.

so that you have an 8½" × 11" page with which to work. In the margins write in directions regarding focus, movement, tone of voice, pitch, volume, and tempo. Highlight or underline your own lines; use color coding if you are reading more than one character or to remind yourself to emphasize a particular word or line.

A portion of Beatrice's monologue from Shakespeare's *Much Ado about Nothing* is shown in Figure 13.1. It was adapted for a reader's theatre presentation called *Shakespeare's Women Talk about Love*. The unifying device or common thread was a bare stage on which several female actors had gathered to audition for a Shakespeare production. As they waited, they discussed love and tried out their prepared audition monologues.

There are many fine plays written specifically for reader's theatre, and many other plays work very well in that kind of

Adrianne, as Beatrice

_____

Yes, faith, it is my cousin's duty to make a curtsy and say,

as Hero, sweetly   "Father, as it please you." But for all that, cousin, let

him be a handsome fellow or else make another curtsy and say,

as self, firmly   "Father, as it please me."

Don't hope to see me fitted with a husband!

Not 'til God make men of some other metal than earth.

to audience   Would it not grieve a woman to be overmastered to a clod of

valiant dust?

To make an account of her life to a clod of wayward marl?

No, I'll none. Adam's sons are my brethren,

And truly I hold it a sin to match in my kindred.

teasing   As for you, cousin, the fault will be in the music

If you are not wooed in good time.

Figure 13.1.
Sample reader's theatre
script.

production. However, if you choose to do so you can create your own book from materials such as collections of letters, speeches, journals, or diaries.

In presenting reader's theatre you have the option to perform in everyday dress, in costume, or in some uniform clothing such as choral robes or formal evening wear. The company budget and the type of material you are performing will help make your decision. Do remember, too, that your publicity should clearly state that the presentation is a reading so that audiences don't arrive expecting a full production.

There are some other conventions of this genre to consider. The book itself should be in uniform folders for all the actors. If you remain onstage the entire time, indicate when you are out of a scene either by sitting down if the others remain standing, or by turning your back to the audience. Individual lecterns or music stands are helpful if the actors are to remain standing or seated in one place throughout. If, however, you choose to do a **staged reading,** the actors will hold their books as they move about the stage in some modified blocking scheme, speaking directly to the other characters. In that case, lecterns or stands are not needed.

Your director will need to decide the focus of your delivery. One choice is to look directly at the audience throughout. Another approach is to turn slightly toward the other characters as you address them. The third choice is to look into what is called "the middle distance," that is, slightly beyond the audience.

Plays Suitable for Reader's Theatre

Some plays written for a reader's theatre style of presentation, or which adapt well to that format, include the following:

Literature on Stage, a collection of five plays adapted by James Carlson and Melvin R. White

A. E. Hotchner's *The White House*

Edna St. Vincent Millay's dramatic poem *The Murder of Lidice,* an account of the destruction of a small Czechoslovak village during World War II

Charles Aidman's adaptation of Edgar Lee Masters's *Spoon River Anthology*

Lorraine Hansberry's autobiographical *To Be Young, Gifted and Black*

Twain by the Tale, sketches, stories, and monologues from the writings of Mark Twain, compiled by Dennis Snee

Susan Griffin's *Voices*

George Orwell's satire *Animal Farm,* adapted by Nelson Bond

The Company of Wayward Saints, George Herman's comedy about a commedia dell'arte troupe that wanders into an allegory

If you decide to adapt material of your own choosing, be sure to select pieces that don't require action, since this will only be a reading.

Considerations in Reading Aloud from Plays

To help prepare for the character you'll be reading, ask yourself the following questions and write down the answers.

1. What is the general nature of my character?
   A. Flat? (two-dimensional, without much defining by the author)
   B. Or round? (fully realized by the playwright through many details offered in the play)
   C. **Static?** (unchanging throughout the play)
   D. Or **dynamic?** (growing and changing in the course of the play's action)
   E. Simple? (easily grasped by the actor and the audience)
   F. Or complex? (Needing thorough study by the actor to present all aspects of the character and requiring careful observation by the audience to fully understand)
2. What is my life history?
   A. What have I been doing prior to the events of the play?
   B. What was I doing just before this moment?
   C. What will I be doing when the play's events are over?
   D. What is my education, religion (if pertinent), social class?
3. What is my attitude toward life?
   A. Accepting?
   B. Hostile?
   C. Trusting?
   D. Skeptical?
   E. Optimistic?
   F. Pessimistic?
   G. Complaining?
   H. Stoic?
   I. Cheerful?
4. In what manner do I behave?
   A. Carefree?
   B. Conventional?
   C. Impulsive?
   D. Eccentric?
   E. Careful?

5. How is the audience meant to respond to me?
    A. Sympathetically?
    B. Unsympathetically?
    C. Objectively?
    D. Compassionately?
    E. Angrily?
    F. Coldly?
    G. Indifferently?

Reading over your responses to these questions should help you determine how to deliver your lines. Of course, once rehearsal is under way, the director will give you specific line readings and suggestions. Nonetheless, you should arrive at the first rehearsal prepared.

THE PROGRAM OF ONE-ACT PLAYS

Putting together a program of three or four short plays can provide a fine evening's entertainment. As with the festival of scenes, it's best if the plays have something in common: a time period, a place, a theme, similar characters, or the same playwright (see Figure 13.3). A program of one-act plays can be cast with different actors for each play or by having the same group of actors move from play to play. If you choose the latter, it does require an intermission between plays to allow for costume changes. In that case it's best to limit the program to three plays and two intermissions, so the audience's patience isn't too greatly tested. Similarly, scene changes should be minimized. Indeed, the unifying device of having all the plays take place in the same setting is extremely convenient.

If you opt to change the setting but want to keep scenery shifts to a minimum, you can use a plain box set with neutral-colored walls and basic doors and windows, and then move in a few pieces of furniture for each new play. Those few pieces, along with the costuming and incidental music, can serve to signal to the audience a new setting and time.

Generally, to preserve the flow of the evening's entertainment, it's best not to have a curtain call after each play. Rather, bring everyone out at the end. Sometimes, however, it may serve the actors and the material better to have the obvious separation of a curtain call. If so, then handle the curtain calls accordingly.

FOOTE NOTE

The short plays performed here represent some of the best of Horton Foote's work. Born in 1916, he is probably most known for his award-winning screen plays, *To Kill a Mockingbird*, *Tender Mercies* and *Trip to Bountiful*. He began his career in theater as an actor which probably explains his devotion to rich characterization and dialogue.

Foote started play-writing in 1939, but really flourished in this role with the advent of television. In fact, two of the one-acts presented here, *The Tears of My Sister* and *A Young Lady of Property*, were written for T.V. in the 1950's (when live drama had to fit into a thirty or sixty-minute time slot). Interestingly, *Blind Date*, which works nicely in this trilogy, was written 30 years later. All three plays examine the traditional roles of Southern women during the first-half of this Century.

Horton Foote has just published his newest collection of plays at age 77.

ACKNOWLEDGEMENTS

The Administration
Donna Magnuson
Don Martin
Judy Myers
Mulryan & York

The Fine Arts Department of St. Scholastica High School

presents

PUTTING OUR BEST FOOTE FORWARD

3 Plays By Horton Foote

Directed by DONNA M. MARTIN

Scenic Design by Alice Tavani

Lighting Design by Bradley J. Floden

November 19, 20 & 21, 1993

• • • • •

Produced in Arrangement with Dramatists Play Service, Inc.

One-Acts by Horton Foote

PLACE: Harrison, Texas
TIME: The 1930's

BLIND DATE
Assistant Director: *Gia Dang*

SETTING: The living room of Robert and Dolores Henry.
DOLORES .... Gracie Bascos
ROBERT .... Jim Rooney
SARAH NANCY .... Erin Dunn
FELIX .... Steven Pazik

THE TEARS OF MY SISTER
Assistant Director: *Julie Hanson*

SETTING: The Monroe Boarding House-Hotel.

SCENE ONE: Late Afternoon of a Summer Day
SCENE TWO: After Supper around 9:00 P.M.
             - the same evening
SCENE THREE: Later that Night

CECILIA MONROE .... Melina Reynoso
MR. WILLIFORD .... David Battaglia
MISS SARAH LEWIS .... Nora Schuette
BESSIE MONROE .... Laura Laarveld
MRS. MONROE .... Clarice Budzilowicz
STACEY DAVIS .... Marc Farne

A YOUNG LADY OF PROPERTY
Assistant Director: *Grace Ann Garcia*

MISS MARTHA DAVENPORT .... Nora Schuette
MR. RUSSELL WALTER .... Rory Leahy
WILMA THOMPSON .... Clarice Budzilowicz
ARABELLA COOKENBOO .... Erin Dunn
LESTER THOMPSON .... Peter Lynch
MRS. LEIGHTON .... Laura Laarveld
MINNA BOYD .... Nicole Gonzalez
MISS GERT .... Heather Crabtree
THIS MAN .... Marc Farne

PRODUCTION STAFF

SCENIC DESIGN .... Alice Tavani
LIGHTING DESIGN .... Bradley J. Floden
STAGE MANAGER .... Leah Cobarrubias
COSTUMES .... Jules Martin
COSTUME ASSISTANT .... Judy Currano
SOUND DESIGN & DIALECT COACH Nancy Burkholder
LIGHTS .... Erin Herrera & Rana Mansoori
SOUND .... Anita Ortiz
MAKEUP & HAIRSTYLES .... Jules Martin
POSTER DESIGN .... Trinh Tran
BANNER .... Kim Blomstrand & Jenny Cummings
TICKETS .... Sr. Victoria Davis, OSB
                          Chika Yoshinaga
PUBLICITY .... Margie Gernhofer
                          Anyshka Anderson
                          Leah Cobarrubias
                          Grace Ann Garcia
                          Trinh Tran

CREWS

COSTUMES .... *Funmi Akinlawon,
        *Morna Brothers, Judy Currano, Anna Rosete

MAKEUP .... Charlotte Broekhuysen,
                Erin Butterworth, Rabia Khaja

SET CONSTRUCTION .... Rooman Ahad,
    Nidhi Agarwal, Kathy Ball, Morna Brothers, Leah
    Cobarrubias, Gia Dang, Grace Ann Garcia, Julie
    Hanson, Erin Herrera, Kammy Leung, Rana Mansoori,
    Monica Luecking, Anita Ortiz, Mary Palmer, Mara
    Salerno*, Kate Santo*, Amber Schwegel*, Michele
    Steele, Theresa Tran.

*Running Crew

Figure 13.2.   Sample program of one-act plays.

Some Unified Selections

Should you decide on an evening of short or one-act plays, the following combinations work well.

Updated Fairy Tales
Ford Ainsworth's *The Bridge* (based on "The Three Billy Goats Gruff")
David Mamet's *Frog Prince*
A. A. Milne's *The Ugly Duckling*

Three by Douglas Parkhirst
This Way to Heaven (a comedy)
Early Frost (a mystery)
Safe Harbor (a romance)

In the Park
Glenn Hughes's *Red Carnations*
Thornton Wilder's *Infancy*
Doris Estrada's *Three on a Bench*

Three Farces
Robert J. Flaherty's *The Party*
George S. Kaufman's *If Men Played Cards As Women Do*
Cleve Haubold's *Shut Up, Martha!*

There are many possible unifying devices and hundreds of plays from which to choose. Play publishers such as Samuel French, I. E. Clark, Dramatists Play Service, Baker's Plays, and the Dramatic Publishing Company have sections of their catalogues devoted to short plays.

COMPETITIVE PLAY FESTIVALS

There are national, regional, state, city, and invitational competitive play festivals held annually. Your director will know whether there are any in your area for which your production is eligible. Some require moving up through the ranks from local to statewide competition, and that is an expense your company may not be willing or able to undertake. If that is so, then check out other possibilities. For example, if there is a college in your area, inquire whether they hold a yearly competition for the local schools. If they don't, urge them to consider doing so.

Your own company could sponsor a competition with other schools in your area. Friendly competition gives companies a chance to see what is new in educational theatre, as well as an opportunity to meet fellow actors from other schools. In that case, as host school you would participate with a presentation, but you would not compete. If each competing school pays an entrance fee, the money can serve to finance any prizes you award—trophies, plaques, certificates, books on theatre, or collections of plays—and to pay an honorarium to the judges you ask to attend. Perhaps the contest could be hosted by a different school every year so that all companies could have opportunities to compete.

In general, material done at such school competitions is limited to a one-act play or a scene from the company's mainstage production. If it is a day-long event you can ask participants to bring a sack lunch and your company can provide beverages, or you can ask your school cafeteria management to prepare extra lunches for sale. If you want to raise the entry fee to include money for an evening banquet at which the awards can be presented, you might arrange that through the school cafeteria management or with a local caterer. It's best to keep the whole event at your school. You might want to ask the third-, second-, and first-place winners to give an encore performance in the evening for a local audience.

TOURING SCENES

Your company may have staged scenes around school or at local organizations as preopening publicity for your mainstage production. If so, you know which scenes work well and can be easily transported. If there still is time in the school year, try taking your scenes on the road as a community service to convalescent homes, senior citizens' centers, children's hospitals or day-care facilities. Probably these will be among your best audiences, appreciative of your kindness and enthusiastic about your performance. Often, it is difficult to let go of a wonderful production, and this last tour can be a very satisfying way to end a season.

SUMMARY

. . . .

If you have time for another production after your mainstage production, you can choose among producing original work; a festival of scenes, particularly one with a unifying device such as a theme; a reader's theatre presentation; or a program of one-acts. If there are no competitive play festivals in your area, consider sponsoring one of your own. Finally, if you are going to tour with scenes from your mainstage production, be sure the scenes can be presented successfully on their own.

*S*ome of the trends in theatre emerging in the last few years seem destined for further development and application. The technological advances in sound, lighting, and staging make possible highly sophisticated integrations of actors and mixed media. The growing popularity of site-specific entertainments should continue; not only are there plays being written to be performed at a specific site, such as an ice-skating rink or a warehouse, but productions are also being mounted at a site suggested by the material. For example, a reading of Molly Newman and Barbara Damashek's *Quilters* could be staged in a dairy barn draped with the work of the local quilting society, or a performance of John Olive's *The Voice of the Prairie* could take place around a campfire in a campground.

The one-man or one-woman show also is growing in popularity. An actor made up and costumed to look like Emily Dickinson or James Thurber or Teddy Roosevelt reminisces about his or her life, reads from letters, and tells stories—all in character. Actors love the challenge and audiences seem to appreciate the insight into a famous person. In addition, it is an inexpensive show to present.

Nonconventional treatment of classic plays continues to outrage or delight audiences: *Romeo and Juliet* at a disco, John M. Synge's *The Playboy of the Western World* set in the Appalachians, and Chekhov's *The Cherry Orchard* set in a San Fernando Valley, California, orange grove are a few examples. Some people

call it change for the sake of change; others call it making the work newly relevant. In any case, it continues alongside the conventional staging of such classics.

As musicals have moved away from the concept of musical comedy, more serious works are being adapted into musicals. Charles Dickens's *Oliver Twist* and *The Mystery of Edwin Drood,* Gaston Leroux's *Phantom of the Opera,* Victor Hugo's *Les Miserables,* and Lorraine Hansberry's *A Raisin in the Sun* already have been staged in musical form. Almost nothing seems beyond the abilities of determined songwriters and producers.

For many years Broadway plays were bought by Hollywood producers eager to make movies that would seize upon the interest already created by a long New York run. For a while now that trend has been reversed as we see successful Hollywood films being made into Broadway musicals. The list is already long: *Fame, Singing in the Rain, Beauty and the Beast, Sunset Boulevard, Seven Brides for Seven Brothers, The Thin Man, Breakfast at Tiffany's,* and *Meet Me in Saint Louis.*

Perhaps the most important new trend is the way ethnic groups are finding their own voices in the theatre. In Australia, aboriginal playwrights are writing not only about their history and their creation myths, but about the aboriginal experience of today. Jack Davis's *The Dreamers, No Sugar,* and *Barungin* have been presented in major cities such as Melbourne and Perth. Richard Walley wrote *Munjong,* which premiered at the Victorian Arts

Center in Melbourne, and co-founded the Middar Aboriginal Theatre in Western Australia.

In Southern California, an outspoken new generation of Hispanic playwrights is carrying on the tradition begun by Luis Valdez of *Zoot Suit* and El Teatro Campesino fame. Valdez himself also is involved in television and film projects, and the touring company of Teatro Campesino has presented plays by Evelina Fernandez and Josefina Lopez.

Ran Avni's Jewish Repertory Theatre (JRT) explores the search for Jewish identity in American culture. In fifteen years it presented over sixty-five productions, including Nahma Shandow's hit musical *Kuni-Leml.* Citing the difference between Yiddish theatre and JRT, Avni explained to writer Fran Siegel that Yiddish theatre often took a George Bernard Shaw or a Shakespeare play and simply did it in Yiddish, whereas JRT selects plays that speak to a theme or issue or character in the Jewish experience and does them in English.

The enormous success of August Wilson, who is writing a series of plays on the black experience in each decade of this century, includes Pulitzer Prizes, Tony Awards, critical acclaim, and enthusiastic audiences. David Henry Hwang's drama *M. Butterfly,* which won a Tony Award, Drama Desk Award, and Outer Critics Circle Award as best Broadway play, has been seen as a metaphor for the perception of East Asian culture by the West. At Perseverance Theatre in Juneau, Alaska, a production of Earl Atchak's *In Two Worlds* weaves Cup'ik dance, drumming, and audience participation through traditionally staged scenes to tell the story of rural natives enticed, then bewildered, by a federal land claims settlement that brought sudden wealth to Alaska's tribes in the 1970s.

A Daly City, California, workshop for young Filipino-Americans yielded scenes chronicling the experiences of several Filipino families living in San Francisco. A team of seven writers then worked with director Chris B. Millado to shape the material into *Kin,* a two-hour production presented by the Teatro ng Tanan at the Fort Mason, California, Cowell Theatre.

In summary, flashy mixed media presentations, site-specific performances, new looks at older works, and a great diversity of cultures finding their own voice—that's what the future seems to hold for theatre.

Writing Projects

1. Write a ten-minute sketch for two to four actors based on one of the following conflicts:
   a. Family loyalties versus peer pressure to break rules
   b. Going away to college versus staying at home and attending a local college
   c. Confronting a friend you saw shoplifting
   d. Whether to tell a friend her boyfriend/his girlfriend is unfaithful
   e. A boy and girl each want to break up without hurting the other
2. Using a book of scenes or a collection of plays, put together a proposed festival of scenes based on one of the following themes:
   a. Being an outsider
   b. The quest for fame or fortune
   c. Finding the perfect girlfriend or boyfriend
   d. Discovering the truth about life or about other people
   e. Misunderstandings
3. List some plays that could comprise an evening of one-act plays of the same type, for example, ghost stories or animal stories; that offer different views of the same situation, for example, thwarted young lovers or lonely older people; or that lead from one time period to another in the same setting.
4. Choose a play that would work well in a reading and prepare a page of the book for readers' theatre.
5. Drawing from letters, speeches, or journals, prepare a five- to ten-minute reading.

Activity Projects

1. Using the material developed in the project above, or another company member's material, present it as a reading.
2. Take one of the original works created in the first Writing Project listed above and cast and direct it for presentation to the company.
3. With a small group from the company, improvise upon a well-known fairy tale. Try to give it an original twist—like "So You Think You Know the Story of Cinderella?"
4. Arrange a tour of scenes from your mainstage production.
5. If there is no play competition in your area, write a proposal for your company to sponsor such an event.

The Playwright

British playwright Alan Ayckbourn is known for his witty, brilliant farces. Having written more plays than Noël Coward and as many as Shakespeare, already Ayckbourn would have a place in theatre history based on sheer numbers alone. Popular as well as successful, his work has been translated into twenty-four languages and performed around the world.

Ayckbourn was born in London to a symphony violinist father and a novelist mother. In school he wrote poetry and joined the drama club, where he was encouraged by a teacher who loved the theatre. After leaving school he worked as a stage manager and eventually as an actor. According to Ayckbourn, he began to take an interest in writing and directing when he realized that his acting ability was only average.

Ayckbourn's ongoing association with England's Stephen Joseph Theatre in the Round began in the 1960s while he still was a drama producer for the British Broadcasting Corporation. By 1970 he had taken over as full-time artistic director at the theatre and began to expand the seasonal theatre into an almost year-round operation. All the while he has adhered to the basic tenets laid down by founder Stephen Joseph: new work, a company structure, and playing in the round.

Ayckbourn never has felt obliged to rebel against the concept of the "well-made play." He says he has a tidy mind and likes symmetry, feeling that if a play's structure is right, it can sustain an evening's entertainment. He reminds people that the term *playwright* suggests the act of crafting a play.

Ayckbourn's love for puzzles and games is evident in his playing with shape and form in *The Norman Conquests*. This ambitious production is a trilogy of plays, all set in the same cottage on the same weekend with the same cast of three couples. The three plays can be seen in any order and each stands on its own, although it's even more enjoyable to see all three within a short period. The twist is the way Ayckbourn has interwoven the three plays. Events occurring in one play are referred to in another and audiences enjoy the thrill of recognition as they discover what was happening in another room at the same time.

Ayckbourn says his plays' chief objective is laughter, explaining, "There is nothing I want to say that can't be said through laughter. . . . I find laughter arising from understanding and recognition between the audience and the stage characters is the most rewarding." For the past few years critics have found a serious thread running through Ayckbourn's recent plays, but in all cases the serious content continues to be conveyed in a lighthearted farcical manner, answering some questions while raising others. That's good theatre.

Appendix

Plays Suitable for Educational Theatre

ABBREVIATIONS

Code:			
M	=	number of men characters	
W	=	number of women characters	
int	=	number of interior sets required	
ext	=	number of exterior sets required	
con	=	contemporary costume styles	
per	=	period costume styles (this includes earlier time periods in the twentieth century, "uniform costuming" indicates all in the same color or same style)	
Baker	=	Baker's Plays	
Clark	=	I. E. Clark, Inc.	
Cuesta	=	Cuesta Company of Players	
DPS	=	Dramatists Play Service	
Dramatic	=	Dramatic Publishing Co.	
French	=	Samuel French, Inc.	
Music	=	Music Theatre International	
Players	=	Players Press, Inc.	
R-H	=	Rodgers and Hammerstein Repertory	
T-W	=	Tams-Witmark Music Library	

ADDRESSES

Baker's Plays
100 Chauncy St.
Boston, MA 02111
(617) 482-1280

I. E. Clark, Inc.
P.O. Box 246
Schulenberg, TX 78956
(409) 743-3232

Cuesta Company of Players
1145 Fourth Street
Baywood Park, CA 93402
(805) 546-3182

Dramatists Play Service, Inc.
440 Park Avenue South
New York, NY 10016
(212) 683-8960

Dramatic Publishing
  Company
311 Washington St.
Woodstock, IL 60098
(815) 338-7170

Samuel French, Inc.
45 West 25th St.
New York, NY 10036
(212) 206-8990

Music Theatre International
119 West 57th St.
New York, NY 10019
(212) 868-6668

Players Press, Inc.
P.O. Box 1132
Studio City, CA 91614
(818) 789-4980

Rodgers and Hammerstein
  Repertory
460 Park Avenue
New York, NY 10022
(212) 541-6600

Tams-Witmark Music Library
757 Third Ave.
New York, NY 10017
(212) 688-2525

FULL-LENGTH PLAYS

The Admirable Crichton — J. M. Barrie (comedy); 13M, 12W; 1 int, 1 ext; per, 1900s; French. The butler Crichton insists that class distinctions should be maintained, but when he and his employers are shipwrecked it is Crichton who must save them with his resourcefulness.

The Adventures of the Speckled Band — Tim Kelly (thriller); 6M, 8W; 1 int; per, Victorian; Clark. Locked "safely" in her room, Julia Stoner is murdered. Sherlock Holmes and Doctor Watson must solve the mystery before the killer strikes again.

Ah Wilderness! — Eugene O'Neill (comedy); 9M, 6W; 3 int, 1 ext (can also be done with backdrop and detail scenery); per, 1900s; French. A joyful celebration of family life and young romance. (may need deletions)

Anastasia — Guy Bolton (drama); 8M, 5W; 1 int; per, 1920s; French. Several years after the Russian revolution a young girl is presented to the Imperial Grandmother as her long-lost granddaughter, Anastasia. Is she really Anastasia, or just the dupe of a clever schemer who wants to get his hands on the deposed czar's fortune?

Androcles and the Lion — George Bernard Shaw (comedy); 14M, 2W; 1 int, 2 ext; per, ancient Rome; French. Kindly Androcles removes a thorn from a lion's paw and is later repaid when the grateful lion refuses to injure Androcles in battle.

Angel Street — Patrick Hamilton (thriller); 2M, 3W; 1 int; per, Victorian; French. Tension mounts as a murderer nearly succeeds in convincing his wife that she is insane. Filmed as "Gaslight."

Anne of Green Gables — Alice Chadwicke (comedy); 4M, 10W; 1 int, per, 1900s; French (request nonmusical version). When the Cuthberts decide to adopt an orphan boy to help with the farmwork, they are at first dismayed, then charmed, when the irrepressible Anne Shirley enters their lives.

Arms and the Man — George Bernard Shaw (comedy); 5M, 3W; 2 int, 1 ext (may use scrim or forestage for ext); per, 19th century; French. Raina Petchoff has the delightful dilemma of choosing between her "chocolate cream soldier" and her fiancé, a dashing but impractical cavalryman.

Arsenic and Old Lace – Joseph Kesselring (farce); 11M, 3W; 1 int; con (could also be costumed in period; play was first performed in the 1930s–'40s); DPS. One of the most popular plays of all time, it features two dear old ladies who gently murder lonely old men to end their loneliness.

As You Like It – William Shakespeare (comedy); 16M, 4W; 2 ext (may use different areas of the same outdoor scene); per, Renaissance; French, Baker. For a shortened, simplified version, Cuesta. Rosalind and her cousin Celia run away to the forests of Arden where they encounter country folk and find romance.

Auntie Mame – Jerome Lawrence and Robert E. Lee (comedy); 28 M, 12W; Acting edition has suggestions for simplified staging; per, 1920s to the present; DPS. The madcap adventures of a scatterbrained and warm-hearted woman who is devoted to her young nephew. Many of the smaller parts can be doubled.

The Bachelor and the Bobby-Soxer – F. Andrew Leslie (comedy); 16M, 9W; unit set; con (or, because of the "bobby-soxer" reference, per, 1940s); DPS. A judge orders a playboy to entertain her younger sister so the teen will lose her infatuation for the older man.

The Bad Seed – Maxwell Anderson (thriller); 7M, 4W; 1 small girl; 1 int; con; DPS. Little Rhoda Penmark is sweet and charming on the surface, but underneath she is the essence of evil as she causes the death of anyone in her way.

Bell, Book and Candle – John Van Druten (comedy); 3M, 2W; 1 int; con; DPS. The sparkling story of a modern-day witch whose love spell gets out of hand.

Belles on Their Toes – William Roos (comedy); 12M, 6W; 1 int; per, 1920s; Dramatic. This sequel to *Cheaper by the Dozen* picks up after Father's death as Mother and the Gilbreth children survive one crisis after another with love and good humor.

Belvedere – Gwen Davenport (comedy); 5M, 4W, 2 children; 1 int; con; French. A novelist hires himself out as a baby-sitter and writes a book about his adventures.

Bernardine – Mary Chase (comedy); 13M, 6W; unit set or backdrop and detail scenery; con; DPS. The fantasies and realities of teenagers on the verge of adulthood.

Blithe Spirit —Noël Coward (farce); 2M, 5W; 1 int; con (or the elegant styles of the late 1930s in which it originally played); French. An eccentric medium seems to have caused a man's late wife to materialize and plague his present marriage.

The Boy with Green Hair —F. Andrew Leslie (comedy-fantasy); 9M, 1W, 7 boys, 3 girls; 1 int; con (time of play follows closely after a war); DPS. An orphan boy clings to the hope that his parents will return from war to claim him. His grandfather helps him to face reality and to find hope for the future.

But Why Bump Off Barnaby? —Rick Abbot (mystery-farce); 4M, 6W; 1 int; con; DPS. When Barnaby Folcey is murdered at a family gathering at Marlgate Manor, it turns out he had a motive to murder everyone else—but no one had any reason to want him dead.

The Cave Dwellers —William Saroyan (comedy); 9M, 5W; bare stage; con; French. A group of penniless people with unquenchable spirit camp on the stage of a soon-to-be-demolished theatre.

The Chalk Garden —Enid Bagnold (drama); 2M, 7W; 1 int; con; French. An eccentric English woman lives with her granddaughter and devotes her life to her garden. A new governess with an air of mystery about her helps both women find happiness.

Charley's Aunt —Brandon Thomas (farce); 6M, 4W; 1 ext, 2 int; per, Victorian; French. An Oxford student is persuaded to impersonate a friend's wealthy aunt from Brazil, so that the friend can meet his sweetheart with the proper chaperone.

Cheaper by the Dozen —Perry Clark (comedy); 9M, 7W; 1 int; per, 1900s; Dramatic. An efficiency expert runs his family of twelve children with all kinds of labor-saving devices.

The Chicago Gypsies —V. Glasgow Koste (comedy-drama); 1M, 6W; backdrop and detail scenery; per, 1930s; Dramatic. Winner of the Distinguished Play award of the American Alliance for Theatre and Education, the play is about the migratory life of the child in a show business family during the Great Depression.

Come Over to Our House —Marrijane and Joseph Hayes (comedy); 8M, 10W and extra girls; 1 int; con (or the 1940s fashions of the original); French. Jay Eldridge's flair for music lands him in the school vaudeville and a surprising number of amusing scrapes.

The Crucifer of Blood — Paul Giovanni (mystery); 11M, 1W; unit set; per, Victorian; French. Sherlock Holmes unravels the puzzle of the sign of four.

The Curious Savage — John Patrick (comedy); 5M, 6W; 1 int; con; DPS. A kindly widow is committed to a sanitorium by her greedy stepchildren, but she and her newfound friends outwit the family.

Cyrano de Bergerac — Edmond Rostand (comedy-drama); 10M, 5W, extras; 2 int, 3 ext; per, 17th century France; DPS. An ugly poet swordsman helps another man win the girl he himself loves.

Daddy Long-Legs — Jean Webster (comedy); 6M, 7W, 6 children (only appear in first act and can be played by small girls of any age); 4 int; con (or may be costumed in the time period it was written, earlier in this century); French. An orphan is sent to college by a benefactor she has never met and writes him letters of her progress addressed to her "Daddy Long-Legs."

Dark of the Moon — Howard Richardson and William Berney (fantasy); 12M, 13W, 3 int, 4 ext (may be simplified); per, late nineteenth century; French. Dramatization of folk tale about Barbara Allen and the witch boy who loved her.

Dear Ruth — Norman Krasna (comedy); 5M, 5W; 1 int; per, 1940s; DPS. A young girl carries on a romantic correspondence with a soldier using her older sister's name. When the young man calls to meet "Ruth" hilarious complications develop.

The Desk Set — William Marchant (comedy); 8M, 8W; 1 int; con; French. Workers in the reference department of a television network fight being replaced by machines.

Done to Death — Fred Carmichael (mystery-comedy); 8M, 8W; 1 int; con; French. While five mystery writers wrestle with the problems of writing a television mystery series, real murders happen around them.

Dream Girl — Elmer Rice (comedy-fantasy); 25M, 7W (men may be doubled); area staging with wagons; con; DPS. A charming but overly imaginative girl escapes into her daydreams to find romance and success.

The Enchanted Cottage — Arthur Pinero (fantasy); 5M, 4W, extras; 1 int, 1 ext; con or any period directly following a war; Baker. A disfigured war hero and a homely servant girl find beauty in each other through the magic of their love.

Ethan Frome — Owen and Donald Davis (drama); 7M, 4W; 2 int, several simple ext; per, 1900s; DPS. The stark tragedy of a New England man who falls in love with the young woman who has come to take care of his semi-invalid wife.

Everybody Loves Opal — John Patrick (comedy); 4M, 2W; 1 int; con; DPS. Three crooks hide out in the home of a friendly recluse where their schemes to do her in for her insurance are thwarted in a comic and satisfying manner.

Everyman — Anonymous (medieval morality play); 11M, 6W; area staging; per, medieval (could also be done in con); French nonroyalty. The character of Everyman takes a journey to the unknown and along the way encounters people in his life.

Family Portrait — Lenore Coffee and William Cowen (Biblical drama); 12M, 10W; 1 int, 3 ext; per, first century AD; French. The effect of the life of Jesus upon the common people of His time.

The Farmer's Daughter — F. Andrew Leslie (comedy); 11M, 3W; 1 int; con; DPS. An unspoiled girl from the country triumphs over some crooked big city politicians.

Father of the Bride — Caroline Francke (comedy); 11M, 7W, extras; 1 int; con; DPS. The simple wedding Mr. Banks plans for this daughter Kay mushrooms to gigantic proportions.

The First Actress — Ben Orkow (drama); 11M, 2W, 3 boys (the men can be doubled); open stage with props; per, 16th century England; DPS. A young girl sets out to be an actress in a time when women were not allowed on the stage.

George Washington Slept Here — Moss Hart and George S. Kaufman (comedy); 9M, 8W; 1 int (but it undergoes changes as the farmhouse is renovated); con; DPS. The Newton family is less than enthusiastic about the tumbledown Revolutionary War farmhouse they've moved to.

The Girls of the Garden Club — John Patrick (comedy); 2M, 17W; 1 int; con; DPS. A group of women whose lives revolve around their garden club must choose a new president.

The Glass Menagerie — Tennessee Williams (drama); 2M, 3W; unit set to represent areas of the house and ext; con; DPS. The now-classic tale of the Wingfield family and the arrival of the Gentleman Caller.

Green Grow the Lilacs — Lynn Riggs (drama); 10M, 4W, extras; area staging; per, American pioneer; French. The play on which the musical *Oklahoma!* was based. The romance of Laurey and Curly blooms amidst the realities of ranch life.

The Happiest Millionaire — Kyle Crichton (farce); 9M, 6W, 1 int; per, World War I; DPS. The wealthy and eccentric Anthony Biddle of Philadelphia almost wrecks his daughter's forthcoming marriage because he hates to see the family circle broken up.

The Happy Time — Samuel Taylor (comedy); 8M, 4W; 2 int; 1920s; DPS. A warm, humorous and uninhibited family teaches its youngest member to love and know truth.

Harvey — Mary Chase (comedy); 6M, 6W; 2 int; con; DPS. The now famous story of Elwood P. Dowd and his friend, an invisible six-feet-tall white rabbit.

The Hasty Heart — John Patrick (comedy-drama); 8M, 1W; 1 int; per, World War II; DPS. A wounded soldier who has withdrawn from others is changed by the sympathetic treatment of his fellow patients.

The Heiress — Ruth and Augustus Goetz (drama); 3M, 6W; 1 int; per, 1850s; DPS. A shy and plain girl falls in love with a fortune hunter but rejects him when she learns the truth.

Hobson's Choice — Harold Brighouse (comedy); 7M, 5W; 2 int; con (or can be done in 1900s style of the original story); French. This is the source of the musical *Walking Happy*. The eldest daughter of a tyrannical merchant marries her father's apprentice and helps him to set up a rival shop.

Holiday for Lovers — Ronald Alexander (comedy); 4M, 5W; 4 int; con; DPS. A family vacation brings good times and romance.

Home Is the Hunter — Helen MacInnes (comedy); 7M, 4W, extras; 2 int; per, ancient Greek or con; French. The story of Ulysses' homecoming from the Trojan War. He is accompanied by Homer, who manages to fall asleep at the most important part of the action.

Home Sweet Homicide — Craig Rice (mystery); 8M, 6W, extras; 1 int; con; Dramatic. While their widowed mother writes mystery stories to support the family, her children manage to solve a mystery of their own and find a suitor for mom.

The Hound of the Baskervilles —F. Andrew Leslie (mystery); 6M, 3W; 1 int; per, turn of the century; DPS. Sherlock Holmes and Dr. Watson unravel the case of the gigantic hound terrorizing the Baskerville family.

The Imaginary Invalid —Molière, trans. M. Stone (farce); 8M, 4W; 1 int; per, 17th century France; French nonroyalty. The story of a hypochondriac and his cure.

The Importance of Being Earnest —Oscar Wilde (farce); 5M, 4W; 1 or 2 int, 1 ext; per, Victorian; French. Much confusion and humor result from two double identities.

The Invisible Man —Eddie Cope (comedy-thriller); 4M, 7W; 1 int; con; Clark. Six home economics students take over the running of an isolated hotel where one of their guests turns out to be the Invisible Man.

I Remember Mama —John Van Druten (comedy); 9M, 13W; unit set; per, 1900s; DPS. The heartwarming story of an immigrant family in San Francisco.

It Happens Every Summer —David Rogers (comedy); 7M, 13W, extras; 1 int; con; Dramatic. A group of college girls selected from all over the country come to New York to work as guest editors for a fashion magazine.

Jane Eyre —Jane Kendall (drama); 4M, 9W; 1 int; per, late 18th century; Dramatic. Charlotte Brontë's story of an orphan who becomes governess to the daughter of a strange but captivating man.

Jenny Kissed Me —Jean Kerr (comedy); 4M, 10W; 1 int; con; DPS. An elderly priest and some young friends try to help Jenny find the perfect husband.

Joan of Lorraine —Maxwell Anderson (romantic drama); 18M, 5W; bare stage with detail scenery; con and per, medieval; DPS. A group of present-day actors rehearsing a play about Joan of Arc come to understand the meaning of faith.

Junior Miss —Jerome Chodorov and Joseph Fields (comedy); 11M, 6W; 1 int; con or, for period charm, the 1940s of the original production; DPS. The popular play about the antics and imaginative schemings of teenagers.

Juvie —Jerome McDonough (drama); 5M, 10W; 1 int; con; (about 60 min) Clark. Set in a juvenile detention center, this prizewinning play honestly depicts the lives of kids who are scared, lonely, and locked up.

Kind Lady — Edward Chodorov (melodrama); 6M, 8W; 1 int; con; French. A courageous woman outwits a group of crooks who are trying to convince the world she is insane.

Laburnum Grove — J. B. Priestley (comedy-mystery); 6M, 7W; 1 int; con; French. A man who leads a quiet life among sponging relatives suddenly announces that he is the leader of a counterfeit ring.

Ladies in Retirement — Edward Percy and Reginald Denham (mystery); 1M, 6W; 1 int; con; DPS. Devotion to her dependent sister leads a woman to murder.

The Lady's Not for Burning — Christopher Fry (poetic-comedy); 8M, 3W; 1 int; per, 15th century; DPS. The romantic entanglements of a man who wishes to die and a woman who doesn't.

Leading Lady — Ruth Gordon (comedy-drama); 11M, 9W; 2 int; per, 1900s; DPS. Life in the American theatre at the turn of the century.

Let's Murder Marsha — Monk Ferris (comedy); 3M, 4W; 1 int; con; French. A housewife addicted to reading murder mysteries overhears what she thinks is a plot against her life.

The Liar — Carlo Goldoni new trans. Tunc Yalman (comedy); 10M, 4W, extras; unit set; con or per, 16th century Venice; DPS. The classic comedy about a young man who seems unable to tell the truth and the complications this causes his family.

Life with Father — Howard Lindsay and Russel Crouse (comedy); 8M, 8W; 1 int; per, 1880s; DPS. Father seems to rule the family with an iron hand, but Mother gets her way with a smile.

Life with Mother — Howard Lindsay and Russel Crouse (comedy); 8M, 8W; 2 int; per, 1880s; DPS. A continuation of the adventures of the Day family.

Liliom — Ferenc Molnar (fantasy); 17M, 5W, extras; 1 int; 4 ext; con or per, 1900s; French. This is the story the musical *Carousel* was based on. A shiftless young braggart marries a servant girl, and after his death he is allowed to return to earth to do one good deed to redeem himself.

Little Moon of Alban — James Costigan (drama); 10M, 8W; unit set; per, 1920s in Ireland; French. An elegant plea for understanding in the time of the Irish Rebellion.

Little Women – Kristin Lawrence (drama); 9W; 1 int; per, American Civil War; Dramatic. The famous Louisa May Alcott book brought to the stage. The March family copes with life while Father serves in the war.

The Loud Red Patrick – John Boruff (comedy); 4M, 5W; 1 int; per, 1912; French. Patrick Flannigan wants all family matters settled by parliamentary principles, but the system backfires when his young daughter wants to get married.

The Magician's Nephew – Aurand Harris (drama-fantasy); 3M, 3W, 3 talking animals; area staging; con and fantasy; Dramatic. C. S. Lewis's story of a boy and girl who adventure through the enchanted lands of Queen Jadis and free them from her spell.

Making It! – Hindi Brooks (drama); 7M, 10W; 1 int; con; Clark. A group of students in a high school for the performing arts have their hearts set on making it in the world of theatre.

The Male Animal – James Thurber and Elliott Nugent (comedy); 8M, 5W; 1 int; con or per, late 1930s; French. A mild professor deals effectively with an ex-football hero rival and a threat to academic freedom.

The Man Who Came to Dinner – Moss Hart and George S. Kaufman (comedy); 15M, 9W, extras; 1 int; con or per, 1940s; DPS. A famous but irascible writer is confined by injury to the home of a midwestern couple, where he disrupts family life with his eccentricities.

The Many Loves of Dobie Gillis – William Davidson (comedy); 6M, 12W; 1 int; con; Dramatic. Max Shulman's famous creation Dobie and his friends go to college.

The Matchmaker – Thornton Wilder (farce); 9M, 7W; 4 int; per, 1880; French. A rich banker hires a female marriage broker to find him a bride, but ends up snagged by the woman herself.

Meet Me in St. Louis – Christopher Sergel (comedy); 7M, 9W; 1 int; per, 1900s; Dramatic. Sally Benson's famous tales of family life in St. Louis at the time of the World's Fair of 1903.

The Member of the Wedding – Carson McCullers (drama); 6M, 7W; unit set; con; DPS. A study in loneliness of an overimaginative young girl in Georgia.

A Midsummer Night's Dream – William Shakespeare (comedy); 13M, 4W, 4 either M or W, extras; area staging; con and fantasy or per, ancient Greece and fantasy or per, Renaissance and fantasy or romantic-summery; Dramatic, Baker. Cuesta (shortened, simplified version). Various pairs of lovers quarrel and make up while townspeople plan a play for the wedding feast of their duke.

The Miracle Worker – William Gibson (drama); 7M, 7W; unit set; per, 1882; French. The dramatization of Anne Sullivan's courageous struggle to teach the blind and deaf Helen Keller.

The Mousetrap – Agatha Christie (mystery); 5M, 3W; 1 int; con; French. The long-running thriller about a group of people snowbound in a remote hotel while a murderer is on the loose.

Mrs. McThing – Mary Chase (fantasy); 9M, 10W; 2 int; con; DPS. A whimsical tale of the education of Mrs. Howard V. Larue III by her nine-year-old son and a little witch-girl.

Much Ado About Nothing – William Shakespeare (comedy); 14M, 4W, extras; backdrop and detail scenery; con or per, Renaissance; French, Baker, Cuesta (shortened, simplified version). A quarrelsome pair unites to save her friend from disgrace and find themselves in love.

Murder on the Nile – Agatha Christie (mystery); 8M, 5W; 1 int; con or per, 1930s; French. A group of people on a paddle steamer trip on the Nile encounter murder.

My Sister Eileen – Joseph Fields and Jerome Chodorov (comedy); 21M, 6W (some doubling possible); 1 int; con; or per, 1940s; DPS. Two girls from Ohio find life in the big city of New York wild and wonderful.

My Three Angels – Sam and Bella Spewack (comedy); 7M, 3W; 1 int; per, 1910; DPS. Three convicts in French Guiana become the good angels to a sadly harrassed family.

New Beat on an Old Drum – Kurtz Gordon (comedy-drama); 5M, 7W, extras; unit set for int/ext; con; DPS. A young schoolteacher and her teenaged niece outwit a tricky real estate developer.

Nicholas Nickleby – Tim Kelly (drama); 15M, 15W (some doubling); area staging; per, Victorian; Dramatic. The Charles Dickens novel adapted to an easily staged two hours. Nicholas attempts to protect his sister, earn a living, help his friends, and thwart a villain.

The Night Is My Enemy – Fred Carmichael (suspense drama); 5M, 5W; 1 int; per, 1900; French. A blind girl finds herself stalked by a mentally unbalanced killer.

Nothing But the Truth – James Montgomery (comedy); 5M, 6W; 2 int; con; French. Bob Bennett bets his friends he can tell nothing but the truth, and it proves not only difficult but embarrassing.

No Time for Sergeants – Ira Levin (comedy); 34M, 3W; unit set; con, military; DPS. A good-natured country boy comes in conflict with the Air Force way of doing things.

On Borrowed Time – Paul Osborn (fantasy); 11M, 3W; 1 ext; con; DPS. A young boy and his grandfather hold Death captive in a tree.

On the Razzle – Tom Stoppard (comedy); 15M, 10W, extras, musicians (for one scene, may be faked with miming and pre-recorded tape); unit set for int/ext; per, 1900s, French. Shares a source with *The Matchmaker,* but is not a version of that play. While their boss wines and dines his intended in the city, his clerks decide to have a day on the town themselves.

One Foot in Heaven – Anne Coulter Martens (drama); 8M, 10W; detail scenery or unit set for 1 int; per, 1910; Dramatic. An Iowa minister moves into a rundown parish but manages to revitalize his congregation.

Onions in the Stew – Betty MacDonald (comedy); 7M, 11W; 1 int; con; Dramatic. An adventurous family samples the delights and headaches of country living on an island in Puget Sound.

Our Girls – Conrad Seiler (farce); 6M, 5W; 1 int; con; DPS. Three boys must masquerade as their sisters to win an inheritance.

Our Hearts Were Young and Gay – Jean Kerr (comedy) 7M, 10W; unit set; per, 1920s; Dramatic. The Cornelia Otis Skinner and Emily Kimbrough book brought to the stage. Two independent girls face typical tourist problems on a trip to Europe.

Our Town – Thornton Wilder (drama); 17M, 7W, extras; bare stage and props; per, 1900s; French. The life of the people of Grovers' Corners followed through flashbacks and looks into the future.

Out of the Frying Pan – Francis Swann (comedy); 7M, 5W; 1 int; con or per, 1940s of the original; French. Six stagestruck youngsters plot to meet the famous producer who lives in their building. Fast-paced and full of good-natured fun and strong characterizations.

Outward Bound — Sutton Vane (comedy-drama); 6M, 3W; 1 int; con; French. A group of passengers on a cruise ship slowly realize they all are dead and are headed for some kind of judgment day.

Papa Is All — Patterson Greene (comedy); 3M, 3W; 1 int; con; French. A Pennsylvania Dutch family is ruled tyrannically by the father, whose influence over the family finally is broken.

The Playboy of the Western World — John M. Synge (comedy); 7M, 5W; 1 int; per, Irish country earlier this century; French. A young man finds himself the hero of a remote village after telling tales of having killed his father.

Play On! — Rick Abbot (comedy); 3M, 7W; 1 int; con; French. A theatre company struggles to put on a play in the face of difficulties from the author, who keeps revising the script.

Pollyanna — Catherine Chisholm Cushing (comedy); 5M, 6W; 2 int; per, 1900s; French. Based on the novel by Eleanor H. Porter. An orphan comes to live with her aunt and changes the whole town from gloomy to glad.

Pride and Prejudice — Jane Kendall (comedy); 5M, 11W; 1 int; per, 18th-century England; Dramatic. From the Jane Austen novel about five sisters seeking husbands.

Pygmalion — George Bernard Shaw (comedy); 6M, 6W; 3 int, 2 ext. (can be done with detail scenery); per, 1900s England; French. A phonetics professor bets he can transform a cockney flower seller into a lady and pass her off in high society. The play on which the musical *My Fair Lady* was based.

Quality Street — J. M. Barrie (comedy); 6M, 9W, extras; 2 int; per, 1800s England; French. A young woman pretends to be her even younger niece in order to win back a former fiancé.

The Rainmaker — N. Richard Nash (comedy); 6M, 1W; 1 int; con-western; French. A con man offers to bring rain to a drought-stricken town but ends up bringing help of another kind.

The Reluctant Debutante — William Douglas Home (comedy); 3M, 5W; 1 int; con; French. Mother's matchmaking attempts fail as her daughter finds her own Prince Charming.

Remains to Be Seen — Howard Lindsay and Russel Crouse (mystery-comedy); 16M, 3W; 1 int; con; DPS. A jazz drummer and a band singer are caught up in the search for the killer of a rich but unmourned reformer.

Ring Around the Moon — Jean Anouilh, translated by Christopher Fry (sophisticated comedy); 6M, 7W; 1 int; con-elegant; DPS. A satirical comedy about mistaken identities and romance.

The Rivals — Richard Brinsley Sheridan (comedy); 9M, 4W; unit set; per, 18th century England; French. Confusions among the aristocracy. Contains the famous character of Mrs. Malaprop.

Romanoff and Juliet — Peter Ustinov (comedy); 9M, 4W; unit set; con; DPS. The son of a Russian diplomat and the daughter of an American diplomat fall in love, with a happier outcome than that of Shakespeare's lovers.

A Roomful of Roses — Edith Sommer (comedy-drama); 3M, 5W; 1 small boy; 1 int; con; DPS. An estranged mother and daughter are reunited and find a new world of friends.

The Royal Family — George S. Kaufman and Edna Ferber (comedy); 11M, 6W; 1 int; con; French. The Cavendish family has dominated the American stage for years. The granddaughter first rebels, then follows the tradition.

Sabrina Fair — Samuel Taylor (comedy); 7M, 7W; 1 int; con; DPS. The well-educated young daughter of the family chauffeur captures the heart of a cynical tycoon.

Send Me No Flowers — Norman Barasch and Carroll Moore (comedy); 9M, 3W; 1 int; con; French. a hypochondriac believes he is dying and so is determined to find a second husband for his wife.

Seven Keys to Baldpate — George M. Cohan (mystery); 9M, 4W; 1 int; con; French. A writer goes away for the weekend to write and finds his privacy invaded by a series of strange people.

She Stoops to Conquer — Oliver Goldsmith (comedy); 15M, 4W; 1 int; per, 18th century England; French nonroyalty. A young lady finds herself posing as a servant in her own home to win a young suitor's love.

The Silver Whistle — Robert E. McEnroe (comedy); 10M, 5W; 1 ext; con; DPS. An amiable con man goes to live in a home for the aged and changes the lives of all he meets.

The Skin of Our Teeth — Thornton Wilder (fantasy); 5M, 5W, extras; 1 int, 1 ext; per, various ages through history; French. The story of the Antrobus family, and, incidentally, of mankind, down through the ages.

The Solid Gold Cadillac — Howard Teichmann and George S. Kaufman (comedy); 11M, 6W; various simple sets, may use detail scenery; con; DPS. A little old lady who owns a few shares of stock ends up in control of the company when the shareholders revolt against the corrupt directors.

The Spiral Staircase — F. Andrew Leslie (thriller); 4M, 4W; 1 int; con; DPS. The young companion of a bedridden old woman finds that she is the next intended victim of an unbalanced killer.

Stage Door — Edna Ferber and George S. Kaufman (comedy-drama); 11M, 21W; 1 int; con; DPS. *Directions for staging in single setting and for making slight alterations to accommodate a high school production will be sent free on request.* The classic story of young hopefuls in a New York City theatrical boarding house.

Stardust — Walter Kerr (comedy); 7M, 11W; 1 int; con; Dramatic. The students at a dramatic academy await the arrival of a famous actor who will guest star in one of their productions. Justly popular for its spoof of "The Method" in acting.

Story Theatre — Paul Sills (fables); 5M, 3W; bare stage with projections; various costumes, animals etc.; French. Clever renderings of stories from the Grimms and Aesop.

Tall Story — Howard Lindsay and Russel Crouse (comedy); 22M, 8W; simple interiors; con; DPS. The star basketball player at a small college finds his life complicated by the faculty, his girlfriend, and some crooks who want him to throw the big game.

The Teahouse of the August Moon — John Patrick (comedy); 18M, 8W, 3 children; 1 goat; area staging; army and oriental costumes; DPS. An officer in the Army of Occupation on Okinawa helps a village become self-supporting through the operation of a teahouse.

Ten Little Indians — Agatha Christie (mystery); 8M, 3W; 1 int; con; French. At a house party on an island the guests are murdered one by one.

Three Men on a Horse — John Cecil Holm and George Abbott (comedy); 11M, 4W, 3 int; con; DPS. A timid man finds he has a gift for picking winners at the race track.

Thurber Carnival — James Thurber (comedy revue); 5M, 4W; simple settings; various costumes; French. Sketches adapted from the short stories and cartoons of James Thurber.

Tiger at the Gates —Jean Giraudoux, translated by Christopher Fry (drama); 15M, 7W; bare stage with gates; per, ancient Greece; French. The story of the fall of Troy as the Greek forces are camped outside the city.

Time Out for Ginger —Ronald Alexander (comedy); 5M, 5W; 1 int; con; DPS. A family protests that their lives are being disrupted when one of the daughters tries out for the high-school football team.

Tom Sawyer —Joseph George Caruso (comedy); 13M, 6W, extras, doubling possible; area staging; per, 19th century America; Clark. Mark Twain's famous characters in various adventures.

Treasure Island —Ara Watson (drama); 18M, 2W; unit set; per, Victorian sailors, pirates; DPS. The Robert Louis Stevenson novel adapted to the stage. A coming of age story complete with maps, hidden treasure, and the infamous Long John Silver.

Twelve Angry Men —Sherman Sergel (drama); 15M, 1 int; con; Dramatic. The jury in a murder trial struggles to reach a just verdict. May be done as *Twelve Angry Women* with an all-female cast.

Two Blind Mice —Samuel Spewack (comedy); 14M, 4W; 1 int; con; DPS. Two nice old ladies run a forgotten bureau, the Office of Medicinal Herbs, in Washington, D.C.

The Unexpected Guest —Agatha Christie (thriller); 7M, 3W; 1 int; con; French. A man is murdered on a country estate, and the most obvious suspect is a man who was reported dead two years before.

The Uninvited —Tim Kelly (thriller); 4M, 6W; 1 int; con; DPS. Stage adaptation of Dorothy Macardle's famous novel. Cliff End House holds a fascination for young Stella, but danger from the past awaits her there. The playscript clearly describes all the tricks needed for the ghost's appearance and other mysterious occurrences.

What a Life —Clifford Goldsmith (comedy); 8M, 10W, extras; 1 int; con; DPS. Perennial favorite Henry Aldrich gets in and out of several amusing scrapes.

What Every Woman Knows —J. M. Barrie (comedy); 7M, 4W; 4 int; per, 1900; French. An ambitious Scot marries a plain woman in exchange for the opportunity for an education, and later discovers that he loves her.

The Wind in the Willows — Alan Bennett (comedy); 25 characters, most can be played by either sex, doubling possible; area staging; animal costuming; French. Kenneth Grahames's characters Toad of Toad Hall, Rat, Mole, and Badger brought to the stage.

The Winslow Boy — Terence Rattigan (drama); 7M, 4W; 1 int; per, 1900s; DPS. A boy is unjustly expelled from military school and his family fights the case with all their means.

Years Ago — Ruth Gordon (comedy); 4M, 5W; 1 int; per, 1900s; DPS. A girl finally convinces her parents to allow her to try for a career on the stage.

Yellow Jack — Sidney Howard (drama); 26M, 1W; unit set; per, 1900 military; DPS. A dramatization of the experiments in Cuba which led to the discovery of the cure for yellow fever.

You Can't Take It with You — Moss Hart and George S. Kaufman (comedy); 9M, 7W; 1 int; con or per, the 1930s of the original production; DPS. The Sycamores, a family of happy individuals, find themselves in hilarious conflict with the conformist Kirbys. A staple of educational and community theatre. As much fun to do as to see.

READER'S THEATRE

Abe Lincoln in Illinois — Robert E. Sherwood (biography); 25M, 7W; platform; choral robes, evening dress or per, 19th century; DPS. The critical years of Lincoln's early manhood up to his election as president shown in a series of scenes.

Animal Farm — Nelson Bond (satire); 5M, 2W; bare stage; uniform costuming works best; French. George Orwell's tale of tragedy in a mythical barnyard becomes a fable for our times.

Back to Methuselah — Arnold Moss condensed version of George Bernard Shaw's cavalcade of mankind (drama); 17 readers; bare stage; uniform costuming; French. Beginning in the Garden of Eden, the play moves to a projection of the future—30,000 years from now.

The Hollow Crown — John Barton (historical); 3M, 1W, 3 singers; bare stage; evening dress or uniform costuming; French. The four readers present the royal writings from William I of England to Queen Victoria. The singers provide interludes with songs from the appropriate time periods. The singing may be eliminated or taped music substituted.

John Brown's Body —Stephen Vincent Benet (historical); 2M, 2W, may use more, plus chorus which speaks and sings; bare stage; choral robes or evening dress; DPS. Beginning with John Brown's attack on Harper's Ferry and going through the Civil War, the story is told from the point of view of a Union soldier and a Confederate soldier.

The Lark —Jean Anouilh, adapted by Lillian Hellman (drama); 15M, 5W; platform; con or per, medieval or uniform costuming; DPS. The interrogation, trial, and execution of Joan of Arc.

The Night Thoreau Spent in Jail —Jerome Lawrence and Robert E. Lee (biographical); 11M, 5W; platform; per, 19th century American or uniform costuming; French. An account of Henry David Thoreau's act of civil disobedience.

Poe! Poe! Poe! —Kathryn Schultz Miller (life and writings of Edgar Allan Poe); 2M, 2W, may use more; bare stage; per, 19th century or evening dress; Clark. Poe himself relates some of his most famous tales and poems.

The Roses of Eyam —Don Taylor (drama); 20M, 10W, 2 small children, extras; platform; choral robes or per, 17th century England; French. The true story of the village of Eyam that, stricken with the plague, sealed itself off from the rest of the country to prevent the spread of the disease. As the characters die the actors should leave the stage so that at the end the few who are left emphasize the tragedy.

Telling Wilde Tales —Adapted by Jules Tasca (the fairy tales of Oscar Wilde); flexible casting; platform; evening dress or uniform costuming; Baker. Not only for children, the Wilde tales teach hope and generosity and understanding. Includes "The Happy Prince," "The Star Child," and "The Nightingale and the Rose."

A Tide of Voices —Suzanne Granfield (historical); 4M, 1W, 1 singer, 1 guitarist; bare stage; per, Revolutionary War or evening dress or uniform costuming; French. The first seventeen months of the Revolutionary War are presented in touching vignettes.

Twain by the Tale —Dennis Snee (Revue); flexible casting, 5 actors minimum; bare stage; uniform costuming; French. Mark

Twain stories, sketches, and monologues show the wit and timeless perceptions of the writer.

Voices —Susan Griffin (drama); 5W; platform; con; French. A play in poetry about five women who neither know each other nor speak to each other—rather, they are telling their life stories to the audience (for a mature company).

Whisperings in the Grass —Suzanne Granville (historical); 5M, 1W, 1M singer/guitarist; bare stage; per, pioneer or uniform costuming; French. A group of inexperienced people begin the journey westward on the Oregon Trail.

The White House —A. E. Hotchner (historical); 7M, 3W; platform; evening dress or uniform costuming; French. From Washington to Wilson, the personal trials, tribulations, and tragedies of America's First Families.

The World of Carl Sandburg —Adapted by Norman Corwin (the prose and poetry of Sandburg); 2M, 1W; platform; evening dress or uniform costuming; French. The best of the Pulitzer Prize winner's verse and prose, including some unpublished works.

ONE-ACT PLAYS

Act Three, Scene Five —Terence Ortwein (comedy-romance); 1M, 4W; bare stage with rehearsal furniture; con; Baker. Five students are rehearsing Act 3, Scene 5 of *Romeo and Juliet,* but egos, inexperience, and jealousies are getting in the way.

Antic Spring —Robert Nail (comedy); 3M, 3W; no scenery required; con; French. Six oddly assorted young people go on a picnic and the result is great merriment.

The Apollo of Bellac —Jean Giraudoux, translated by Maurice Valency (satire); 9M, 3W; 1 int; con; French. A shy young woman learns that she can win any man she wants by comparing him to the nonexistent statue of the Apollo of Bellac.

The Bald Soprano —Eugene Ionesco (absurdist comedy); 3M, 3W; 1 int; con, maid's uniform, fireman's uniform; French. a satirical look at social conversation.

The Bishop's Candlesticks —Norman McKinnel (drama); 3M, 2W; 1 int; per, 18th century France; French. The famous scene from Victor Hugo's *Les Miserables* where the Bishop befriends the convict Jean Valjean.

The Bride Comes to Yellow Sky — Frank Crocicco (comedy); 4M, 1W; 1 int; per, The Old West; DPS. The Marshall of Yellow Sky brings home his bride to encounter an aging desperado.

The Cinderella Syndrome — V. Glasgow Koste (comedy); 5W; 1 int; con; Baker. Based on the famous story, this play is not specifically for children. It is a fresh look at kinship—mothers, stepmothers, and godmothers.

The Comedian — Tim Kelly (drama); 6M, 6W; bare stage; con; Baker. A group of young actors rehearses a play about the martyred St. Genesius, patron saint of actors and theatre. Each member of the cast plays a character of today as well as a character in ancient Rome. Easily staged.

A Cup of Tea — Ruth Sergel (drama); 2M, 4W; 1 int; con; Dramatic. Adapted from the Katherine Mansfield story of a selfish society woman who withholds help from a starving girl in order to buy an expensive trinket for herself.

Early Frost — Douglas Parkhirst (thriller); 5W; bare stage with props; con; French. Young Alice discovers a mystery while playing in her aunts' attic.

The Emperor's Nightingale — Dan Totheroh (comedy); 9M, 3W, extras; bare stage with props; Chinese costuming; French. The Hans Christian Andersen fairy tale about the emperor who loves the singing of the nightingale in his garden.

Feathertop — Maurice Valency (fantasy); 7M, 3W; unit set; per, 18th century America; DPS. Feathertop is a scarecrow, fashioned by a witch, who goes out into the world and succeeds.

The Frog Prince — David Mamet (comedy-fantasy); 2M, 2W; 1 ext; fairy-tale costuming or con; French. The old tale is told with modern sensibility and quite a few laughs.

The Ghost Story — Booth Tarkington (comedy); 5M, 5W; 1 int; con; Baker. Home from college, George longs to be alone with his girl, so he tries to frighten her friends away with a ghost story.

Goodbye to the Clown — Ernest Kinoy (drama); 3M, 3W; 2 int; con; French. Peggy insists on the presence of the clown, an imaginary playmate. As she is able to face the death of her father she is also able to say goodbye to the clown.

Guests of the Nation – Neil McKenzie (drama); 7M, 1W; unit set; Irish and English military uniforms; DPS. English soldiers are captured by Irish revolutionaries and the men become friends, but then the brutalities of war intrude.

The Happy Journey to Camden and Trenton – Thornton Wilder (comedy); 3M, 3W; bare stage with chairs; earlier 20th century American; French. A family journeys by car to visit a married daughter.

If Men Played Cards As Women Do – George S. Kaufman (comedy); 4M; 1 int; con; Baker. Classic sketch about men who act as they think women do at the bridge table.

If Women Worked As Men Do – Ellen Goodfellow (comedy); 4W; 1 int; con; Baker. A satire on the businessman's excuse of "a hard day at the office."

I'm a Fool – Christopher Sergel (comedy); 4M, 4W; bare stage with props; per, 1900s; Dramatic. The adaptation from Sherwood Anderson's short story about a stablehand who pretends to the beautiful girl he's just met that he's a wealthy horse owner.

Impromptu – Tad Mosel (drama); 2M, 2W; 1 int; con; DPS. Four actors sit on a darkened stage awaiting the stage manager. Without his authoritative presence they are merely characters in search of a play.

In the Zone – Eugene O'Neill (drama); 9M; 1 int; sailor costumes; DPS. Sailors open a shipmate's private box of letters and are ashamed at having treated him so shamefully.

The Long Christmas Dinner – Thornton Wilder (drama); 5M, 7W; 1 int; since the play's time covers ninety years and the actors have no time for costume changes, some festive "timeless" clothing is best; French. The history of a family told through a series of Christmas dinners.

The Lottery – Brainerd Duffield (drama); 8M, 5W, extras; bare stage; con; Dramatic. Adapted from Shirley Jackson's shocker about how a village ensures a good harvest.

The Man in the Bowler Hat – A. A. Milne (comedy); 4M, 2W; 1 int; con; French. The ordinary lives of John and Mary are filled, for a while, with excitement.

The Marriage Proposal – Anton Chekhov (comedy); 2M, 1W; 1 int; con or per, 1900s Russia; French nonroyalty. A nervous young man intends to propose to an attractive young woman, but instead gets into an argument with her.

A Minor Incident – Hindi Brooks (romance); 3M, 1W, extras; 1 ext; per, 1960s hippie; Clark. A young man and woman meet when their cars collide and class differences disappear as attraction takes over.

A Minuet – Louis N. Parker (drama); 2M, 1W; 1 int; per, 19th-century France; French. A French aristocrat and his estranged wife are reunited as they both await the guillotine. A powerful verse play.

The Monkey's Paw – W. W. Jacobs and Louis N. Parker (thriller); 4M, 1W; 1 int; con; French. A family is given a monkey's paw with mysterious powers.

Mooncalf Mugford – Brainerd Duffield and Helen and Nolan Leary (drama); 2M, 3W; 1 ext; con; Dramatic. Mooncalf is considered crazy because he talks to his dead friends and sees dragons in the ocean. He finally persuades his wife to join him in a land of dreams.

A Night at an Inn – Lord Dunsany (thriller); 8M; 1 int; con or per, early 19th century; French. The story of the retribution sent by an Eastern idol on some thieves who have stolen his ruby eye.

Nightmare – LeRoma Greth (thriller); 2M, 4W; 1 int; con; Dramatic. A young girl home from school for the summer finds her family and home strangely changed.

The Old Lady Shows Her Medals – J. M. Barrie (drama); 2M, 4W; 1 int; per, World War I or any wartime; French. An old woman invites a young soldier to spend his leave with her because she has no children of her own.

The Open Window – James Fuller (comedy); 1M, 3W; 1 int; con; Dramatic. The famous Saki short story of the young lady who convinces a visitor that he's seeing ghosts.

Pantaloon – J. M. Barrie (commedia); 4M, 1W; 1 int; commedia costumes; Players. The happiness of Harlequin and Columbine is threatened by the manipulative Clown.

Pullman Car Hiawatha – Thornton Wilder (drama); 15M, 18W; 1 int; con; French. The passengers in a Pullman railroad car are shown in their thoughts as the train passes through the countryside. Philosophical content.

Red Carnations – Glenn Huges (comedy); 2M, 1W; 1 ext; con; French. A delightful satire on romantic encounters.

Rest in Peace – Pat Cook (fantasy-spoof); 4M, 3W; 1 int; con and hospital uniforms; Dramatic. A patient mistakenly thinks he has died and he gets to hear what others really think about him.

Riders to the Sea – John M. Synge (drama); 1M, 3W; 1 int; per, early 20th-century Ireland; French, Baker. Baker's calls this the best one-act ever written. An old woman grieves over her five sons lost at sea while the sixth and last son prepares to go to sea.

The Rising of the Moon – Lady Gregory (comedy); 4M; 1 ext; con or per, early 20th century Ireland; French nonroyalty. A ballad singer encounters the policeman sent to arrest him, but they become friends. Even the promise of a reward does not keep the policeman from letting the man escape.

The Road to Corinth – Alan L. Steinberg (comedy); 4M, 8W; 1 int; per, ancient Greece; Players. Two bit players in a bad production of a Greek classic decide to take over the play, but in the end come to appreciate even their small contribution to the play.

The Slave with Two Faces – Mary Carolyn Davies (fantasy); 3M, 4W; 1 ext; con; French. A beautiful allegory that takes place in a forest. Two girls expect to meet Life and come to understand that one can be the master of Life or the slave of Life.

Suppressed Desires – Susan Glaspell (satire); 1M, 2W; 1 int; con; baker. Misapplied Freudian psychology almost results in divorce.

The Terrible Meek – Charles Rann Kennedy (religious drama); 2M, 1W; 1 int; per, first century A.D. Israel; French nonroyalty. The effect of the crucifixion of Jesus on a Roman captain, a soldier, and an unknown woman. The play is acted in total darkness until the dawn arrives.

This Is a Test – Stephen Gregg (comedy); flexible casting 13–15 actors, either sex; 1 int; con; Dramatic. The characters have only sixty minutes to complete a test that will predict their futures.

Trifles – Susan Glaspell (drama); 3M, 2W; 1 int; con; Baker. The wife of a murdered farmer is arrested on suspicion. Two neighbor women suppress evidence that could convict her.

The Trysting Place — Booth Tarkington (comedy); 4M, 3W; 1 int; con or per, 1920s; Baker. Four couples arrange to meet in the same hotel lobby and complications develop before each man can meet the intended partner.

The Twelve Pound Look — J. M. Barrie (satire); 2M, 2W; 1 int; con; French. A pompous man hires a temporary secretary, who turns out to be his former wife who had left him as soon as he had saved the twelve pounds to buy a typewriter.

The Ugly Duckling — A. A. Milne (comedy); 4M, 3W; 1 int; royal costumes; Baker. A man and woman, each fearing they are too plain for the other, arrange for an impersonation, but in a chance meeting fall in love anyway.

Undertow — Anne Weatherly (drama); 9W; 1 int; con; Baker. A young woman's jealous sister nearly destroys her happiness.

The Valiant — Holworthy Hall and Robert Middlemass (drama); 5M, 1W; 1 int; con; Baker. On the day of his execution a prisoner receives a visit from a young girl searching for her long-lost brother.

Who Am I This Time? — Kurt Vonnegut (comedy); 3M, 7W; area staging; con; Dramatic. An insecure young man and a shy young woman find themselves when they are on stage.

OF MULTICULTURAL INTEREST

The Amen Corner — James Baldwin (comedy); 4M, 10W; unit set; con; French. Love and forgiveness prove a necessity in the African American family, church, and community.

Cotton Patch Gospel — Tom Key, Russell Treyz, and Harry Chapin (musical); flexible casting; unit set; con-rural South; Dramatic. The gospel is presented in a setting of rural Georgia with country music songs.

Dear Me, the Sky Is Falling — Leonard Spigelgass (comedy); 5M, 7W; 1 int; con; French. Molly Goldberg is a Jewish matriarch who fearlessly takes on all the problems of the neighborhood.

The Diary of Anne Frank — Frances Goodrich and Albert Hackett (drama); 5M, 5W; 1 int; per, World War II; DPS. A young Jewish girl and her family are in hiding to escape the Nazis.

In White America — Martin B. Duberman (historical); 3 black (2M, 1W), 3 white (2M, 1W); platform; uniform costuming; French. The absorbing story of the African American in this country from slavery to Little Rock.

Kumi-Leml — Nahma Sandrow (musical farce); 6M, 2W; unit set; per, 1880s; French. An Orthodox Jewish father thinks he has found the perfect match for his young daughter, but she has her heart set on someone else.

Lady Precious Stream — S. I. Hsiung (romantic drama); 5M, 5W, extras; traditional Chinese scene and costumes; French. A lovely blend of fidelity, love, treachery, and poetry.

Martin Said So — Wanda Schell and Kenny Bento (drama); 3M (black), 3W (black), 2M (white); 1 int; con; Clark. When her great-granddaughter refuses to serve on a committee to celebrate the birthday of Dr. Martin Luther King, Jr., the woman decides to give the girl some glimpses of her heritage.

Purlie Victorious — Ossie Davis (comedy); 6M, 3W; 2 ext; per, early 19th-century southern U.S.; French. All the clichés about the old South are given a comic twist.

Raisin — Robert Nemiroff and Charlotte Zaltzberg (musical); 9M, 6W, chorus, extras; unit set; con; French. Lorraine Hansberry's *Raisin in the Sun* set to music.

Raisin in the Sun — Lorraine Hansberry (drama); 7M, 3W; 1 int; con; French. A poor black family in Chicago achieves greater maturity and dignity as they struggle to use $10,000 of insurance money wisely.

Remember My Name — Joanna Halpert Kraus (drama); 5M, 5W; area staging; per, World War II France; French. A young girl struggles to survive the Nazi threat in wartime France.

Spirit of Hispania — Jules Tasca (drama and comedy); 24M, 19W (if each tale is cast separately); bare stage and props; various costuming, including animals; Baker. Five short Hispanic plays that explore Latin American culture. Also available in Spanish.

A Star Ain't Nothin' But a Hole in Heaven — Judi Ann Mason (drama); 3M, 4W; 1 ext; per, 1960s rural Louisiana; French. A young black girl raised by her uncle and aunt must choose between accepting a scholarship to a northern college or staying in her hometown.

A Tale of Chelm — Arnold Perl (one-act farce); 5M, 3W; 1 ext; DPS. Yiddish tale of an angel, in charge of the distribution of souls, who accidentally spills her bag of stupid souls over one particular village.

Tevya and His Daughters — Arnold Perl (drama); 6M, 6W; bare stage; per, early 1900s Russia; DPS. Perl based his play on the stories of Sholom Aleichem and also gave permission for the musical *Fiddler on the Roof* to be based on the same stories. Tevya is concerned with making a good match for his two eldest daughters.

To Be Young, Gifted and Black — Lorraine Hansberry (autobiographical); flexible interracial casting; platform; con; French. A fast-paced, powerful, touching, and hilarious kaleidoscope of scenes from the life of the prize-winning playwright.

Yellow Jacket — George C. Hazelton and Benrima (Chinese fantasy); 17M, 12W, extras; 1 int; Chinese costuming; French. A young man passes through the stages of his life, finding adventure, excitement, satisfaction, and, at least, meaning.

MUSICALS

All American — Mel Brooks, Charles Strouse, and Lee Adams; 6M, 6W; con; Dramatic. A European professor is hired by a small college. His encounters with his adopted country, students, and fellow faculty lead all to greater understanding.

Anne of Green Gables — Donald Harron and Norman Campbell; 12M, 17W; per, 1900s; French. Musical version of Lucy Montgomery's story of the orphan girl who rises from destitution to happiness by virtue of her personality and determination.

Annie — Thomas Meeham, Charles Strouse, and Martin Charnin; 23M, 16W; per, 1930s; T-W. Optimistic Little Orphan Annie and her dog Sandy overcome the miseries of the Great Depression when rich Daddy Warbucks adopts her.

Annie Get Your Gun — Irving Berlin, and Herbert and Dorothy Fields; 22M, 13W, 2 children; per, late 1800s Wild West Show; R-H. Sharpshooter Annie Oakley becomes a success in Buffalo Bill's famous western show and falls in love with Frank Butler, her sharpshooting rival.

Anything Goes – Cole Porter, Guy Bolton, P. G. Wodehouse, Howard Lindsay, and Russel Crouse; 12M, 10W, chorus; per, 1930s; T-W (sophisticated). A young man disguises himself to be near the girl he loves as she sails to wed an English nobleman.

Babes in Arms – Richard Rodgers and Lorenz Hart; 19M, 6W, chorus; R-H; con. A group of teenagers, left on their own by their traveling actor parents, decide to put on a show to prove their own abilities.

Bells Are Ringing – Betty Comden, Adolph Green, and Jule Styne; 21M, 8W; T-W; modern. Ella works for a telephone answering service and gets involved in her customers' lives. She falls in love with Jeff, a down-in-his-luck writer, and sets out to help him.

Best Foot Forward – John Cecil Holm, Hugh Martin, and Ralph Blane; 12M, 10W, chorus; T-W; 1930s college setting. Undergraduates of Winsocki U. invite a famous Hollywood starlet to the big dance. The boys' rivalries and their girlfriends' jealousies cause confusion.

Big River – Roger Miller and William Hauptman; 22M, 10W, extras, doubling possible; per, mid-19th century rural America; R-H. Mark Twain's *Huckleberry Finn* adventures.

Bloomer Girl – Sig Herzig, Fred Saidy, Harold Arlen, and E. Y. Harburg; cast 28; T-W; 1880s. The play deals with the early American Suffragette movement and the scandal caused when Harriet Bloomer invents a new type of female undergarment.

The Boy Friend – Sandy Wilson; Music; 1926; 8M, 8W; a spoof of 20s musicals. Polly attends a fashionable finishing school when she falls for Tony, a delivery boy. She pretends to be a working girl until she learns that Tony is really a nobleman.

Brigadoon – Alan Jay Lerner and Frederick Loewe; 13M, 5W; 18th-century Scotland and con. Tommy and Jeff get lost on a hunting trip and find themselves taken back in time when they discover a Scottish village that comes into being for only one day each century.

Bye Bye Birdie – Michael Stewart, Charles Strouse, and Lee Adams; 20M, 22W; T-W; con. Conrad Birdie, an Elvis-type singer, has been drafted, and his manager concocts a final publicity stunt; he will kiss a typical teenage girl farewell on national TV.

Calamity Jane — Charles K. Freeman, Sammy Fain, and Paul Francis Webster, based on the movie; cast 19; T-W; the Dakota Territory, 1876. Jane rides and shoots like a man, but she hankers to be a lady after she meets a handsome lieutenant. She tries to make herself over but then realizes it is Wild Bill Hickock that she loves.

Call Me Madam — Irving Berlin, Howard Lindsay, and Russel Crouse; 16M, 4W; Music, modern. Sally Adams, the American ambassador to the tiny country of Lichtenberg, is involved in intrigue when a member of her staff falls in love with the country's Princess and she finds herself attracted to the Prime Minister.

Camelot — Alan Jay Lerner and Frederick Loewe; 16M, 6W; T-W; medieval England. King Arthur must deal with the treachery of his nephew Mordred and the problems of the knights of his Round Table. His dreams of a peaceful world based on chivalry are destroyed when Queen Guinevere falls in love with Sir Lancelot.

Carnival! — Bob Merrill and Michael Stewart; cast 20; T-W; con. Lilli, a lonely orphan, joins a third-rate European traveling circus and is infatuated with a handsome magician. A crippled and bitter puppeteer loves her, but can only express himself through his puppets.

Carousel — Richard Rodgers and Oscar Hammerstein; 16M, 4W; R-H; 1880s New England. Billy Bigelow marries Julie. His inability to express love or to provide for her leads to attempted robbery and his death. An angel helps him return to make retribution to Julie and his daughter.

Cinderella — Richard Rodgers and Oscar Hammerstein; 2M, 5W; R-H; fairy-tale fantasy. The classic story of the rags-to-riches girl is complete with wicked stepmother, ugly stepsisters, a fairy godmother, and a handsome Prince Charming.

Curley McDimple — Mary Boylan & Robert Dahdah; 3M, 4W, 1 child; French; 1930s, a satire on "Shirley Temple–type" movies. A curly-haired orphan teams up with a down-and-out dance team, and they become big-time vaudeville stars before Curley is reunited with her long-lost rich grandfather.

Dames at Sea — George Haimsohn, Robin Miller, and Jim Wise; 3M, 3W; French; a parody of 1930s movie musicals. A sweet hometown girl comes to New York to be a dancing star. She steps in for an ailing star, saves the show, and achieves her goal.

Damn Yankees — George Abbott, Douglas Wallop, Richard Adler, and Jerry Ross, 18M, 6W, chorus; Music; 1950s. A middle-aged fan of the Washington Senators makes a pact with the Devil who transforms him into a young long-ball hitter who can lead the Senators to victory over the NY Yankees in the World Series.

Desert Song — Otto Harbach, Oscar Hammerstein, Frank Mandel, and Sigmund Romberg (operetta); 11M, 7W, dancers and singers; 5 int, 5 ext; French. A girl, longing for adventure, doesn't realize that her mild-mannered suitor actually is the heroic Red Shadow, leader of the Riff uprising in Morocco.

Donnybrook! — Robert McEnroe and Johnny Burke, 9M, 5W; French; con; Ireland. An American boxer comes to Ireland to settle down and, with the help of a matchmaker, marries a spirited colleen but antagonizes her fierce-tempered brother in doing so.

Ernest in Love — Anne Croswell and Lee Pockriss; 10M, 6W; Music; Victorian England, based on Oscar Wilde's *The Importance of Being Earnest*. Two young gentlemen create confusion by inventing fictitious relatives and dual identities.

Fade Out – Fade In — Betty Comden, Adolph Green, and Jule Styne; cast 26; T-W; 1930s Hollywood. Hope Springfield's rise from being an usher in a movie house to becoming a legendary film star provides slapstick satire.

The Fantasticks — Tom Jones and Harvey Schmidt; 7M, 1W; Music; simple, open staging. Two fathers pretend to feud so that their offspring will be attracted to each other. When they hire a bandit to stage a kidnapping, the girl falls in love with her captor instead.

Fiddler on the Roof — Joseph Stein, Jerry Bock, and Sheldon Harnick; 12M, 10W, chorus; Music; 19th century Russia. Tevye, a Jewish dairyman, follows the dictates of "tradition," but he must learn to adapt to his daughters' different views of life and contend with Russian pogroms.

Finian's Rainbow — Burton Lane, E. Y. Harburg, and Fred Saidy; 24M, 4W; T-W; modern. To the mythical Missitucky, U.S.A.; comes the Irishman Finian, who buries some gold stolen from a leprechaun. Greed and the appearance of the leprechaun cause problems.

Fiorello! – Jerome Weidman, George Abbott, Jerry Bock, and Sheldon Harnick; cast 35; T-W; early 20th century. New York City's most famous mayor, Fiorello LaGuardia, must fight Tammany Hall politicians, police corruption, and sweatshop factory owners.

First Impressions – Abe Burrows, Robert Goldman, Glenn Paxton, and George Weiss; 14M, 12W; French; from Jane Austen's *Pride and Prejudice,* early 19th-century England. Mrs. Bennett wishes to marry her five daughters to men of status and wealth. Happily, the girls succeed in spite of her.

Flower Drum Song – Richard Rodgers and Oscar Hammerstein; 11M, 7W, chorus; R-H; modern San Francisco Chinatown. Mei Li, a mail-order bride, is rejected by her intended husband, who sells her contract to Wang Ta's father. Wang spurns her, but eventually realizes she is the girl for him.

Frank Merriwell – Skip Redwine, Larry Frank, and Heywood Gould; 7M, 6W; 1890s, a parody on boys' adventure stories. Frank, a good, clean, thrifty, trustworthy, and reverent college boy, must foil a sinister plot to blow up the country.

George M! – Michael Stewart, John and Fran Pascal, and George M. Cohan; cast 35; T-W; 1878–1937. Cohan's life is traced from his birth into a vaudeville family to becoming America's "Yankee Doodle Kid," despite his ambition that causes conflict in his private life.

Girl Crazy – George and Ira Gershwin, Guy Bolton, and Mack McGowan; 16M, 12W, chorus; T-W; con. A rich playboy is sent West by his father, hoping the rough life will straighten the young man out. Instead, he starts a dude ranch and imports chorus girls.

Goldilocks – Jean Kerr, Walter Kerr, Leroy Anderson, and Joan Ford; 8M, 3W; French; 1920s, a satire on Hollywood. A silent movie producer, obsessed with doing a stupendous Egyptian movie, keeps his backers and his star by a series of conniving schemes.

Good News – Laurence Schwab, B. G. DeSylva, Lew Brown, and Ray Henderson; 10M, 5W; French; 1920s college setting.

323

A campus football hero can't play in the big game unless he passes his astronomy exam. A demure coed tutors him, and he ends up winning the game and the girl.

Greenwillow — Frank Loesser and Lesser Samuels; Music; rustic, rural fantasy. For generations the eldest son of the Briggs family is cursed by the "call" to wander. Gideon loves Dorrie, but he will not follow his heart because one day his "call" will come.

Guys and Dolls — Frank Loesser, Jo Swerling, and Abe Burrows; 15M, 4W, chorus; Music; New York City, 1950s. A Salvation Army sergeant, determined to save her mission from closing, accepts the help of a local gambler who has romance in mind. A comic subplot concerns a night club singer's attempts to get her longtime boyfriend to the altar.

Half a Sixpence — Beverley Cross and David Heneker; 12M, 11W; Dramatic; 1900, England. Kipps, an apprentice in a draper's shop, dreams of being wealthy. A surprise inheritance realizes his dream, but he gives up his new life to return to his sweetheart.

Hallelujah, Baby! — Arthur Laurents, Jule Styne, Betty Comden, and Adolph Green; Music; early 20th century to modern times. Georgina, dissatisfied with the kind of servile life blacks have been forced to live, comes into conflict with her mother who is satisfied with the *status quo.*

Happy Hunting — Howard Lindsay, Russel Crouse, Matt Dubey, and Harold Karr; 6M, 5W, chorus; Music; con. A rich Philadelphia hostess is determined to snare a titled husband for her daughter Beth, but she finds herself falling in love with the royal duke she has "purchased" for Beth.

Hello, Dolly! — Michael Stewart and Jerry Herman, based on Thornton Wilder's *The Matchmaker;* 8M, 6W, chorus; T-W; the Gay '90s. Dolly Levi, a matchmaker, finds a wife for the miserly merchant, Horace Vandergelder, but when the girl prefers Horace's clerk, Dolly is forced to change her calculations.

Henry, Sweet Henry — Nunnally John and Bob Merrill, based on the novel *The World of Henry Orient;* 8M, 8W; French; modern. Two teenage girls decide that a debonair, avant-garde composer is the man of their dreams and set out to secretly follow him everywhere.

Here's Love — Meredith Willson and Valentine Davis; 10M, 10W, chorus; Music; based on the film "Miracle on 34th Street"; con. When Doris hires an old man named Kris Kringle to enact Santa Claus for Macy's Department Store, she finds she may be dealing with the legendary elf himself.

High Button Shoes — Stephen Longstreet, Jule Styne, and Sammy Cahn; cast 19; T-W. Charming turn of the century romp featuring a Keystone Kops ballet.

High Spirits — Hugh Martin and Timothy Gray; 3M, 7W; T-W; based on Nöel Coward's *Blithe Spirit;* con. During a séance, the first wife of Charles is accidentally called back from the dead, causing his current wife to be none too pleased. (Rigging for flying sequences required.)

How to Succeed in Business Without Really Trying — Frank Loesser, Abe Burrows, Jack Weinstock, and Willie Gilbert, 18M, 8W, chorus; Music; satire on big business. J. Pierrepont Finch overcomes all obstacles on his climb to a position of power, not due to any work on his part, but rather by being sneakier than those who try to stop him.

The Human Comedy — William Dumaresque and Galt MacDermot; (folk opera); 12M, 10W, extras; unit set; French. William Saroyan's novel about small-town life during World War II, adapted to the stage.

Into the Woods — Stephen Sondheim and James Lapine; 9M, 12W; some parts are doubled; fairy-tale costuming; Music. The first act works out the familiar fairy tales, while the second act tells what happened afterward.

Irene — Hugh Wheeler, Harry Tierney, Joseph McCarthy, and Joseph Stein; cast 14; T-W; 1919. Enterprising Irene runs a piano store. Called to the Marshall mansion, to tune their piano, she meets the young heir who is impressed by Irene's head for business as well as her looks.

Kiss Me, Kate — Cole Porter and Bella and Samuel Spewack, based on Shakespeare's *The Taming of the Shrew;* 10M, 3W; T-W; modern and Shakespearan. Fred needs his ex-wife for his musical version of the Bard's *Shrew.* When she threatens to walk out, he relies on the aid of two gangsters to keep her in the show.

Legend of Sleepy Hollow — John P. Donaldson and Herbert S. French; 9M, 7W, several children; French. Taken from Washington Irving's story of Ichabod Crane's rivalry with Brom Bones for the love of Katrina Van Tassel.

Li'l Abner — Norman Panama, Melvin Frank, Johnny Mercer, and Gene dePaul, based on Al Capp's cartoon strip; cast 46; T-W. Dogpatch's citizens are caught in Gen. Bullmoose's scheme to turn Mammy Yokum's tonic into a secret weapon. (The political satire needs to be updated.)

Little Mary Sunshine — Rick Besoyan; 6M, 3W; French; a spoof of operettas. A lovely heroine, a stalwart captain of the Colorado Rangers, and a villainous Indian are involved in a complicated and funny plot.

Me and My Girl — L. Arthur Rose, Douglas Furber, and Stephen Fry; 11M, 8W, chorus; French. A young cockney turns out to be heir to a title and wins over the aristocrats with his brash charm.

The Me Nobody Knows — Robert Livingston, Herb Shapiro, Will Holt, and Gary William Friedman; cast of 12, both sexes; French. Adapted from the writings of ghetto children, their thoughts, dreams, and observations. Music has rock flavor.

Meet Me in St. Louis — Hugh Wheeler, Hugh Martin, and Ralph Blane; cast 20; per, 1900s; T-W. Musical version of the Sally Benson novel and Christopher Sergel play that provided a nostalgic look at a St. Louis family in the time of the World's Fair.

Mr. President — Irving Berlin, Howard Lindsay, and Russel Crouse; Music; modern. A fictitious American president, his wife, and two children must deal with national and world crises as well as cope with family problems.

The Music Man — Meredith Willson and Franklin Lacy; 13M, 19W, chorus; Music; Iowa, 1912. Harold Hill, a fast-talking charlatan, fleeces the citizens of River City by promising to teach their children how to play band instruments. In the end, he is transformed by the love of the town librarian.

My Fair Lady — Alan Jay Lerner and Frederick Loewe, based on George Bernard Shaw's *Pygmalion;* cast 23; T-W; Edwardian England. To win a wager, Henry Higgins takes Eliza, a Cockney flower girl, and transforms her into a lady, elegant enough to be mistaken for a princess at an embassy ball.

No, No, Nanette — Otto Harback, Frank Mandel, Vincent Youmans, and Irving Caesar; 3M, 7W, chorus; T-W; 1920s.

Nanette seems to have everything: money, a loving family, and the handsome Tom. What she really wants, however, is to be like her flapper girlfriends and to go to Atlantic City.

Oh! Kay – George and Ira Gershwin, Guy Bolton, and P. G. Wodehouse; T-W; 1920s. Kay and her brother have taken up bootlegging to improve the family finances and are using the estate of wealthy Jimmy Winter as a cache.

Oklahoma! – Richard Rodgers and Oscar Hammerstein; 9W, 14M, chorus; R-H; the Oklahoma Territory. Laurey must decide between the charming but exasperating Curly and the surly farmhand, Jud, as to who will escort her to the box social.

Oliver! – Lionel Bart, based on Charles Dickens' *Oliver Twist*; 9M, 7W, chorus; T-W; 19th-century London. The orphan Oliver runs away and is befriended by the Artful Dodger and Fagin, who teach him how to pick pockets.

On a Clear Day You Can See Forever – Alan Jay Lerner and Burton Lane; 16M, 7W; T-W; con. Daisy, under hypnosis, tells Mark, a psychiatrist, of a former life as Melinda in 18th-century England. Mark finds himself in love with Melinda, while Daisy falls in love with Mark.

110 in the Shade – N. Richard Nash, Harvey Schmidt, and Tom Jones; cast 19; T-W; con West. Starbuck, a con man, arrives and claims he can end the drought that is parching the country. Unattractive Lizzie is scornful, but soon comes to realize that love can make a plain person beautiful.

The Pajama Game – George Abbott, Richard Bissell, Richard Adler, and Jerry Ross; 10M, 6W, chorus; Music; con. Sid, the foreman of a pajama factory, is caught in a management and labor dispute, especially after he falls in love with a union organizer.

Peter Pan – J. M. Barrie, Carolyn Leigh, Mark Charlap, Jule Styne, Betty Comden, and Adolph Green; 28 characters, both sexes; French; 19th century and fantasy. Peter, the boy who refused to grow up, encounters the evil Captain Hook, pirates, Indians, and three English children. (Rigging for flying sequences is required.)

The Pirates of Penzance – W. S. Gilbert and Arthur Sullivan (operetta); 14M, 14W, some doubling; 2 ext; per, Victorian, pirate, police; T-W. The Sergeant-Major's daughters find romance with some not-very-wicked pirates.

Plain and Fancy —Joseph Stein, William Glickman, Arnold Horwitt, and Albert Hague; 19M, 11W; French; con and Amish. While visiting in Pennsylvania, a New Yorker learns about Amish speech, dress, and lifestyle, as well as witnessing a barn raising and a "shunning."

Redhead —Herbert and Dorothy Fields, Sidney Sheldon, David Shaw, and Albert Hague; 8M, 7W, chorus; Music; Victorian England. Essie, who works in a wax museum, has visions that get her into trouble when they show her the fiendish strangler who is terrifying London.

The Roar of the Greasepaint—The Smell of the Crowd — Leslie Bricusse and Anthony Newley; cast 5; T-W; fantasy. Overbearing "Sir" and humble "Cocky" meet to play *The Game*. Cocky can't win because Sir keeps changing the rules until Cocky begins to assert himself.

Robert and Elizabeth —Ronald Millar, Ron Grainer, and Fred Morrit, based on the play *The Barretts of Wimpole Street,* 30M, 10W; French; London, 1845. A tyrannical father holds his children's lives in a tight grip, but his authority is bested when his daughter, Elizabeth, falls in love with the poet, Robert Browning.

The Secret Garden —Marsha Norman and Lucy Simon; 12M, 10W, extras, some doubling; backdrop and detail scenery, projections; per, 1900s; Music. A young orphan comes to live with her reclusive uncle and manages to bring him back into world through their mutual love of a beautiful garden.

Seventeen —Sally Benson, Kim Gannon, and Walter Kent, based on Booth Tarkington's novel; 13M, 12W; French; Indiana, 1907. Willie Baxter falls for a summer visitor, the baby-talking Lola. He must contend with other suitors, his parents, and his pesky little sister.

1776 —Sherman Edwards and Peter Stone; 25M, 2W; Music; American Revolution. John Adams, Benjamin Franklin, Thomas Jefferson, and other founding fathers quarrel and compromise during a hot summer to achieve agreement.

She Loves Me —Joe Masteroff, Jerry Bock, and Sheldon Harnick; 9M, 8W, small chorus; 1 int, 2 side settings; per, 1930s; T-W. Two people who work together dislike one another, not knowing each is the other's pen pal.

Shenandoah — Gary Geld, Peter Udell, James Lee Barrett, and Philip Rose; 11M, 3W; Music; Civil War era. A farmer tries to keep his sons out of war, but after one is killed by raiders and another is kidnapped, he finds he must become involved.

Show Boat — Jerome Kern and Oscar Hammerstein, based on Edna Ferber's novel; R-H; 1890s to 1920s. Magnolia leaves her father's show boat to marry a handsome gambler. After he deserts her, she returns; years later, they are reunited.

Silk Stockings — Cole Porter, George S. Kaufman, Lueen McGrath, and Abe Burrows; cast 32; T-W; con. A beautiful Russian, in Paris, falls in love with an American. Fearing defection, the Soviets send three agents to bring her back, but they too are transformed by Western freedom.

Skyscraper — Peter Stone, Sammy Cahn, and James Van Heusen; 11M, 5W; French; modern. A spirited young woman takes on city government when her antique brownstone in New York is threatened by the building of a new skyscraper.

The Sound of Music — Richard Rodgers, Oscar Hammerstein, Howard Lindsay, and Russel Crouse; 9M, 14W; R-H; Austria, late 1930s. Maria becomes governess to the motherless Von Trapp children, who are enchanted by her. Their father falls in love with her, but all must flee when the Nazis take over.

South Pacific — Richard Rodgers & Oscar Hammerstein; 22M, 13W, chorus; R-H; WW II Navy nurse Nellie Forbush falls in love with planter Emile DeBecque, despite their difference in age, but she rejects him when she learns he has half-caste children. She comes to learn that love is stronger than prejudice.

The Student Prince — Sigmund Romberg and Dorothy Donnelly; cast 20; T-W; 19th-century Heidelberg. The operetta about a prince who falls in love with a commoner while attending a famous German university. Duty calls, and he must leave his love behind. Good singing voices are required.

A Tree Grows in Brooklyn — Betty Smith, George Abbott, Arthur Schwartz, and Dorothy Fields, French; early 20th century. A young girl grows to maturity in a colorful Irish-American family. Based on the famous novel.

Two by Two — Richard Rodgers, Peter Stone, and Martin Charnin; 4M, 4W; R-H; Biblical. Noah must contend with his youngest son who neither wishes to marry the girl of Noah's choice nor to board the ark before the onset of the Flood.

The Unsinkable Molly Brown – Meredith Willson and Richard Morris; 28M, 9W, Music; 19th & 20th centuries. Molly marries Leadville Johnny Brown who strikes it rich. Her attempts to enter high society cause problems, but not even the sinking of the *Titantic* can keep her down.

Walking Happy – Roger O. Hirson, Ketti Frings, Sammy Cahn, and James Van Heusen; 14M, 7W; French; 19th-century England. The daughter of a shoemaker rebels against her stern father, opens her own shop, and marries his humble bootmaker, transforming the lad in the process.

West Side Story – Arthur Laurents, Leonard Bernstein, and Stephen Sondheim; 22M, 15W; Music; con. Tony, a member of the Jets, falls in love with Maria, sister of the leader of the Puerto Rican Sharks. He is caught between his new emotions and his old loyalties.

Where's Charley? – Frank Loesser and George Abbott, based on the play *Charley's Aunt;* 8M, 3W, chorus; Music; Victorian England. Jack convinces Charley to masquerade as his own aunt, a rich widow from Brazil. When Jack's father arrives, Charley must play both himself *and* his aunt.

Wildcat – N. Richard Nash, Carolyn Leigh, and Cy Coleman; cast 17; T-W; American West. A beautiful, red-haired oil prospector competes with rough and tumble oil riggers to bring in a gusher.

Wish You Were Here – Arthur Kober, Joshua Logan, and Harold Rome; 5M, 2W, chorus; Music; con. Teddy can't decide whether to go ahead with her marriage, so she joins her girlfriend at Camp Carefree. When she meets Chick, her confusion about her future increases.

The Wiz – William F. Brown and Charlie Smalls, based on *The Wizard of Oz;* T-W; fantasy. The well-known story of Dorothy, the Scarecrow, the Tinman, and the Cowardly Lion is retold from a modern perspective with an African American cast.

The Wizard of Oz – Frank Gabrielson, Harold Arlen, and E. Y. Harburg; cast 11, both sexes; T-W; fantasy. The most famous version of Dorothy's journey through Munchkinland and the Land of Oz, containing all the well-known songs.

Wonderful Town – Joseph Fields, Jerome Chodorov, Leonard Bernstein, Betty Comden, and Adolph Green, based on the play *My Sister Eileen;* cast 42; T-W; 1930s. Ruth and Eileen leave Ohio and come to New York to achieve careers. They endure the indignities of big city life and eventually are rewarded with success.

You're a Good Man, Charlie Brown —Clark Gesner, based on the comic strip "Peanuts"; 4M, 2W; T-W; con. An average day in the life of that famous loser, Charlie Brown, is enacted with his pals, Snoopy, Linus, Lucy, Schroeder, and Patty.

Glossary

abstract set A set that uses drapes, free-standing doors, and window frames to convey the idea of a setting, without any actual set construction.

act A major division of a play.

acting area The space, be it stage, platform, or floor, set aside for performing the play.

action The movement in the play from the initial entanglement to the resolution.

actor One who performs a role or represents a character in a play. The term now is used both for male and female.

actor-proof Well written enough to survive even a poor performance.

ad-lib To improvise something—dialog, stage business—not given specifically in the script but indicated by such directions as "The crowd ad-libs surprise."

amphitheatre A large, oval-shaped building with no roof and tiers of spectator seats.

antagonist The character who provides the obstacle to the protagonist's objective in the play.

apron The area of the stage in front of the curtain line.

arena stage An open space at floor level with the audience seated on all sides of the acting area.

arras set A set that uses a cyclorama curtain rather than scenery.

aside Words spoken by an actor so that the audience can hear them but, by convention, the other actors can't.

assistant director   The person who assists the director by keeping the blocking plot, making note of all script changes, working with the actors to help them learn lines, prompting the actors in the first rehearsals off book, and acting as messenger to backstage crews when the director is conducting rehearsals.

audition   The opportunity to read for a part in a play.

avant garde   Literally, the advance guard, especially in the arts. In theatre, those on the cutting edge whose work is experimental and unorthodox.

backdrop   A flat surface the width of the stage, usually made of canvas, hanging from the flies at the rear of the staging area and painted to represent the desired setting.

backstage   The area behind the set or backdrop that is not seen by the audience.

ballad opera   A production in which sections of dialogue alternate with lyrics set to already-popular songs.

bit part   A small role consisting of a very few lines and a brief appearance on stage.

black box   A small theatre without a proscenium arch in which the interior—walls, ceiling, floor—is painted black.

blackout   A lighting cue that requires the lighting technician to totally darken the entire stage in a split second.

blocking   Determining the basic movements of the actors during a play, including entrances, exits, and crosses.

blocking plot   A series of diagrams of the stage floor with the blocking marked.

book show   A musical play that has a plot and spoken dialogue.

box set   A setting of three walls and a ceiling, leaving the fourth wall to be imagined by the actors. As nearly as possible the set represents a real room.

break a leg   A traditional greeting to an actor, given just before a performance.

Bugaku   The earliest form of Japanese theatre, it is a series of austere dances accompanied by drums, flutes, and gongs.

burlesque A type of comedy in which characters, stage business, dialogue, and costumes are so exaggerated as to destroy any illusion of reality.

call The time established for the actors and techies to report to their stations before a performance.

callback The second stage in the audition process, in which actors who are under serious consideration for a role are asked to return for further readings or interviews.

call board A bulletin board placed backstage upon which schedules, announcements, and even reviews are posted for cast and crew.

cast All the actors performing in a given play.

casting The process of auditions and interviews by which the director selects the cast for a play.

catharsis The sense of release felt by the audience at the end of a tragedy.

catwalk A metal bridge in the flies, near the roof of the stage.

centering An actor's term for concentrating, focusing on the work at hand and being in character.

character role A major role in a play, but not one of the romantic leads. Often used to describe a character unlike the actor playing the role in terms of age, voice, or physical characteristics.

cheat To turn the body out, partially toward the audience, while appearing to talk directly to another character on stage.

chorus In Greek drama, the group of performers who sang and danced between the episodes of the play. Now commonly used to designate a group of performers who sing, dance, or recite together in a production.

cold reading An audition where the actors are asked to read from a script without any preparation.

collaborative theatre A situation in which the actors and director, and sometimes the playwright as well, work together to develop the book for a play.

comedy Generally, a play of a happy nature, light of spirit, and amusing dialogue, in which any serious disaster is averted.

335

comedy of manners A comedy in which the manners and mores of a given segment of society are held up to ridicule.

commedia dell'arte Sixteenth- to eighteenth-century Italian comedy of an improvisational nature using stock characters.

community theatre Amateur productions by residents of a locality, generally cast by open auditions.

comp A complimentary, or free, ticket to a show.

company A group of actors and technicians who join together to produce a play. The members function as a team.

complication An incident that further tangles the plot.

concentration The actor's focus on the moment of the play in which he or she is acting.

confidant (fem. **confidante**) A close friend of the principal character.

conflict The opposition to the protagonist in a play. It may be circumstances or people.

costume Clothing worn by the actors during a performance.

costume building The actual sewing together of a costume.

costume plot A list of costumes and accessories, indicating when and by whom they will be worn, and notes about quick changes and the like.

costume shop The area where the costumes for a play are built, maintained, and stored.

crash box A narrow, high-sided wooden box with a lead weight at the bottom and a close-fitting lid, placed just offstage, into which an actor or props person can hurl a glass or plate to create the sound of breakage.

critic A writer who evaluates and analyzes plays according to accepted aesthetic principles.

cross A stage direction meaning to move across the stage from one side to the other.

cross over A stage direction meaning for one character to cross the stage from one direction while another crosses from the other direction.

cue A signal from the stage manager to actor, stage crew, props person, sound or lighting technician that some predetermined action, such as an entrance or a sound effect, is required. Also used by actors to mean the line immediately before their own.

curtain call   The moment at the conclusion of the performance when the cast bows to the audience in acknowledgment of the applause.

cyclorama (cyc)   A fabric drape hung from the flies to create a semicircular backdrop for a performance.

dance captain   The leader of the chorus in a musical show, also responsible for teaching steps to the dancers after the choreographer has demonstrated them.

declaim   To act using broad gestures and overly dramatic line readings.

decor   The "look" of the show, including the costumes, set, furnishings, and props.

decorum   A manner appropriate to the time, place, and characters of the play.

detail scenery   Small, easily changed pieces of scenery in a larger formal setting, or placed in front of a setting and removed at a scene or act change.

deus ex machina   A god introduced into the middle of a conflict who uses supernatural means to solve all the problems of the characters in the drama.

dialogue   Speech between two or more characters.

dimmer   An electronic device to raise or lower the intensity of a stage light.

director   The person responsible for the direction of the actors in a play, that is, the one who determines such matters as tempo and interpretation.

doubling   The playing of more than one character in a play by the same actor.

dress parade   A wardrobe check during which the actors wear their various costume changes through a kind of parade that enables the director and costumer to check the colors under lighting, as well as the fit and appropriateness of each costume.

dress rehearsal   The last rehearsal before a play is performed for the public. It is done in full costume and technical effects, with no stopping for mistakes.

dutching   To glue a strip of canvas over the crack between two flats in order to provide a seamless set.

dynamic character   One who grows and changes throughout the course of the play.

educational theatre   Theatre connected with school and having educational, rather than commercial, goals.

emotional recall   An acting technique using some personal emotion to trigger emotion in a scene onstage.

ensemble playing   The type of acting in which a cast works as a team to create a total effect rather than a group of individual performances.

entanglement   The events that complicate the plot of a play.

exposition   Information relayed to establish location, time, circumstances, and background for the play.

extravaganza   An elaborate, lavish, spectacular production, usually musical, with a large cast, expensive costumes, and grand sets.

fade   A gradual dimming of the stage lighting. Also a gradual change in music volume.

farce   An extreme form of comedy that depends on quick tempo and flawless timing by the actors.

flat   The basic unit of stage scenery. It consists of a wooden frame with canvas or muslin stretched to fill it and a wooden crosspiece for backing.

flies   The area above the stage, hidden from the audience by a border or drapery, to which scenery can be flown, or lifted clear of the stage.

focus   The adjustment of the size and shape of a beam from a stage light *or* the direction the beam is aimed. Also, the direction of an actor's attention, action, or line delivery.

gel   A very thin sheet of gelatin, available in a wide range of colors, set in a frame, and mounted in front of a stage light in order to color the beam directed onto the set.

genre   Type—in this case, a type of drama. The main genres of drama are tragedy, comedy, melodrama, and farce.

gobo   A disc of heat-resistant material into which a pattern has been cut. When placed over the lens of an ellipsoidal spotlight, the pattern is projected onto a backdrop.

greenroom   A room backstage or nearby where actors wait for their entrance cues. Also, a place to assemble after a performance to hear the director's notes.

ground row   Small scenery standing independently onstage, such as a hedge or fence.

hero (fem. **heroine**)   The protagonist of a play.

house   The seating area of a theatre; also, the audience itself.

housekeeping   Keeping the work areas in a theatre clean and organized, as well as keeping tools in good repair.

house left/right   Directions viewed from the perspective of the audience.

house manager   One who oversees or runs the box office of a theatre, hires and instructs the ushers, and attends to the safety and comfort of the audience.

improvisation   A spontaneous scene or episode created by an actor or actors without a script.

inflection   Vocal modulation, variety in pitch.

ingenue   The young, attractive, innocent female lead in a play, and generally the romantic interest.

juvenile   The male counterpart to the ingenue and her partner in the romantic plot.

Kabuki   A type of Japanese theatre consisting of three types of plays: historical, dance-plays, and domestic dramas.

lazzo (plural **lazzi**)   The bits of comic business and gimmicks performed by the clown characters in the commedia dell'arte.

lead   The principal actor in a production.

lighting instrument   The lamp, reflector, lens, and housing which together make up the piece of equipment used to light a stage.

lighting plot   The detailed plan by the lighting designer that indicates the position and type of each lighting instrument to be used in a production, as well as a cue sheet for the technician running the lights in performance.

line reading   The manner in which an actor delivers a line: the inflection, tone, volume, and pace used.

load-in   The positioning of the set on the stage.

makeup   The cosmetics that actors wear onstage.

mainstage production   The major production of the school term.

mansion setting   The use of a series of simple constructions on small platforms, each one representing a different locale.

mask   To use flats or drapes to block the sightlines of audience members so they cannot see beyond the set of a play.

melodrama   Drama originating in nineteenth-century England that relies heavily on sensationalism and sentimentality.

message plays   Plays that propose solutions to problems.

mixed media performance   A presentation that mixes live performers with electronic elements such as projected slides, films, video tapes, and recorded music.

monologue   A work written to be performed by just one person.

motivation   The reason a character does something.

musical theatre   A type of entertainment containing music, songs, and, usually, dance.

Noh   A highly stylized form of Japanese theatre.

notes   Director's comments, given after a rehearsal or performance, discussing what was good and what still needs work.

notices   The singling out of an actor or actors for special mention in the published review of a play.

obstacle   A character or situation in a play that creates conflict, that delays or prevents another character from achieving an objective.

on/off book   When an actor has his or her lines memorized, the actor is off book. When an actor still needs the script, the actor is on book.

participatory theatre   A type of play that involves the audience in the performance.

performance space   The area, be it stage or platform or room, where a play is performed.

periaktos A three-sided prism made of flats and mounted on casters so that it can be turned to show a different background on each side.

period piece A play from another era that has remained popular over time, performed in the style, costumes, and sets representing the period it depicts.

plot The events of a play; the story.

practical scenery/props Scenery and props that actually work on stage: a stove that cooks, a book that can be read.

prepared audition An audition where an actor presents material that has been thoroughly prepared and memorized.

press kit A folder or large envelope containing black-and-white photographs, a cast list, a description of the play, and all the details of performance, sent out to publications in order to gain publicity for a show.

principals The leading characters in a play, or the leading actors in a company.

prior life The presumed life of a character before his or her appearance in a play.

producer The person who puts together a theatrical production: obtains the financial backing, leases the rights to the play, rents the theatre, hires the director, designers, house and stage crew, supervises the advertising and budget, and, sometimes, hires the cast.

prompt book The stage manager's copy of the script in which are noted all the blocking and technical cues.

properties plot The list of all properties used in the play.

props fabrication The sculpting, molding, or constructing of the props needed for a production.

props table The area where all the show's props are collected and arranged.

proscenium arch The picture frame through which an audience watches a play in a proscenium arch theatre.

protagonist The principal character, around whom the action of a play revolves.

public service announcement (PSA) Announcements concerning upcoming productions, broadcast on radio and television stations as a service to the community.

read in   To read from the house the lines of absent actors.

read through   When the actors sit down together to read through and discuss the play with the director. This usually is done at the first company meeting following selection of the cast.

reader's theatre   A performance at which the play is read aloud to an audience, rather than memorized and presented off book.

realism   An attempt in theatre to represent everyday life and people as they are or appear to be, through careful attention to detail in motivation of character, costuming, setting, and dialogue.

repertoire   All the parts an actor has played, or all the plays or songs with which an actor is familiar.

reviewer   One who writes an opinion of a performance for publication in a magazine or newspaper, or for broadcasting on radio or television.

revival   A play performed sometime after its original production in a faithful recreation of the original.

revue   A production featuring a collection of songs, dances, and sketches, but no plot.

royalty payment   The fee paid to a playwright for permission to perform his or her play.

run through   A rehearsal at which an entire scene, or act, or play is done without stopping for corrections.

satire   A type of comedy that uses wit, irony, and exaggeration to expose individual or institutional folly, vice, or stupidity.

scene   A division of an act in a play.

scene shop   The backstage area where the scenery for a play is built and painted, where the tools and materials are stored, and where a setting can be assembled on a trial basis.

scenery   The background forms—walls, archways, sky, trees, skyline, stairs—that provide the setting for a play.

scrim   A sturdy dark blue gauze hung as a drop in front of a set.

sculpting   A props fabrication technique using urethane foam or some other medium that is shaped and worked into a desired form, such as a loaf of bread.

set piece   A piece of scenery designed to stand by itself.

set-ups   Staged situations that make intriguing photos for publicity.

shaping   A prop fabrication technique suitable for creating small items that will not be handled in the course of the play. Plasticine is the medium often used.

Shingeki   Japanese "new theatre," dealing with contemporary issues.

sidekick   The male counterpart of the soubrette in a musical.

sightlines   Imaginary lines from the audience to the stage. Directors must plan the blocking to meet the sightlines of the audience and set designers must ensure that backstage areas are masked from every area in the house.

sit on book   To prompt actors in rehearsal by feeding them their lines as needed.

sketch   A short piece or skit, complete in itself, that is presented within a longer work, such as a revue.

soubrette   The vivacious, pert, usually comic female, often the confidante of the ingenue, or an actor who plays such parts.

stage business   All the actions, excluding blocking, performed by an actor on stage.

stage directions   Notes provided in the script of a play, generally in italics or parentheses, to indicate blocking, line readings, business, or directions for effects.

stage left/right   Directions from the perspective of the actor on stage.

stage manager   The person responsible for overseeing all the backstage elements of a production.

staged reading   A performance in which the actors hold their books and read from them, but move about the stage in a modified blocking scheme and address the other actors when they speak lines to them.

star turn   Playing a part on a different level from everyone else in the play so that one stands out; also, calling undue attention to oneself and not acting as part of the ensemble.

static character   One who remains the same throughout the entire course of the play.

stock character   One who represents a particular personality type or occupation.

strike   To dismantle the setting of a play and reduce it to its basic elements at the end of a run. To strike the set in midperformance is to clear away one setting to make room for the next act's scenery.

subtext   The thoughts, feelings, and reactions implied but never stated in the dialogue of a play.

supporting roles   Characters in a play who are not the leads but interact with them and have some part in the conflict or the working out of the resolution.

technical rehearsal   A rehearsal devoted to trying out the technical aspects of a production: scenery changes, costume changes, sound and lighting effects, complicated props.

technicians   Those who carry out the technical responsibilities in a production.

theatre games   A type of improvisation carefully structured by the director to achieve a specific objective in rehearsal, such as establish trust.

theme   What the play means, as opposed to what happens in it.

Tony Awards   Nickname for the Antoinette Perry Awards given annually for the best theatre work on Broadway.

tragedy   A serious play that ends unhappily.

tragic hero   The central figure in a tragedy, who falls from a high position in society because of a tragic flaw in character. His fall usually has tragic results for his kingdom or country.

tribute   A gift, floral or commemorative, given to the director and the assistant director by the entire company after the final performance.

typecasting   The casting of roles in a play by choosing actors who most closely resemble the physical and personality descriptions of the characters.

understudy   One who is prepared to take over an important role should the actor playing the role miss a performance.

unit set   An arrangement of scenery in which some or all of the pieces can be used in different combinations for different scenes.

upstaging   Standing upstage of an actor forcing him or her to turn away from the audience in order to exchange dialogue, also, using any kind of stage business to draw attention away from another actor in a scene.

villain   The evil character who opposes the hero or heroine.

voice projection   Control of the voice's volume so that even those in the last row of the house can hear and understand every word of dialogue in the play.

wings   The area immediately offstage left and right where actors stand to await their cues.

workshop production   A work in progress. The playwright and director, and sometimes the actors themselves, continue to work on a play even as they perform it for an audience.

Index